UNITED STATES NAVY DESTROYERS OF WORLD WAR II

UNITED STATES NAVY DESTROYERS OF WORLD WAR II

by
JOHN C. REILLY Jr.
edited by
Frank D. Johnson

BLANDFORD PRESS
POOLE · DORSET

First published in the UK 1983 by Blandford Press,
Link House, West Street, Poole, Dorset BH15 1LL.

Copyright © 1983 Blandford Books Ltd. Reprinted 1985

Distributed in the United States by
Sterling Publishing Co., Inc.,
2 Park Avenue, New York, N.Y. 10016.

ISBN 0 7137 1026 8

British Library Cataloguing in Publication Data

Reilly, John C.
  United States Navy Destroyers of World War 2.
  1. United States. *Navy* – History
  2. Destroyers (Warships) – History
  3. World War, 1939–1945 – Naval operations, American
  I. Title   II. Johnson, Frank D.

Typeset in Singapore
by Polyglot Pte Ltd
Printed by BAS Printers Ltd.,
Over Wallop, Hampshire
Bound by Robert Hartnoll Ltd. Bodmin, UK

Third Printing
Printed by Arcata Graphics
Kingsport, TN.

Contents

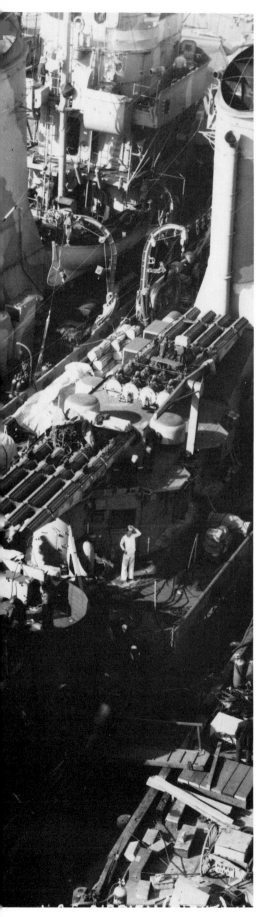

O'Brien (**DD-415**) and *Walke* (**DD-416**), of the *Sims* class, seen on **16 December 1941**.

Frontispiece
Abner Read (**DD-526**), a low-bridge *Fletcher* class, seen on **13 June 1943**.

Preface

Navies have long made good use of small fighting ships. From classical antiquity to the days of sail, fleets found their own need for ships designed for speed or for work in restricted waters where their bigger consorts could not go. While it would be an exaggeration to trace a line of descent from the Roman *liburnian* through the brig and the sloop-of-war to the fleet destroyer of World War II, the versatility and seamanship displayed by these small ships and the men who manned them might well be thought of as part of the heritage of the modern destroyer.

The torpedo, of course, brought the destroyer into being. Various schemes for bringing explosive charges into contact with the underwater hulls of ships had been thought of since David Bushnell's submersible *Turtle* of 1776 and Robert Fulton's prototype towing torpedo of the early 1800s. Contact mines and spar torpedoes appeared during the Crimean War and the American Civil War and although the mine came to stay, it was a totally passive weapon; its victim had to come to it. The spar torpedo had mobility but proved at least as dangerous to hunter as to victim. The Luppis-Whitehead 'fish torpedo' of 1866 offered new horizons in destructive power. Self-propelled 'automobile torpedoes' were eagerly developed by large and small navies, to whom it seemed a threat or a welcome equalizer depending on the perspective of the nation involved. As a result of the development of the Whitehead torpedo, steam torpedo boats were built in quantity and grew in size through the latter part of the nineteenth century.

The United States Navy's destroyers, from their beginning in the early 1900s through the end of World War II, may be thought of as forming four fairly distinct generations. The first of these was made up of sixty-eight raised-forecastle 'broken-deckers' which spanned the period of growth and transition from coal to oil, reciprocating engines to geared turbines, and 18-inch compressed-air guncotton torpedoes to 21-inch air-steam weapons with TNT warheads.

The mass-produced 'flushdeck' destroyers of the *Wickes* and *Clemson* classes, completed during World War I and the early postwar years, formed a second generation. Designed and built for surface action in support of a battle line, their arrangement of single-purpose guns and broadside torpedo tubes was inherited from their ancestors.

After a 'holiday' of more than ten years, the result of tight postwar budgeting, a Third Generation began to appear. Built under the legal limitations of the London Treaty, these ships incorporated some new wrinkles in ordnance, engineering, and hull design and represent a break with the generations which preceded them. This new generation had two branches; 1,500-ton fleet destroyers with dual-purpose gun batteries and 1,850-ton leaders with their antiaircraft capability deliberately waived in favor of the heaviest obtainable surface firepower. The last ships of the former group, completed after the expiration of the Treaty, included a modest increase in displacement.

The fourth step in this evolution began shortly before World War II, when the first of three major groups of bigger standard fleet destroyers was designed and ordered. The *Benson* and *Gleaves* classes, with the later *Fletcher*, *Allen M. Sumner*, and *Gearing* classes, traced their ancestry to the Treaty-built ships of the 1930s but included such improvements as superior seakeeping ability, better resistance to damage, heavier short-range antiaircraft batteries and antisubmarine armaments, and — in the *Allen M. Sumner*s and *Gearing*s — designed provision for the use of radar. These ships served with honor through World War II; many of them continued to carry on into more recent times in the United States Navy and in a number of foreign fleets, something of a testimonial to the practicality of their design and the ruggedness of their construction.

This work is intended to provide a general idea of the third- and fourth-generation destroyers with which the United States Navy fought its share of World War II, and of the process by which each successive class of ships came to be. It is not a history of destroyer operations; this was well done a generation ago by Theodore Roscoe in his *United States Destroyer Operations in World War II* (Annapolis, Maryland: United States Naval Institute, 1953). Samuel Eliot Morison's *History of United States Naval Operations in World War II* (Boston, Massachusetts: Little, Brown & Co, 1947–62; 15 volumes) is an essential basis for any study of wartime destroyer service. The voluminous war diaries and operational reports of individual destroyers and of force and fleet commanders in the Operational Archives Branch of the Naval Historical

Center (Washington Navy Yard, Washington, DC) are a treasure trove of raw material for future study and analysis.

One rather conspicuous omission will be apparent; very little will be said of the famous 'flushdeckers', the four-stack destroyers of the *Wickes* and *Clemson* classes which served in considerable numbers through World War II. These well-known ships have already been described and illustrated by Commander John Alden in his *Flush Decks and Four Pipes* (United States Naval Institute, 1965), and there is little to be gained by duplicating what has already been well done.

The continuous back-and-forth of discussion and paperwork from one segment of the Navy to another may well seem confusing. This is, though, how ships were designed and modified. The track of a class' design sometimes suggests a soccer game as it passes from place to place and back again, but this is the way of any large organization. The treatment of this process may seem a bit impersonal. We will see how the General Board did this, the Bureau of Ordnance took exception to that, and the Commander Destroyers, Scouting Force, offered comments. In examining this process, the names of people are generally not included, except in instances where the persons involved are very well known, or where someone is being quoted as an individual. The time period considered here extends over fifteen years, and frequent reassignment of persons who attend meetings or sign correspondence on behalf of offices or bureaus would give this work an extensive and confusing cast of mostly unfamiliar characters.

The organization of the Navy during this time requires some explanation (see Appendix C). The Secretary of the Navy was a civilian member of the President's cabinet and had final powers as far as the Navy Department was concerned. The Chief of Naval Operations (CNO) was, before the United States entered the war, the senior flag officer and was responsible to the Secretary for the planning and overall direction of the Navy's military functions. Each of the technical Bureaus which will be encountered here — Construction and Repair, Engineering, and Ordnance — had a Bureau chief, a flag officer, who reported directly to the Secretary; CNO had no command authority over the Bureaus. The main strength of the forces afloat was organized, before Pearl Harbor, into the United States Fleet. This was divided, along tactical lines, into a Scouting Fleet and a Battle Fleet, renamed Scouting Force and Battle Force in 1931. Within each Force, type commanders directed the administration and readiness of ships of particular types. Since destroyers were assigned to both forces, there were two flag officers — Commander Destroyers, Battle Force (ComDesBatFor), and Commander Destroyers, Scouting Force (ComDeScoFor) — whose opinions were solicited when comment was desired from the Fleet concerning new designs or changes to existing ones. These officers, and others in the chain of command, might also address high command on their own initiative about matters of concern.

The Office of the Chief of Naval Operations was organized into a number of divisions. The Fleet Training Division and the Fleet Maintenance Division were both involved in efforts to bring the operating forces to the best possible degree of readiness. Fleet Training was responsible for performance, while Fleet Maintenance took care of material; both were involved in formulating and altering ship concepts. The War Plans Division developed policies in support of war planning, and was asked to look at concepts in the context of possible operations.

Much of the Navy's administration was carried out by boards and committees, long a feature of naval administration. The General Board, the most important of these, was established in 1900 and served as an advisory body to the Secretary of the Navy. One of its continuing functions during the time surveyed here was the formulation of recommended shipbuilding programs and determination of military characteristics for new ships. When each year's proposed building program was under consideration, the Board, through a process of hearings, discussions, and exchange of correspondence with the Bureaus and the fleet, eventually compiled a set of characteristics — such as qualities of size, speed, armament, endurance, and the like — desired for new ships. These went to the Secretary for approval; he was under no obligation to accept the Board's recommendations, but could send them back for reworking.

After he had finally approved a set of military characteristics, these were then sent to the technical Bureaus for design refinement and contracting. A set of contract plans — general-arrangement drawings — and specifications formed the basis for competitive bidding by private builders or an order to navy yards, or sometimes a combination of the two. One of the builders, commercial or Navy, was selected to prepare the detailed working plans for construction. At any point in this process, and even while actual construction was going on, changes could be, and often were, made at the Department's discretion or with its approval. There were, thus, numerous differences — sometimes major ones — between an original contract plan and the finished ships in a given program.

A detailed discussion of the Navy Department's organization, and of the roles of the various Bureaus and offices in the design and construction of ships, can be found in Rear Admiral Julius A. Furer's *Administration of the Navy Department in World War II* (Washington, DC: Government Printing Office, 1959), and in Vice Admiral Edwin B. Hooper's *The Navy Department: Evolution and Fragmentation* (Washington: Naval Historical Foundation, 1978), pp 14–18.

American naval ships of this period are identified both by name and by hull number, and both are used in this work. An American hull number is not quite the same thing as a British pennant number. It begins with two or more letters which indicate the type of ship in question. For instance, DD stands for Destroyer; DM for Light Mine Layer (a destroyer with mine tracks installed); APD for High-Speed Transport (a destroyer or destroyer escort modified to land troops or underwater demolition teams); and so on. The basic type symbol for Destroyer (DD) will be seen throughout; others are defined in context, so no elaborate explanation is needed here. The letter type symbol is combined with a consecutive number to identify a given ship. Thus, *Porter* (DD-356) is the three hundred and fifty-sixth destroyer authorized for construction since these numbers began to be used. In American practice a ship, or a class of ships, may be identified by the entire name-number combination. It may also be described by name or by number alone; one sees many references, in publications and in documents, to, say, the *Gridley* class, or the DD-445 class. When ships are funded for construction, they are assigned numbers and these numbers are used to identify and file plans and correspondence dealing with them from the beginning. Names are selected later, before or during construction. Classes, as the table in Appendix D will show, are not always grouped together in the numbering sequence. This can be the result of changes in design after a building program is voted and numbers are assigned; construction of 'follow-on' ships under a subsequent fiscal-year program; or — during the war years — of allocation of building contracts out of a strict design-progression sequence for the sake of expediting completions. Examples of all of these will be found further on.

This work is principally based on the records of the General Board of the Navy and the wartime records of the Office of the Chief of Naval Operations, both held by the Operational Archives Branch of the Naval Historical Center, Washington, DC, and on the records of the Ships' Histories Branch of the Naval Historical Center, as well as on material in the author's collection. Any opinions or conclusions expressed here reflect no official position of the Naval Historical Center or of the Department of the Navy.

I would like to express my thanks to my wife, who put up with a great deal of domestic clutter while this was being done. My sincere gratitude also goes to Mrs Agnes Hoover, of the Naval Historical Center's Curator Branch, and Miss Barbara Gilmore, Mrs Gerri Judkins, Mrs Nina Statum, and Miss Martha Crawley, all of the Operational Archives Branch, for their essential assistance, and to Mr Robert J. Cressman for the use of some of the results of his extensive photo-archival research. Illustrations used here are US Navy official material, from the author's collection unless otherwise identified. (Some of the photographs bear contemporary shipyard photograph identification labels, applied to photographs of modifications, and new equipment and armament installations taken as part of the normal modification or overhaul process, and to the general recognition photographs taken for updating purposes when work had been completed). Any errors, whether of commission or of omission, are solely mine.

John C. Reilly Jr

1
Early Torpedo Boats and Destroyers

If we are to have a Navy for war-like operations, offensive and defensive, we certainly ought to increase both the number of battleships and torpedo boats.

President Grover Cleveland, 1894

After a variety of early torpedo-boat experiments, a 'first-class torpedo boat' was authorized by the Congress of the United States in 1886. This ship commissioned in 1890 as *Cushing* (Torpedo Boat No. 1), a name destined to live on in the tradition of the American destroyer. Between 1896 and 1900 thirty-one more torpedo boats were ordered. These were a rather motley array of fourteen different classes, built to American as well as foreign inspired designs ranging from 100 to over 228 feet in length. These craft were generally 'short-legged', frail and rather undependable machines. Patrol and escort operations, which later came to epitomize 'destroyer work', were handled during the Spanish-American War by more seaworthy gun-boats and converted yachts rather than by the torpedo boats then in commission, these craft being relegated to carrying dispatches. For the first time, though hardly for the last, other ships had to be pressed into service to supplement surface torpedo craft.

Torpedo boats grew in size and power as their numbers increased. The heated-air torpedo was soon followed by the air-steam version with greater range and explosive-carrying capacity. Torpedo boats were seen to be a viable menace to the battle line and self-defense measures — searchlights and small caliber rapid-firing guns — were deemed inadequate. The eventual approach to fleet defense took the form of an enlarged torpedo boat, bigger and faster for seaworthiness and firepower, armed with guns heavy enough to kill torpedo boats before they could close to firing range. Britain began to introduce these ships, dubbed 'torpedo-boat destroyers' by Sir John Fisher, in 1894 when HMS *Havock* was commissioned. Other powers followed and in 1898 the US Congress authorized sixteen of the new ships. On 19 May 1902 *Decatur* (Torpedo-Boat Destroyer No. 5) was commissioned and became the first American destroyer to go into active service. (American type designations were spelled out until 1920 when the more familiar type symbol DD was adopted to designate destroyers).

Delving far back into the pedigree of the American destroyer, the long, sleek lines and narrow beam of US torpedo boats of the late 1890s spawned a need for a larger craft of essentially the same shape which could protect the battle line from such craft as that pictured here. Thus was born the 'torpedo boat destroyer'. Eventually, the torpedo boat and torpedo boat destroyer would merge into the modern 'destroyer'. Seen here is the USS *Shubrick* (Torpedo Boat No. 31) late in her career during the early 1900s.

The immediate forerunners of the famous 'flushdeck four pipers' were such ships as the destroyer *Shaw* of the *Sampson* class, pictured here at dockside at Mare Island, California shortly before the US entry into World War I. The forward 4-inch and one-pounder guns can be seen clearly in this early example of shipyard photography. Like most ships of her time, *Shaw* was equipped with a windshield to provide her open bridge with some weather protection. Wartime experience would soon show, however, that this was not enough for work in more rigorous climates.

By the end of 1903 all sixteen of the '1898 boats' were with the Fleet. After some hesitation, more destroyers were authorized in 1906 and a process of development began. Guns and torpedo tubes increased in size, as did the ships themselves. Turbines replaced reciprocating engines in the 1906 ships as the constant emphasis on the destroyer's need for speed prompted ceaseless experimentation in the area of more powerful and reliable power plants. Oil fuel was not only conducive to improved efficiency, but it allowed a destroyer to refuel at sea while underway, something a coalburner could not do. By 1916 reduction gearing had been introduced to destroyer construction.

The United States' entry into World War I gave the destroyer force its first taste of real war. In accordance with what was to be a continuing fact of destroyer life, the type was handed a new task. Depth charges and primitive hydrophones were installed and the destroyer became an antisubmarine vessel. Director control of destroyer guns, a British development, improved the 'tin can's' chances of landing shells on the target. Gyrostabilization of the director sight made it easier for the director pointer to stay on target, and the American mechanical rangekeeper — a parallel development to the Royal Navy's Dumaresq — produced deflection orders. All this was primitive, but, nonetheless, a start.

2
The Flushdeckers

If there has ever been such a thing in the history of the United States Navy as a typical American class of ship, the flush-deck destroyers of World War I come closest to filling the bill.

Commander John D. Alden, *Flush Decks and Four Pipes* (Annapolis, 1959)

The result of the wartime construction program in which capital ships were set aside to expedite the building of antisubmarine vessels, the flushdeckers were the first mass-produced American destroyers. Six *Caldwell* class prototypes, authorized in 1915, embodied a number of design differences thought worthy of service testing. Long before they were completed, the pressure of events dictated a wholesale expansion of the the American naval shipbuilding program. By the Armistice, 172 of these ships had been laid down and 37 of them had been commissioned. Ninety-six more were begun shortly afterward; five were cancelled before their keels were laid but by 1922 a total of 268 of the new ships were in commission. Like earlier American destroyers, these ships were designed for speed and fuel economy. Their high length-to-beam ratio gave them the best possible radius with the speed needed for torpedo attack. However, this suited them poorly for antisubmarine work where agility was needed. Wartime calculations, for instance, showed that the average flushdecker had a much wider 180-degree turning radius at higher speeds than did a contemporary battleship.

During the postwar years budget cuts soon led to the inactivation of many oilburning destroyers, with the scrapping of the older coal-fired ships as well as the now-weary torpedo boats. The United States' destroyer

Top
USS *King* (DD-242), a representative 'flushdeck' destroyer of the World War I building program, is seen about 1930 with a canvas target slung between her stacks for offset gunnery practice. These ships were the US Navy's entire destroyer force until well into the 1930s, and many served through World War II.

Bottom
Flushdeckers lay a smoke screen during fleet exercises. Through the years destroyer missions have steadily evolved. When this photograph was taken, battle line defense and massed torpedo attack were considered the destroyer's principal reasons for existence.

force now consisted of the active flushdeckers; from 1923 through to 1930 an average of 101 to 106 destroyers were in commission. A variety of proposals were introduced during the 1920s to remedy the flushdeckers' defects, since no money was forthcoming for new construction. These included reducing the number of funnels to conserve precious deck space, as well as relocation of guns and some torpedo tubes on the centerline. With no money available, all such schemes were retired to the archives.

Postwar operations found destroyers taking offensive fleet operations as their principal role. Studies of the Battle of Jutland, in which aggressive destroyer action had affected the outcome, had a powerful influence on naval thinking. Fleet exercises emphasized the role of the destroyer, both in screening its own battle line and in gaining an advantageous position from which to launch large-scale torpedo attacks. The battleship-destroyer combination continued to dominate the tactical thought of the day. The converted aircraft carrier *Langley* joined the fleet in 1922, and the former battlecruisers *Lexington* and *Saratoga*, converted as carriers, went into commission late in 1927. As carrier operations became part of the picture, destroyers found another task; accompanying the 'flattops' to serve as 'plane guard and antisubmarine escort.

During the 1920s a number of flushdeckers were converted to fast minelayers, designed to race into position ahead of an enemy's battle line and sow drifting mines in his path as well as to plant more conventional moored minefields in hostile waters where other minelayers could not live. Radio installations were added during these years as were radio direction finders.

Through the 1920s the Navy struggled to keep the destroyer force as battle-ready as possible in spite of deterioration from hard service and scanty funds. The London Treaty, in effect at the end of 1930, placed a numerical ceiling on destroyer strengths. Worn-out ships, active since their completion, were discarded wholesale and replaced

Top
In a fine view of flushdeckers on maneuvers between the wars, USS *Zane* (DD-337) has her boats swung and ready for lowering. Besides making it difficult to keep forces up in numbers, between-the-wars belt-tightening even showed itself in such areas as speed limitations to conserve fuel.

Bottom
A testimonial to the durability of early American destroyer designs were the four-stackers transferred to England prior to the US entry into the war. These ships continued to serve under British crews as convoy escorts throughout the war. Pictured here is HMS *Buxton*, ex-USS *Edwards* (DD-265).

Top
Paul Jones (DD-230) has her four 4-inch guns, but six tubes have been removed in favor of 20 mm AA guns and K-guns. She has an SC air-search radar and an SO surface-search unit. Her Vickers-pattern gun director can be seen on top of the wheelhouse.

Bottom
Former American flushdeckers, traded to Britain in 1940 in exchange for base rights in the Western Hemisphere, were modified in varying degrees in Royal Navy service. HMS *Ramsey*, the former USS *Meade* (DD-274) here wears Admiralty dazzle camouflage and has a British Type 277 radar in the 'lantern' over her bridge. This was a WS (Warning of Surface Craft) radar, or what the US Navy would call a surface-search equipment. *Ramsey* still has American 4-inch 50-caliber single-purpose guns, but carries only one triple torpedo tube, relocated on the centerline.

by sister ships taken from the reserve fleet, refitted and reactivated by the ships' crews and fleet tenders. The London Treaty placed limits on the size and power as well as the numbers of destroyers allowed. It defined a destroyer as a surface warship of 1,850 standard tons or less and with no guns over 5.1 inches or 130 mm. ('Standard' displacement, a typical legal compromise, is the weight of a ship fully manned, armed, and ready for sea but without fuel or reserve feed water on board. It was drawn up at the Washington Conference as acceptable both to powers who considered steaming endurance vital and those whose needs were more tactical than

strategic. It supplanted, as a design datum, 'normal' displacement which had come into use during the early years of the American steel navy in the late 1800s. That formula had changed several times, but was generally based on full-load displacement minus a specific fraction of fuel and consumables. It was used as an estimated 'fighting displacement' for calculating the design waterline and — in bigger warships — the placement of armor.) The United States was allotted 150,000 tons of destroyers; sixteen percent (24,000 tons) of these could be larger 1,850-ton ships if desired, while the rest were limited to 1,500 tons apiece.

13

3

New Destroyer Construction Begins

The fleet's primary weapon is still the big gun. Whether the destroyer aids the gun by actually torpedoing enemy capital ships or by *threat* of torpedo attack *forces* him to maneuver to his disadvantage, to break off gunfire, to lose his target by the use of smoke, or to cover the retirement of the fleet in the face of superior force, the destroyer is fulfilling its battle mission which is to assist the big guns in imposing their will on the enemy. . . . Seakeeping qualities are a *sine qua non* to the fleet destroyer if it is to be an efficient auxiliary to the big gun in battle.

Lieutenant Commander H. J. Wright, USN, letter to the *United States Naval Institute Proceedings*, LXI (July 1935)

By the late 1920s France, Britain, Italy and Japan had new destroyer building programs underway. Even Germany, restricted by the Versailles Treaty, had built a dozen seagoing *Torpedobooten* of the *Wolf* and *Möwe* classes. Japan was hard at work on the new 'Special Type', the *Fubuki* class and its descendants. France was building not only conventional destroyers, but ships of over 3,000 tons with 5.5-inch guns, 'light cruisers' in Treaty terms, but superdestroyers in armament and tactical concept. The flushdeckers of the United States Navy had been reasonably adequate by the standards of World War I, but by now were being left far behind. Clearly, something better was needed.

Early in 1927 an informal study was begun aimed at producing a new design incorporating a high-pressure steam plant and embodying the results of postwar operating experience and technical developments. It was hoped that Congress might fund two or three such ships.

Calculations were developed around the concept of a 325-foot, 1,600-ton, 36-knot vessel armed with four 5-inch/51-caliber single-purpose guns of the type then in use in battleships for torpedo defense, one 3-inch/50-caliber antiaircraft gun, smaller anti-aircraft machine guns and twelve 21-inch torpedo tubes. It was assumed that the entire battery should be located on the ship's centerline. This was difficult to provide for, especially with the 5-inch guns which would require power hoists. Previous design discussions had recognized that it was militarily desirable to place the torpedo battery on the centerline, but this could not be done in earlier destroyers. It now seemed possible to mount centerline tubes with an adequate arc of train to either side, but the deck space available would make it necessary to develop a 6-tube mount to get the same 12-tube battery mounted in the flushdeckers. A tentative plan envisioned a superimposed three-over-three tube arrangement.

The first plans were sent to the Fleet for comment. By now the concept had hardened into a 34-knot ship with machinery similar to that of the flushdeckers, but with high-pressure boilers and twin rudders for better maneuverability. The planned battery remained at four 5-inch/51-caliber guns, one 3-inch/50-caliber gun and two 6-tube mounts.

Comments from prospective 'customers' varied. The Commander Destroyer Squadrons, Battle Fleet, held that the 'building of new destroyers should be urged upon Congress at an early date in order that we may not lose the art and for replacement purposes, following the policy being followed now by all the other great powers. Although we have a numerical destroyer superiority, it consists of many vessels most deficient in many essential military qualities and all of whom are ageing year by year.' He liked the centerline torpedo battery, better for daylight attacks when all tubes could be trained in the same direction; it still permitted half of the tubes to be trained to each beam at night or in poor visibility. The firing of large controlled torpedo spreads would be complicated, involving rather intricate arrangements of gyro angles; ComDesBatFlt felt it might be better to mount four triple tubes on the centerline. This should be done easily if 5-inch/25-caliber dual-purpose guns, already installed in battleships and cruisers for air defense, were used instead of the 5-inch/51. This would eliminate the need for the 3-inch AA gun, provide a higher rate of gun fire, and allow the 5-inch battery to be used for fleet air defense. The Commander in Chief, Battle Fleet, remarked that the new design represented a 'marked improvement' with its centerline battery and reduced number of stacks. He also preferred the 5-inch/25 to the 5-inch/51: 'the increased need for anti-aircraft fire in screening duties, as well as in normal duty . . . , renders it very important that an efficient anti-aircraft battery be carried.'

The understanding within the Office of the Chief of Naval Operations (OPNAV) was that these ships would, at first, serve as squadron flagships. As more were built, they would then replace flushdeckers in division service. Antisubmarine work was thought a minor consideration since most such duty would be carried out by supporting forces rather than by the Battle Fleet. The design thus emphasized high-speed seakeeping, as had earlier American destroyer designs, rather than maneuverability.

After studying the design, the Bureau of Ordnance agreed that the 5-inch/25 was preferable to the 5-inch/51. The high initial velocity of the 51-caliber gun was desirable, but the existing 4-inch destroyer gun already had a greater range than could be practically used with existing fire-control gear. The Bureau felt that a fire-control system for destroyers should be light, compact, and simple, emphasizing ruggedness in view of the hard riding and rough handling expected. It would be pointless, they concluded, to incorporate gun performance beyond the ships' control capabilities.

Ordnance objected to the great rotating weight of a loaded 6-tube mount. It would be very difficult, they felt, to handle such a mount in a destroyer. Either the improved triple mount designed for new-construction heavy cruisers, or a new quadruple mount, would be preferable. In any case, the Bureau recommended that all torpedoes be carried in tubes rather than designing a smaller battery with reloads, as tubes weighed little more than any other type of satisfactory torpedo stowage.

While this discussion proceeded, the Bureau of Aeronautics produced a design of its own in March 1927. This was a modified flushdecker, with everything between the stacks and the after deckhouse removed and a turntable catapult installed. Two reconnaissance floatplanes were to be accommodated. The catapult featured six torpedo tubes, three below and to each side of the catapult track. Six reloads were to be stowed in corresponding positions beneath the after end of the catapult, making reloading (theoretically) quick and easy. The Navy's General Board (its deliberative body which formulated military characteristics for proposed new construction) had favored the combination of destroyer and scout plane since the early 1920s, when flushdecker *Charles Ausburn* tried out an experimental arrangement in which a 'plane was carried above the forward gun mount and lowered into the sea by a boom. This effort, however, came to nothing. Congress simply had no intention of funding such projects.

In September 1927 the General Board recommended a five year building program which included characteristics for a 1,850-ton destroyer leader. This, again, was a type long considered. During 1919–20 numerous 'leader' concepts were sketched, varying considerably in configuration but most being based on a 360-foot hull with four 5-inch/51-caliber guns and six to twelve tubes. These had been nothing more than drawing board studies, serving only to keep officers and designers thinking beyond the flushdecker. The Secretary of the Navy approved the new design, which called for four 5-inch/51s on the centerline with at least six AA machine guns and four triple torpedo tubes without reloads. The type was to have a 35 knot trial speed and 'to maintain as high speed as is practicable in heavy weather with special attention to handiness'. Depth charges were included and the bow was to be reinforced for ramming submarines!

Discussion continued through 1928. The Chief of Naval Operations' Director of War Plans did not care for the 5-inch/25 AA gun, which many considered a suitable improvement on the flushdeckers' 4-inch/50. Its trajectory was too high, he felt, for effective use by destroyers against others of their kind at more than 5,000 yards; a higher-powered, flatter-trajectory 5-inch gun was needed. A squadron of destroyers armed with high-powered 5-inchers might be used to advantage to clear the way for conventional destroyers in

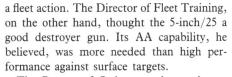

a fleet action. The Director of Fleet Training, on the other hand, thought the 5-inch/25 a good destroyer gun. Its AA capability, he believed, was more needed than high performance against surface targets.

The Bureau of Ordnance advocated construction of heavy destroyer leaders with better heavy-weather gunfighting capabilities. Foreign navies were producing large destroyers, and the ability of this kind of ship to use its guns in seas that made smaller ships' batteries inoperable was worth having. Leaders could not only counter an enemy's torpedo attacks — the 'torpedo-boat destroyer' concept revisited — but would be essential to defeat the bigger foreign ships. A big ship was indicated, able to make good speed in a seaway and to fight her guns effectively when lighter destroyers could not. The 5-inch/51 was better for this work than the 5-inch/25, with a flatter trajectory and a longer danger space at predicted battle ranges, although the shorter gun's air-defense capacity and 25 per cent faster rate of fire were of clear value.

Some officers pointed out that the destroyer leader would be used in fleet antisubmarine screens which would, in the foreseeable future, become antiaircraft screens as well. A dual-purpose battery would then become a neces-

sity. Others seemed to think the gun question a bit overdrawn since the destroyer type's principal *raison d'etre* was still considered by many to be the torpedo attack.

15

4

The Farragut Class

A perfect ship of war is a *desideratum* which has never yet been obtained; any near approach to perfection in one direction inevitably brings with it disadvantages in the other.

British Admiralty committee on ship design, quoted in Chief Engineer J. W. King, USN, *The War-Ships and Navies of the World* (Boston, 1880), 208

No construction money was forthcoming from Congress so matters lapsed until 1930 when discussion of new designs resumed. As before, a number of views and concepts were presented. The Bureau of Construction and Repair developed three designs; a 1,850-ton leader and 1,500-ton and 1,375-ton destroyers. These were to be of more rugged construction than the flushdeckers with higher freeboard for better seakeeping and four centerline 5-inch/25-caliber guns as the main battery. The leader mounted two centerline quad torpedo tubes with provision for quick reloading. The 1,500-tonner had two centerline triples while the small ship included four waist triples. Some officers favored two destroyer types, large 'defensive' ships with heavy gun batteries and small, fast 'offensive' destroyers emphasizing torpedo power. The tentative characteristics drawn up by the General Board in December 1930 called for twelve tubes and four to six guns, dual purpose 'if practicable', with a top speed of 35 knots and a radius of 6,500 miles at 12 knots.

Discussion focused on some of the technical and tactical changes of recent years. The chance of a major fleet action was more remote than before and the modern destroyer was four or five times more likely to use its guns than its torpedoes. Carrier torpedo-bomber squadrons were now operational and the aircraft, being a faster torpedo-launching platform than the destroyer, rendered the destroyer's tubes somewhat less of a factor than they had been before. New destroyers should, it was felt, compare with the best foreign practice with preferably six but no less than five guns of at least 4.7 inches. These guns and their optimum location should be given priority over other considerations. Various arrangements of gun mounts and triple or quadruple torpedo tubes were considered

before final selection. It was suggested that, if later wartime needs so dictated, the after 5-inch gun might be replaced by another bank of torpedo tubes.

On 28 February 1931 the appropriation act for Fiscal Year 1932 was signed into law. This provided for the construction of five new destroyers, the first since World War I. Contract plans and specifications were drawn up and approved by July and contracts were let for *Farragut* (DD-348) and four sisters. Orders were placed for three more in September 1932 under the 1933 program.

Primarily due to the long period between building programs, rather than a gradual developmental process, the *Farragut* class represented a sharp break with the earlier trend of US destroyer design. After a gap of more than ten years in new construction, this was to be expected in the light of foreign developments. The *Farraguts* were raised-forecastle ships with five of the new 5-inch/38-caliber guns and two quadruple torpedo tubes. Close-in antiaircraft armament, four .50-caliber machine guns with simple 'iron sights', was as insignificant as that of any foreign contemporary. The 5-inch battery was controlled by a newly developed director which incorporated an optical rangefinder and an electromechanical computer, or 'rangekeeper' as the Navy then called them. Target range and bearing were determined by the director and fed into the rangekeeper along with the ship's own course and speed, plus corrections for such factors as wind; a gyroscope mechanism, called a 'stable element', introduced continuous corrections to compensate for the pitch and roll of the ship. The computed train and elevation orders were then electrically transmitted to the guns. This Mark 33 director, besides solving the two-dimensional surface gunfire problem, could also handle the

three-dimensional AA control problem. Its rangekeeper, the mechanical 'brain' of the system, could cope with target speeds up to 275 knots or diving speeds up to 400 knots. The 5-inch guns could be remotely controlled unlike the situation in earlier destroyers where gun crews had to 'match pointers' and keep their guns lined up with the director's visually-signalled gun orders. The system designed for the *Farragut* class was still very far from perfect, especially for air-defense. It was, nonetheless, a major step forward.

One might not necessarily think of a destroyer as having much of a potential as a gun platform, but officers at this time disagreed. Lieutenant Commander F. S. Craven, a frequent contributor to discussions of destroyer design, wrote to the General Board that 'director control of gunfire is of great value, not only in bad weather but in bringing the battery (and searchlight) directly and surely to bear on the target intended to be engaged. The importance of this control is seldom realized during peace time because target practices cannot present the problems of target designation that would frequently arise in battle.'[1] In any event, the fleet seemed satisfied with the effectiveness of its gun-and-director combination. By 1941 the Chief of Naval Operations, in discussing the day division battle practices fired by the destroyer force during 1940–41, could note that 'results of these practices indicate that destroyers mounting 5-inch/38-caliber guns can be expected to make early hits on opposing light forces at ranges of 7,000 to 8,000 yards,' though he went on to say that 'range should be closed below 7,000 yards to insure a really destructive effect.'[2] (Average shooting range for long-range gun battle practice in 1940–41 was 7,778 yards for 1,500-tonners and 7,601 yards for 1,850-tonners with 5-inch/38s; flushdeckers with 4-inch/50s fired at an average of 4,744 yards.)

The new design emphasized seaworthiness. Because of the emphasis placed on seakeeping and the need to be able to drive these ships at high speed in heavy seas, the designers made every effort to keep hull stresses as low as possible. Extensive use of welding saved a fair amount of weight, an important consideration when the sum of offensive and operating weights was being calculated as closely as it was in these Treaty-limited ships. Hydraulic steering replaced the steam steering used in the flushdeckers. To obtain drier forward gun positions, the *Farragut* class went back to the raised forecastle that had been a characteristic of pre-World War I American destroyers. Some bow flare improved seakeeping; the designers avoided flaring the bows to such an extent that they would throw too much spray

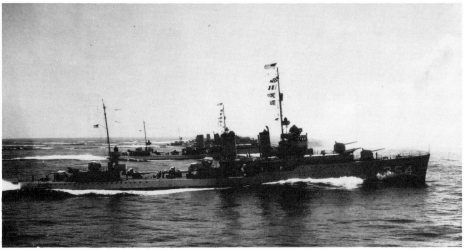

or cause excessive pounding in a head sea. A partial turtleback forecastle, with tumble-home and a pronounced camber reminiscent of the old torpedo boats, had been considered but was dropped in favor of mounting two super-firing 5-inch guns forward of the bridge. Longitudinal hull framing was used for the first time in United States destroyers in lieu of the hitherto-customary tranverse framing, and provided better resistance to hogging and sagging within the stringent weight limits involved. A widened stern was drawn to accommodate depth-charge tracks, or mine tracks should a need arise.

Engineering plants in the *Farragut*s included 650-degree (F.), 400-psi boilers using superheated steam designed to generate more power with a lighter, more compact installation. *Farragut* (DD-348), the lead ship, made 38.6 knots on her preliminary trials.[3]

Such improvements, of course, cost money. The service had been inured to belt-tightening by years of parsimonious budgets which had, as one disgusted officer remarked, developed 'eight-knot minds in thirty-knot ships'. The *Farragut*s, lavish in proportions and equipment by earlier standards, were quickly dubbed 'gold platers' by the fleet.

Farragut (DD-348) and *Dewey* (DD-349), first of the new generation of 1,500-tonners to go into commission, in June and October 1934 respectively, were carefully studied. Criticisms inevitably arose. Their gun and torpedo control installations were called 'elaborate, complicated and expensive'; the ships themselves were called 'too gadgety' and 'too much light cruiser'. The Navy's protracted affair with the four-stackers seems to have resulted in a bit of future shock. The lack of light cruisers during the 1920s and early 1930s had, it was said, 'led to an unhealthy acceptance of destroyers as permanently to fill this role of light cruisers, and has inspired too ambitious developments to that end which are excessive for a destroyer's capabilities as well as its needs.' The Bureau of Ordnance, on the other hand, held that power drives for gun and

Top
Monaghan (DD-354) at Mare Island, 15 February 1942. She is apparently painted in the overall dark sea blue of Measure 11, a color scheme used on many destroyers during 1942. 20 mm AA guns have been mounted forward of the bridge, on platforms around the second stack, and on the after deckhouse. Small, unshaded hull numbers at bow and stern were a feature of camouflage painting.

Bottom
MacDonough (DD-351) on 29 May 1942. She is armed with 20 mm AA guns forward, amidships, and aft but has not received the heavier Bofors gun. Her bridge structure and Mark 33 gun director are seen to particular advantage here.

Opposite top left
Worden (DD-352) in November, 1942, with a pair of twin 40 mm mounts abaft her stack in the place occupied by her fifth 5-inch gun before the AA improvement process was begun. The 5-inch director has been equipped with a Type FD ('Fox Dog') radar.

Opposite top right
A later view of *Monaghan*, taken on 13 October 1942, showing her arrangement of depth-charge tracks and after gun armament. Two side-throwing depth-charge projectors, or 'K-guns', with their loading davits, have been installed to each side of the after deckhouse. An early Type SC air-search radar antenna is at the masthead, with an SG surface-search antenna just below; the gun director has an FD.

Opposite bottom
Aylwin (DD-355) on 25 October 1944, in the pattern camouflage prevalent through the Pacific Fleet during that year. The *Farragut* class did not receive any of the late-wartime AA improvements made to some ships of the later classes.

torpedo-tube mounts, with the new Mark 33 dual purpose gun director, were no more than geared to the needs of modern warfare. Heavier guns and torpedo-tube mounts had to be kept bearing on faster-moving air and surface targets, and the old handwheel system was simply no longer adequate except as an emergency back-up. Efforts had been made to include enough ruggedness in the new gear, and manual operation was still available in case of power failure. This, the designers felt, was a reasonable compromise between military necessity and the demand for across-the-board reliability and redundancy.

The adoption of the 5-inch/38 gun for the new destroyers had been preceded by a good bit of study and debate. The old 4-inch/50 used in the flushdeckers fired fixed ammunition, quick-loading and reasonably easy for one man to handle, and requiring fewer ammunition handlers per gun. Fixed rounds, though, were limited by the maximum weight of a complete round which could be handled without going to some sort of fully-mechanical loading mechanism. Such a thing was years away. Designers and most officers wanted a heavier gun than the 4-inch, comparable to new foreign ordnance, with a higher initial velocity for a suitably flat trajectory. These *desiderata* made semi-fixed ammunition, with projectile and cartridge case handled separately, acceptable. When the new

gun, evolved from the semi-automatic fixed-ammunition 5-inch/25 AA gun, was provided with a troughlike loading tray in which projectile and cartridge case were laid and power-rammed into the chamber, a satisfactorily high rate of fire could be obtained. The gun mounts installed in the *Farragut* class weighed 13.06 to 14.18 tons apiece — heavier than the 5-inch/51 or 5-inch/25, and about three times

the weight of the old 4-inch/50 — but were judged militarily worthwhile, and, as things worked out, were to set the American destroyer on its way to a worthwhile role in fleet air-defense. The 5-inch/38, while ballistically inferior to the 5-inch/51 for surface fire, was better than the 5-inch/25 in this respect and fired a comparable projectile at a comparable rate. Its projectile weighed more than half as

Gun	Type	Initial Velocity (ft-sec)[1]	Range (yds)[2]	Time of Flight (secs)	Maximum Ordinate (ft)[3]	Projectile Weight (lbs)	Weight of Gun and Mount (lbs)[4]
4-in/50	SP	2,900	10,000	19.71	1,630	33	10,140–10,470
			14,000	33.50	4,545		
5-in/25	DP	2,200	10,000	26.10	2,955	50	20,200–20,240
			14,000	46.58	9,400		
5-in/38	DP	2,600	10,000	20.81	1,825	55.18	29,260–30,140
			14,000	35.81	5,645		
5-in/51	SP	3,150	10,000	17.00	1,200	50	22,400–24,600
			14,000	29.16	3,717		

[1] Service charge.
[2] Not maximum ranges, but selected for comparison.
[3] Highest point of trajectory in feet above earth's surface.
[4] Representative weights of *open* mounts.

MacDonough on 1 September 1943, with 20 mm gun tubs forward of her bridge. She has an SG radar with an elongated later-model SC above it; the early SC was something of a disappointment in service and later versions attempted to remedy its deficiencies. The basic radar pattern for wartime destroyers — air search, surface search, and 5-inch fire control — remained the same until 1945 when blind-firing radars for 40 mm guns and height-finding equipments for radar picket ships began to appear.

much again as that of the 4-inch/50, and its velocity, time of flight, and trajectory were little inferior. It had the AA capability that both the 4-inch/50 and 5-inch/51 lacked, and better AA performance than the 5-inch/25.

A weak spot in the original 5-inch/38 system was its thyratron drive, in which large gas-filled tubes amplified the signals received from the gun director to move the gun in train and elevation and keep it on target. Thyratron tubes were fragile, vulnerable to shock and vibration; reports of gunnery practices fired during the 1930s include warnings of the need to keep spare tubes on hand, protected from the shock of the ship's own guns. With the 5-inch battery so dependent on its power drive to function at its designed effectiveness, something more sturdy and dependable was needed. Electric-hydraulic power drives were used in the subsequent *Porter* class; the *Mahan* class reverted to thyraton, but all later destroyers from *Gridley* on had electric-hydraulic gun mounts.

Farragut and *Dewey* conducted experimental firings early in 1935 as part of a comprehensive series of service tests designed to identify difficulties. These gunnery tests indicated that full gun crews could maintain a rate of 14 shots per gun per minute using ready-service projectiles. 'These tests, and Proving Ground data, indicate that the 5"/38 caliber gun is one of the most accurate weapons we have yet built. The battery of these guns, mounted as it is on a hull of excellent sea-keeping qualities, makes possible a volume of fire, an accuracy of fire, and an effective range far in excess of the gun power which has in the past been ascribed to destroyers.'[4] Surface firings were carried out at ranges of 6,330 to 16,141 yards. AA shoots were fired at altitudes of 3,000 to 9,000 feet, but at the unrealistic (even for 1935) target speeds of 70 to 75 knots. The Mark 33 and 5-inch/38 combination was simply not being tested under warlike conditions. This would, eventually, be taken care of under somewhat different circumstances.

Early inclining experiments indicated that damaged stability for these ships, at the 'minimum safe operating displacement' of 1,650 tons, was better than the intact stability of the *Clemson* (DD-186) class, the last group of flushdeckers. Commanding officers of the new ships were cautioned to pay attention to the distribution of fuel oil in the tanks, but were told that water ballasting of fuel tanks was not necessary.

Excessive propeller vibration was encountered by *Farragut*. *Dewey* had a different propeller design, and on her trials was pronounced 'exceptionally free of vibration'. When the same screws were retro-fitted in *Farragut*, the trouble ceased. Engine-room ventilation, something which had plagued designers for decades, was improved after early steaming showed its inadequacy.

The first ships of the class were delivered without depth-charge tracks to save weight. The forces afloat objected, citing the need for peacetime practice and experimentation. During 1935 this decision was reversed, and two tracks were ordered to be fitted to each ship. Track extensions were ordered, but only for the sake of having them available in case of emergency. The comment was made that there would be no question of weight limits if the restrictions of the London Treaty were removed, but the physical question of stability would remain. 'On account of the design characteristics and the refinements of design, there is no margin either of stability or strength that could be sacrificed except as a war time measure.' Later experience was to prove that even the pressure of war could not justify any lack of regard for stability.

Here arose a problem which was to recur. Records indicate that destroyer designers took the London Treaty's limits seriously. Neither in Washington nor in the fleet does there appear any sentiment in favor of slipping any excess displacement by 'on the sly'. But, in staying within Treaty obligations, designers and builders shaved so close to the 1,500-ton or 1,850-ton limitations that virtually no margin — room for growth — was provided. This presented an early problem when the question of depth charges arose. It was to cause further headaches as the stability of finished ships was compared to design calculations. It would complicate things yet again when such unthought-of items as radar and greatly-increased AA armament became part of the outfit of the well-dressed destroyer.

5

First of the 'Leaders': the Porter Class

The greatest fallacy in ship-design is to build ships to counter specific opponents. It had been fallacious in the Napoleonic Wars and it was equally fallacious a century later, for the designed opponents have little likelihood of meeting in battle. The answer is a concentration of lesser ships, just as in 1939 the answer to the *Graf Spee* was not another pocket battleship but three inferior cruisers.

Antony Preston, 'The End of the Victorian Navy.' *The Mariner's Mirror*, LX (November 1974), 377

As we have seen, various 'destroyer-leader' concepts had been toyed with since World War I, apparently stemming from observation of the Royal Navy's flotilla leaders. Five such ships, recommended by the General Board for the Fiscal 1921 program, would have been World War II-size 2,200-tonners with extensive (for their day) radio and radio-telephone plants. The US Navy's lack of light cruisers was reflected in their proposed armament of high-velocity 5-inch/51 guns, and the command and control mission of the ships was underscored when the General Board directed that they carry a 'suitable airplane' for scouting and observation, if such could be developed. Other schemes were investigated, but the same dollar shortage which inhibited construction of conventional destroyers — or, even, improvement of existing ones — also made thought of 'leader' construction out of the question.

Theoretical discussion continued. In the earlier days of the destroyer force, a division commander was simply the senior commanding officer; besides running his own ship, he had to assume tactical and administrative responsibility for up to six ships, with no division staff to assist him. By the mid-1920s division commanders were relieved of individual ship command. Destroyer Squadrons (DesRons), instead of being directed by the senior Division commander as before, also had their own commander.

The question of command facilities remained. Division and Squadron commanders had to exercise command from destroyers, not the roomiest ships under any circumstances. No provision was made for such things as a flag plot. What was needed, some officers thought, was a ship along the lines of the British flotilla leader; able to accommodate a unit commander and his staff, and tactically capable of maneuvering with conventional destroyers and leading torpedo attacks.

In those pre-radar days, information came in by direct observation and by radio. Large optical rangefinders provided reasonably accurate ranges to one's own forces and to the enemy. A running plot of the situation gave the commander the picture he needed for timely decisions. All this added up to weight and space, both at a premium in the existing flushdeckers. 'Destroyer flagships' were widely advocated; the examples of Britain, France and Italy, all of which had or were building large destroyers in some numbers, were cited. So were Japan's *Tenryu* class light cruisers. Reference was even occasionally made to the 'division boats' of the Imperial German Navy, built as early as the 1890s as flagships for a division of seven *Torpedobooten*.

When discussion of leader construction was resumed in 1928, the Director of War Plans in the Office of the Chief of Naval Operations advocated adoption of a ship armed with a more powerful 5-inch gun than the existing 5-inch/25. This gun's high trajectory limited its surface effectiveness to just 5,000

yards, not much of a distance at high destroyer speeds. The continuing lack of light cruisers to 'run interference' for the destroyer squadrons led War Plans to propose using a squadron of heavy destroyers to clear the way with gunfire for a torpedo attack. The Bureau of Ordnance felt that 'the destroyer leader should have more effective gun-fire in heavy weather than the destroyer ... based on the fact that foreign vessels of the same type are provided with 4.7-inch guns and are of sufficient tonnage to give a fairly good gun platform in rough weather. It has been the experience of all of us, in weather that is quite usual at sea, that ... destroyer guns cannot be operated. Under those conditions a vessel with better freeboard and better gun platform could attack with impunity any number of destroyers. It seems ... wise to consider the necessity of furnishing good gun platforms for our destroyer leaders.'[1] (The experience cited here was gained in flushdeckers and their predecessors.) At this point insufficient cruiser strength made many officers look to the heavily-armed large destroyer as an appropriate counter to a potential enemy's big torpedo craft. A 2,000-ton ship, with a good sea speed, would be a 'very much better gun platform' than the existing flushdeckers. Other officers pointed out that destroyer types were still basically 'a primary means of firing torpedoes'. The principal reason, as most seemed to see it, for going to a larger leader type was to produce a more seaworthy ship with adequate accommodations for a squadron commander and his staff, with the plotting and communications facilities needed for tactical control. Torpedo armament took second place to gun fire-power in leader concepts, as the lack of cruisers dictated. Leader characteristics, as framed in May 1928, provided the maximum surface gunfire capability compatible with what was considered reasonable torpedo armament and, after the London Treaty, with a 1,850-ton standard displacement. This concept, developed under the General Board's recommendations of September 1927, began with four single purpose 5-inch guns, at least six AA machine guns, and twelve tubes. Discussion continued through the next two years, and the desired characteristics were gradually hammered out. The gun armament of the hypothetical leader was increased to six, preferably dual-purpose, 5-inchers and the steaming radius was also increased. In August 1930, the Commander in Chief, United States Fleet, strongly recommended development of a destroyer leader.

A conference of officers, held at the Naval War College in Newport, Rhode Island, on 10 November 1930, all but unanimously concluded that 'a specially designed destroyer

Top
The *Farragut*s were followed by the *Porter* (DD-356) class. Designed and built as squadron leaders, they had to depend on the ships around them for long-range AA protection since their 5-inch twin mounts were single-purpose. Armament for this class was discussed at length before the final design was approved, and planners opted for a heavy surface-gunfire capability with the conventional fleet battle in mind, the final decision being influenced by the lack of cruisers to run interference for attacking destroyer squadrons. To get eight guns into a London Treaty displacement of 1,850 tons, a single-purpose capability had to be accepted.

Above
With her four twin gun mounts arranged 2-A-2, and controlled by two elevated directors, *Porter* depended for her air-defense on two .50-caliber guns and the centerline 1.1-inch quadruple AA gun mounts seen forward and aft. These early 1.1-inch installations were not director-controlled, which made them less effective than they might have been. Prewar practices with the .50-caliber machine gun in American warships tended to demonstrate their uselessness as close-in weapons.

22

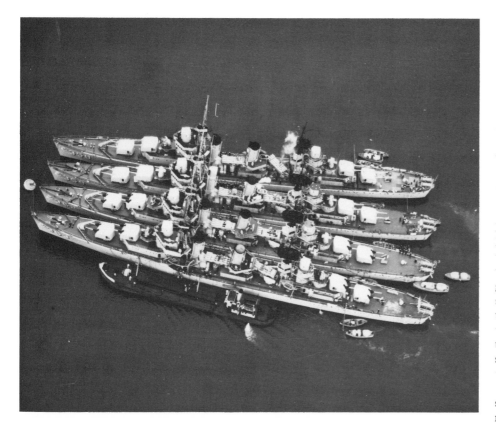

An unusual view of four *Porters* — from top to bottom, *McDougal* (DD-358), *Winslow* (DD-359), *Moffett* (DD-362), and *Balch* (DD-363) — moored to a buoy at San Diego early in 1938. Topside detail, as well as gun and torpedo-tube arrangement, is clearly visible. 1.1-inch AA mounts are carried forward and aft; .50-caliber guns are mounted on the platform around the after stack. *Winslow's* forward stack, cowled back 90 degrees in the hope of deflecting stack gases from the bridge, is unique among the ships of this class.

Opposite
The *Porter* class *Clark* (DD-361) refueling in the Pacific, 1940, showing details of the massive superstructure borne by this class. The coffin-like horizontal objects on the main deck just below the after gun director are aluminum lockers for spare torpedoes. The *Porters* carried two such lockers on each side of the after-deckhouse, and were the only American destroyers of this period to carry reload torpedoes. As the photograph makes clear, this was hardly the kind of rapid-reloading arrangement found in wartime Japanese destroyers. (US Navy, courtesy Robert J. Cressman collection.)

leader for each destroyer squadron is essential if destroyer squadrons are to operate efficiently and effectively in *any* of the many kinds of operations destroyers are used for in war'. One of the participants, Lieutenant Commander Andrew Mack, drew on his experience in a destroyer flagship and on his extended War College study of destroyer attack methods to point out that: 'much has been done in the past five or more years to develop a destroyer attack doctrine which will best enable the combined efforts of the destroyers of our fleet to inflict the greatest . . . damage upon the enemy in . . . action. The methods of massed attack which have been developed are excellent if there is coordination in the attack between the several squadrons. The attacking squadrons arrive in different sectors about the enemy battle line at such times, and fire in such manner, as to cover all possible maneuvers of the enemy.'

Such large-scale coordinated attacks succeeded in peacetime maneuvers because there was no opposition from enemy cruiser-destroyer forces. In war, destroyer attacks would meet resistance which would very likely delay or deflect some of the attackers, or even prevent them from getting into firing position. Any attack plan would necessarily have to be flexible, allowing each squadron commander the maximum degree of initiative in directing his attack. The pace of destroyer combat made the best possible observation and plotting facilities a *sine qua non* for the operational commander. War games demonstrated that attack plans for light forces seldom worked as calculated, and that the actual form of the attack was usually determined by the attack commander at or near the moment of deployment. Better command facilities, Mack felt, would be conducive to more flexible attack doctrine.

A consensus of opinion developed during General Board hearings in November 1930, to the effect that the 'leader' type was not essential and that a large destroyer would be preferable so that a 'heavy destroyer squadron' might be created. Once more, the paucity of light cruisers was asserting itself. The Board believed that, under Treaty limits, maximum offensive power had to be provided in any 1,850-ton destroyers that might be built. To sacrifice hitting power for command facilities, it thought, was not justified.

The Board and the technical Bureaus proceeded with their study, but not until May 1932 did the General Board sent recommended 1,850-tonner characteristics to the Secretary of the Navy for approval.

The Bureau of Construction and Repair had drawn up three schemes. One was a 5-gun leader with flag accommodations. The other two were large-destroyer types with uptakes trunked into a single stack to make room for guns and torpedoes. The first of these had six single gun mounts in a 3-A-3 arrangement; the other had two singles and two twins. All three sketches had two quadruple centerline torpedo tubes. Preliminary outlines had shown various combinations of single and twin mounts or single and dual-purpose guns.

The General Board selected the 3-A-3 scheme for what the Board considered its maximum practical hitting power, and development of plans and specifications began. As design work proceeded, Captain A. J. Chantry, the Design Officer in the Bureau of Construction and Repair, felt that the design's offensive capability would be significantly increased if four twin 5-inch single-purpose gun mounts could be substituted for the six singles originally specified. Machine guns of 1.1-inch and .50 caliber would be depended upon for antiaircraft defense. The elimination of protective plating over magazines, steering gear and wheelhouse, as well as other savings in hull and superstructure weights, would keep the standard displacement within the London Treaty limit. Both Ordnance and Construction and Repair felt the plan workable, and the final design was developed to show eight single-purpose 5-inch/38-caliber guns in four twin gunhouses. The Chief of Naval Operations, in March 1933, recommended the new design to the Secretary of the Navy. After a hearing, the General Board endorsed Chantry's concept. At least eight 5-inch guns, with eight tubes and 'over 35 knots' were to be included, with two 1.1-inch quad AA mounts and two .50-caliber AA machine guns.

Early provision was made for ballistic plating over the wheel-house, magazines, machinery spaces and steering gear. In the final design, in line with Chantry's recommendations, only half-inch STS protection on the main deck over the boilers and engines was retained. Hulls were basically similar in design to that of *Farragut*, though greater use

Above, left, and opposite top
Porter (DD-356) in November 1941. The conspicuous tophamper which characterized this class has been removed. *Porter* retains a 1.1-inch AA mount forward, with .50-caliber guns in tubs amidships. Her boxy single-purpose gun director has a Type FC surface-fire. radar, later redesignated Mark 3. The heavy 5-inch twins of the prewar 'leader' classes gave them a powerful appearance and would undoubtedly have shown their value in a conventional engagement.

Opposite center
Moffett (DD-362) on 26 March 1944, with her original 5-inch battery. She has two 20 mm guns forward, two more on an after-stack platform, and another two abaft the mainmast with a pair of 40 mm twins. Since *Moffett* was assigned to the Atlantic, her close-in AA armament has not been brought to Pacific proportions.

Opposite bottom
Clark (DD-361) off Panama, 26 May 1943; her third 5-inch mount has been replaced by a 40 mm mount.

was made of welding. Provision was made for a 'practically constant' metacentric height by allowing certain fuel tanks to be flooded as soon as expenditure of oil brought displacement below normal; considering the amount of topweight these ships were to carry, this was a virtual necessity.

The original construction program for Fiscal 1934 funded only four of these ships. Franklin D. Roosevelt assumed the Presidency in March 1933, and on 16 June of that year the depression-relief National Industrial Recovery Act (NIRA) was enacted. Roosevelt does not seem to have been a naval expansionist. He was, however, persuaded that an increase in naval shipbuilding would be quickly effective in alleviating unemployment. On the same day that the NIRA was signed F. D. R. set his signature to an executive order allotting $238 million for construction of ships within London Treaty limits.

Selfridge (DD-357) as modernized, April 1944. She retains her eight tubes and mounts 20 mm guns amidships, a quad 40 mm forward, and two 40 mm twins aft. This refit, though expensive, gave these seaworthy, long-legged ships an AA capability fit for war service. Compare *Selfridge* with the further modification given to *Phelps* (DD-360).

This money was applied to the aircraft carriers *Yorktown* and *Enterprise*, plus four cruisers, two seagoing gun-boats, and four submarines. It also permitted the 1934 destroyer program to be increased by four more 1,850-ton leaders, and sixteen 1,500-tonners which would become the *Mahan* class (of course, these were 1933 dollars!).

Bids for the first four destroyer leaders were invited in May 1933, with the circular calling for a trial speed in excess of 35 knots with a radius of no less than 7,500 miles at 15 knots based on 95% of fuel-tank capacity. (To allow room for expansion, oil fuel loadings were calculated at 95% of tank capacities.) The additional NIRA money permitted the new

group of large destroyers to be expanded to eight, and contracts for all of them were signed on 3 August 1933.

When ships of this type were first considered during and after World War I, they were referred to as destroyer leaders. In July 1920, the Secretary of the Navy established a system of standard ship-type designations, using letter symbols to specify types. In an evolved form, this system is still in use today within the US Navy. Under the general type category of destroyers the designation Destroyer Leader (DL) was set up. In later discussions, big destroyers were variously referred to as destroyer leaders or as 'large' or 'heavy' destroyers, indicating a divergence of

Phelps (DD-360) at New York in August 1945 after AA modernization. She has a new bridge, suggesting that used in some destroyer escorts, and a Mark 37 director to control her new 5-inch dual-purpose battery. She mounts a 40 mm quad forward and two aft, with a pair of twins amidships.

opinion among officers about the role of the 1,850-tonner. Now that construction of the type was a serious possibility, the Secretary of the Navy decided, in April 1933, that no official distinction would be made and that the new ships were to be classified simply as destroyers (DD). They thus became the DD-356 class (DD-356 through -363), and the name *Porter* was given to the lead ship of the class. Regardless of their formal designation, the *Porter* class were used as leaders in the pre-war fleet. By 1939 each of the Battle Force's eight destroyer squadrons would be led by a 1,850-tonner.

In their hull and machinery the eight *Porter*s were basically similar in concept to the *Farragut* class except for size. Their gun battery reflected their purpose; as squadron flagships, they were expected to make up for the lack of light cruisers by clearing the way for attacking destroyer divisions in a fleet action and by backing them up in battleline defense with gunfire. The twin 5-inch/38 mounts introduced in this class were single purpose, incapable of high-angle AA fire. At the time, weight limitations made this mandatory. A satisfactory dual purpose twin mount — not yet even designed — would have dictated a ship far heavier than the London Treaty would allow if the desired gun firepower was to be obtained. Since the *Porter*s were to be used with squadrons of destroyers

armed with 5-inch dual-purpose guns, and were to have what designers pronounced a 'very efficient' close-in AA battery — as we have noted, two quad 1.1-inch and two .50-calibers — a single-purpose 5-inch armament was judged acceptable.

Impressive-looking ships with a cruiser-like appearance, the *Porter* class mounted their two quadruple torpedo tubes on the centerline, as in the *Farragut*s. Stowage for four reload torpedoes was provided in aluminum lockers aft on the main deck, but quick-reload gear was absent. The value of these spare torpedoes in an open-sea fleet action would have been dubious, to say the least.

The *Porter* class was unique among American destroyers in having two single-purpose gun directors for their 5-inch batteries. This allowed more resiliency in the face of battle damage and permitted the ships to engage two targets simultaneously under director control, again emphasizing the tactical importance attached to their gunfire capability. As with the *Farragut* class, construction weights were so closely calculated that the approved characteristics did not include permanently-installed depth-charge equipment. The Bureau of Ordnance recommended their installation; Construction and Repair indicated that enough of a margin of weight would be left when the ships were completed to permit inclusion of the tracks with a limited number of charges.

The Chief of Naval Operations concurred, recommending that depth charge tracks be provided for all new destroyers. The acting Secretary of the Navy approved and on 22 March 1934 he ordered BuOrd to design and manufacture tracks and full wartime depth-charge allowances 'as soon as practicable' for all 1,500 and 1,850-ton ships.

The original preliminary design sketch for the *Porter* class showed three boiler rooms and two engine rooms. The accepted contractor proposal substituted two boiler rooms, both — as was customary at this time — arranged forward of the two engine rooms. Two diesel generators, one each forward and aft, were prescribed for emergency use, principally for the 5-inch mounts' unusual power demands.

The eight *Porter*s went into commission between February 1936 and February 1937. A proposal to remove the after gun director was aired in October 1936, but it was never carried out. Weight was not thought critical in these ships at the time, and lessening top-weight would still not make it possible to add additional torpedo tubes as had been done by this time in the design for the later *Somers* (DD-381) class of 1,850-tonners. Bridge structures were found to create serious eddies at high speeds, and early experience with the *Porter*s contributed to the design of the streamlined bridges fitted to the *Sims* (DD-409) and later classes.

6

New Construction Continues

It is a curious paradox that the more colossal we build our ships the finer the measurements we must make to have them work.

Editorial, *Sea Power* magazine (June 1921)

Between 1937 and 1940 the *Farragut* and *Porter* classes were followed into the fleet by another fifty-two 1,500-tonners and five 1,850-ton leaders. These ships followed the broad pattern set by the first two classes. The Fiscal 1934 program, expanded by the funds provided by President Roosevelt under the NIRA in 1933, included sixteen ships of the *Mahan* (DD-364) class.

Fifteen *Mahans* went into commission in 1936 with the last ship following in 1937. As originally designed, they would have essentially duplicated the *Farraguts*. As constructed, they followed the pattern of the slender looking, raised-forecastle two-stacker but with twelve torpedo tubes. Contracts were awarded to three bidders for the first six ships. Since all were to be identical, one of the

builders would typically have had to develop the design and prepare the working drawings for the class. But the conditions under which the ships were designed were difficult; designers and draftsmen were scarce after the long post-World War I building holiday and none of the three shipbuilding firms the Navy had chosen to construct the ships had what the Navy considered an inhouse design organization adequate to the demands of the new destroyer concept. As a result, the New York-based firm of Gibbs and Cox was called upon. Gibbs and Cox had designed passenger ships for the Grace Line, these incorporating advanced engineering plants, and it was decided to design the new DD-364 class around the most modern machinery available. Their engineering plant would clearly be an experi-

ment, but the Navy felt it could not go on building modern destroyers with what was becoming obsolescent steam engineering.

As the engineers at Gibbs and Cox neared the completion of their design task, it was evident that the new ships would represent a considerable advance in propulsion machinery. Their General Electric turbines would turn at a much higher speed than in previous ships (high-pressure turbine speed in *Mahan* would be 5,850 rpm as opposed to 3,460 rpm in the earlier *Farragut*) and could, thus, be more compact. Double reduction gears and 700-degree boilers with economizers rounded out the engineering plant that some critics felt would be overly complex, too crowded for the space allowed, and, thus, difficult to maintain. In service, however, the *Mahans* proved no

Similar in silhouette to the *Porters*, the *Mahan* (DD-364) class were improved *Farraguts* with the midship 5-inch gun moved to the top of the after deckhouse. One quadruple torpedo tube is on the centerline between the stacks, with two more in main-deck waist positions abaft the second stack. *Flusser* (DD-368) is seen here with two .50-caliber guns on an elevated platform forward of the bridge and two more on the after-deckhouse. Like the *Farragut* class, these ships have a single Mark 33 dual-purpose director. The tripod foremast, with a pole mainmast just aft of the second smoke-pipe, is characteristic of this class as built. Laid down during the Depression to provide employment, the *Mahan* class embodied the most modern engineering plant available for service use at the time.

disappointment and were later said to have 'the most rugged and reliable of any main drive installation ever installed in the Navy up to that time.'[1] But the controversy stirred by the design concepts embodied in *Mahan* and her sisters did not stop with the engineering plant.

The original design for the *Mahan* class allowed hull stresses that were higher than those called for in the *Farragut* or *Porter* classes. This was challenged; even if their hull girders did not fail, the new ships would be at a disadvantage when driving into head seas. Since increased propulsive power was being designed into them, it seemed only logical to keep stresses lower than in *Farragut*. In designing the *Farragut* class, it had been necessary to accept higher girder stresses than had been permitted for the flushdeckers in order to provide about 28 per cent better freeboard than in the older ships. Further increases in hull stress were, at least in some circles, thought dangerous.

The Bureau of Construction and Repair accepted what one civilian design engineer called 'very high stresses' to obtain four additional torpedo tubes and an expected smooth-water increase of three or four knots. This, he felt, was 'not suited to the character of service expected of these destroyers', and the added horsepower 'would be valueless a large part of the time should the hull deflect objectionably or vibrate badly when driven at reasonably high speed in moderately rough water'. Reinforcement of the ships' longitudinal framing was advised, the weight required for the reinforcement being subtracted from the allowed weight margin to stay within the 1,500-ton treaty limit. Should the ships prove overweight as completed, triple tubes could be substituted for the two wing four-tube mounts.[2] Another designer suggested deletion of one 5-inch gun with its ammunition, a saving of more than seventeen tons.[3]

Top
Case (DD-370) at Boston, 9 November 1937.

Center
A quartering view of *Tucker* (DD-374). Ships of these classes were built with, or developed, numerous minor differences in appearance. The 26-foot motor whaleboats carried to each side of Mount 53 had to be moved out of the way before that gun could be used.

The ingenuity of the 'old' destroyer Navy was nothing to be underestimated. While on air-sea rescue station east of Wake Island during fleet exercises in June 1940, *Tucker* (DD-374) stretched her fuel supply by rigging sails. Her home-made foresail and mainsail moved her at an estimated 3.4 knots, letting her maintain steerageway as she 'loitered' on station for several days.

Above
Conyngham (DD-371) shows her reduced silhouette on 10 July 1942. Like other *Mahan* class ships, she has been lightened to make room for AA armament. 20 mm guns are installed amidships, on the after-deckhouse, and on a platform built atop the 5-inch gun crew weather shelter forward of the bridge. *Conyngham*'s outline suggests that of the *Porter* class *Clark* except for the disposition of her guns and torpedoes. Ship identification could be a problem unless lookouts were well acquainted with the idiosyncrasies of the various classes.

Conyngham at pierside; the high forecastle bulwark, elevated twin AA-gun platform abaft Mount 52, and windshield topping the pilot house are features of the wartime *Mahan* class.

Shaw (DD-373), ready for service again on 2 July 1942 after having her bow blown off at Pearl Harbor. This and the next two photographs offer an excellent look at a war-modified *Mahan*.

Top
Another view of *Shaw* on 2 July 1942. A quadruple
1.1-inch AA mount is on the after-deckhouse; the device
next to the forward torpedo tube is a machine used in
5-inch loading drills.

Center
Shaw grounded off New Caledonia in January 1943, but
was freed and completed the war. Here she offloads
material into a barge to lighten ship. She has had her
1.1-inch quad replaced by a twin 40 mm mount; the
general wartime destroyer AA plan used 1.1-inch guns as
expedients until sufficient 40 mm guns became available
to replace them.

Bottom right and opposite top
Cassin (DD-372) and *Downes* (DD-375) were sunk in
drydock at Pearl Harbor. Some components from the
wrecks were salvaged, and new ships were built to the
basic *Mahan* class design with the original names and
hull numbers. Compare these views of *Cassin* with other
ships of the class; note such differences as the centerline
torpedo battery and the new bridge with its Mark 37 gun
director.

32

Center
Jouett on 26 March 1945 after her AA modernization. Like the converted *Porter*s, *Jouett* retains eight torpedo tubes but her narrower stability reserve has given her a twin 40 mm mount forward instead of the 40 mm quad installed in the *Porter* class.

Bottom left and bottom right
Conyngham on 22 May 1944, highlighting details of her configuration. She now has two 40 mm twins and directors abaft her tubes, with three 20 mm guns forward of the bridge in a high-low arrangement seen in many destroyers at the time. Two K-guns, with depth-charge stowage racks, appear below the overhang of the after deckhouse. Note the usual shipyard clutter in the destroyer undergoing refit alongside *Conyngham*.

7

More Experimentation

An eighteen-hundred-ton destroyer making thirty knots in rough water behaves in a way to be expected of a ship of her design. The proportion of her length to her breadth is very like the proportions of a lead pencil, and one has only to float a lead pencil in a bathtub and then agitate the water to form a good idea of the antics a destroyer performs in a storm. The higher a gun is mounted above the water's edge, the more efficiently it can be served, so that a destroyer's guns are mounted just as high as is consistent with stability; and on her deck are mounted four ponderous torpedo tubes; and the fire-control system also demands the loftiest position possible. So that a destroyer is liable to roll just as far as is consistent with the limits of safety; she differs from the pencil in that the pencil rolls completely over and over, while the destroyer only very nearly does.

C. S. Forester, *Gold From Crete* (Boston, 1970)

The program for Fiscal 1935 included two 1,850-ton ships and twelve 1,500-tonners. These vessels were planned as slightly modified repeats of the *Porter* and *Mahan* classes. DD-381 and -383 were to be modestly altered *Porters* while DD-380, -382, and -384 to -393 were drawn as improved *Mahans* with lighter tophamper and completely enclosed forward 5-inch gun mounts with integral ammunition hoists incorporating automatic fuze setters. The only 1935 destroyers actually built to their original designs were two ships of the *Dunlap* (DD-384) class, constructed from the *Mahan*-derived plan. Two of the remaining 1,500-tonners (DD-380 and DD-382) were built by Bethlehem Steel at its Quincy, Massachusetts, yard. Bethlehem proposed a new design, with four 5-inch guns instead of five and sixteen torpedo tubes in four main-deck 'wing' mounts, two each to port and starboard. (These ships would come to be known as the *Gridley* class which included only *Gridley* and *Craven*.) Both of the boiler rooms were typically arranged forward of the two engine rooms as in all of the 'goldplaters' and the naval architects at Bethlehem began a brief trend in American destroyer silhouettes when they trunked the uptakes from both firerooms into a single fat stack. This was accepted as an

improvement since it freed valuable deck space. Detailed plans for another eight ships (DD-386–393), ordered from four Navy Yards, were drawn by the Bureau of Construction and Repair in general agreement with Bethlehem's concept but with a number of differences of detail. Propulsion plants resembled those of the *Farragut* and *Porter* classes, reflecting the differences of opinion prevalent in naval engineering circles about the merits of high pressure, high temperature steam and high-speed turbines.

Contemporary sources disagree on the class breakdown of the 1935 single-stack destroyers. Some refer to them all as the *Gridley* class, while others differentiate between the *Gridley* (the Bethlehem-designed DD-380 and 382) and *Bagley* (the Navy-developed DD-386–393) classes. The Navy took the latter course, and that is followed here. This was a bit more than academic hairsplitting, as seen when questions of wartime stability arose.

The two Fiscal 1935 1,850-tonners stimulated the controversy even further. The criticism leveled at the power plants of the *Mahan* class, as Admiral Bowen described it, 'was nothing compared to the storm which broke following the preliminary acceptance trials of the destroyer *Somers* (DD-381) in ... 1937.'

Somers' boiler plant is described[1] as having its origin in the early 1930s when the battleship *New Mexico* (BB-40) was extensively modernized and reboilered. *New Mexico*'s boilers included integral superheaters, with superheaters heated by the same combustion gases as the rest of the boiler. Thus, the amount of superheat varied with the boiler output; it could neither be predicted nor controlled. Working together, Babcock and Wilcox and Foster Wheeler developed a superheat-control boiler in which a dividing wall separated the superheater from the saturated-steam side; each portion of the boiler was heated by its own burners, and superheat could be readily and accurately controlled. The new boilers were also 'air-encased'; that is, they were closed off from the fireroom. This permitted boiler operation with ventilating hatches open, inflicting less heat on the boiler-room crew. These boilers were built into *Somers*, using 850-degree steam at 600 psi, along with General Electric turbines with double-reduction gears, developing 52,000 horsepower. Her boiler plant was operated at 40 per cent overload at Philadelphia Navy Yard before installation without damage. Thus, in emergency, three overloaded boilers could safely do the work of four at normal power; this was seen as a safety factor in case of battle damage. *Somers*' trials were successful. Her full-power speed was 38.5 knots, and her cruising radius was 21 per cent greater than *Porter*'s. Shortly before Pearl Harbor *Somers*' captain was to report that 'up to the present time *Somers*' performance has been about 12% better than expected.'[2]

Like their contemporaries, the *Somers* class — the two ships of 1935, plus three more (DD-394 through -396) authorized for Fiscal 1936 — were originally sketched as *Porters* with somewhat less topweight. As constructed they lacked the 'cruiser' look of the earlier 1,850 ton class. Much simpler in appearance than the *Porters*, *Somers* and her sisters had a pole foremast and mounted a single 5-inch gun director. Combining boiler uptakes into one stack made room on the centerline for three quadruple torpedo-tube mounts, giving the *Somers* class the heaviest torpedo broadside ever mounted in an American destroyer. (The 16-tube *Gridley* and *Benham* classes could fire only eight tubes in one direction. As far as 'throw weight' was concerned, contemporary Japanese destroyers were armed with the heavier Type 93 torpedo, the 24-inch *Long Lance*; one destroyer, *Shimakaze*, carried fifteen Type 93s in three quintuple centerline mounts.)

As in the *Porter* class, *Somers*' 5-inch battery consisted of four twin single-purpose gun mounts, with two quadruple 1.1-inch

automatic AA mounts. This reflected not only the continuing lack of light cruisers (good things were hoped for from the new '10,000-tonners' of the *Brooklyn* (CL-40) and *St Louis* (CL-49) classes, but only nine ships were in the building program and these would not go into commission until 1937–39), but the lack of a dual-purpose 5-inch twin mount that could be built, in what were thought adequate numbers, into a Treaty-sized hull. A 5-inch twin DP mount did not join the fleet until 1939, and then in the two *St Louis* class cruisers. To get even three of these mounts into a destroyer required a lighter mount, with a thinner gunhouse, and a bigger ship. Dual-purpose twins were not to make their appearance in the destroyer force until the completion of the first of the *Allen M. Sumner* (DD-692) class at the end of 1943.

Top
Dunlap and *Fanning* (DD 384-385) made up a two-ship class, the only ships actually built to the improved-*Mahan* design drawn for the twelve 1,500-ton destroyers (DD-380, 382, 384-393) of the 1935 program. These were the first American destroyers to have closed forward gunhouses instead of shields, with integral fuze setters in their projectile hoists. Their light pole foremast and absence of a mainmast help to distinguish the *Dunlap*s from the *Mahan*s as built.

Bottom
A well-known photograph of *Dunlap* 'making knots' on trials. The necessary emphasis on speed in destroyer designs made them less suitable for submarine-hunting than later wartime ships built for that particular purpose.

Right

Ten single-stacked ships of the 1935 program, built to the same general military characteristics, displayed two somewhat different profiles and are variously referred to as one or two classes. *Gridley* (DD-380) and *Craven* (DD-382) were built to detailed plans drawn up by Bethlehem. Their four 5-inch guns were arranged 2-A-2; four quad tubes were mounted amidships, two to each side on the main deck. The *Gridley* class had the same general forward superstructure arrangement used in destroyers of the 1930s through the *Benham* class. Ship's offices and senior officers' quarters are on the forecastle deck. Above this is the charthouse, surmounted by a windowed bridge with open wings. On top of the wheel-house is the Mark 33 gun director, with a signal searchlight and torpedo director mounted to either side. The cylindrical housing on the after torpedo tube protects the position from which both tubes on a side could be aimed and fired in local control.

Bottom

Like their ancestors of torpedo-boat days, the destroyer force of the inter-war years depended on the skill of a special breed of blue-water sailors. Lieutenant-Commander Arleigh Burke poses for a 'family portrait' with the crew of his new *Gridley* class *Mugford* (DD-389). It was in ships like these that Burke and many another destroyerman began to learn the lessons and formulate the ideas that would bear fruit only a few years later in a world war.

Top
Patterson (DD-392) in Puget Sound, *circa* 1937. The *Bagley* class shared the general dimensions and battery of the *Gridley*s. Boiler uptakes are more prominently trunked into the single smokepipe. The small midship structure, a torpedo work-shop and repair-party stowage space, holds the elevated searchlight platform carried on the after-deckhouse in the *Gridley* class.

Left
Mugford at sea; the generous glazing of the wheelhouse was intended to give protection from the weather while still providing the best possible visibility for helmsman and conning officer.

Top
Jouett (DD-396), one of five 1,850-ton 'leaders' of the *Somers* class commissioned in 1937-39. Like the *Porter* class, they were armed with eight single-purpose 5-inch/38s. In other respects they were very different. Three quadruple tubes could be carried on the centerline since boiler uptakes all led into a single stack. Lighter and less cluttered topside, *Somers* and her sisters had a simple pole foremast and one gun director. As in *Porter*, 1.1-inch AA mounts are carried forward and aft. The most advanced — and controversial — feature of their design is not visible. High-speed turbines of domestic design, powered by high-pressure, high-temperature steam from new boilers with superheat control, were strongly attacked. The new plants' defenders contended that they were simpler, more reliable, and more economical; *Somers'* machinery weighed 10 percent less than *Porter'*s.

Center
Another view of *Jouett*, emphasizing her twin 5-inch mounts. This heavy surface battery, combined with a strong torpedo armament, would have made this class useful in the kind of general fleet action widely thought likely during the years between the world wars. They would have been vulnerable to a concentrated aerial attack, against which their powerful gun batteries would have been of little use. Capable of a nominal 35 degree elevation compared to 85 degrees for other destroyer guns, they might have been of some value against torpedo planes although their director was designed solely for surface firing. 1,850-tonners were normally assigned to duty as squadron flagships, operating in company with two four-ship divisions of 1,500-ton destroyers armed with 5-inch dual-purpose guns.

Stability problems did not permit the wartime *Gridley* class to handle 40 mm guns. *McCall* (DD-400) here shows two Oerlikons forward, two amidships, and two on her after-deckhouse.

38

Warrington (DD-383), one of the first two *Somers* class ships built under the 1935 program; the remaining three were funded in Fiscal Year 1936. These 'leaders' presented a much more modern silhouette than did the toplofty *Porter*s. Warrington foundered in an Atlantic hurricane in 1944, the only one of her class lost in World War II.

The *Somers* class followed the same general armament progression as did the *Porter* class. Here *Davis* (DD-395), seen on 23 July 1943 at Charleston, still has her four single-purpose 5-inch mounts but has kept only eight of her original twelve tubes. 20 mm guns are mounted amidships and aft, and *Davis* has the now-customary destroyer radar installation. As in the *Porter* class her fire-control radar is the single-purpose Mark 3.

Somers (DD-381) at Charleston, 1 April 1944. Her configuration is comparable to that of *Davis*. The ships of the *Somers* class had a less topheavy appearance as built when compared to the earlier *Porter* class, but in practice the *Porter*s seem to have had a somewhat better margin of stability.

Top above
Jouett (DD-396), seen at Charleston on 20 April 1944, has had her high after 5-inch mount removed. A 40 mm AA mount replaces it; another 40 mm twin is offset to port abaft the stack, and a third is on the elevated centerline platform forward of the bridge which used to support a quadruple 1.1-inch mount. A low-slung silhouette and prominent, widely-separated, single stack combine with twin gunhouses to identify the *Somers* class.

Center left
An aerial view of *Warrington* (DD-383), 23 April 1943. She is rigged, in most respects, like *Jouett*. 20 mm guns can be seen forward with a 20 mm gun and a 40 mm twin abaft the stack and another 40 mm twin with three 20 mm guns aft.

Center right
Davis (DD-395) at Charleston, 18 November 1944. Like most of the *Porter* class, *Davis* has received a new dual-purpose 5-inch battery.

Ralph Talbot (DD-390), with a *Bagley* class sister alongside, at Mare Island on 11 April 1942. Details of bridge arrangement and layout of guns and tubes are of interest, as are the ships' closed-shield Mark 33 directors. Pairs of 20 mm guns are located forward, amidships, and aft. The prominently-trunked, flat-sided single stacks are identifying touches.

Jarvis (DD-393) on 8 May 1942, three months before her loss south of Guadalcanal. Though she lacks surface-search radar — the SG was introduced later in the year — she already has an SC, with an FD on her gun director. Like other 1,500-tonners, she has had an anchor removed to compensate for new equipment.

Opposite bottom
Fanning (DD-385) in April 1942, maneuvering at speed with *Balch* (DD-363) with *Benham* (DD-397) or *Ellet* (DD-398) in the background on the way toward Japan with the carrier *Hornet* to launch Lieutenant Colonel James Doolittle's B-25 bombers. Wartime modifications to the *Dunlap* class generally followed the pattern of the 'parent' *Mahan* class. Prewar doctrine called for the *Porter* and *Somers* class 'leaders' to operate with destroyers armed with dual-purpose 5-inch batteries, but this was of little avail under Pacific-war conditions. The four ships of the *Gridley* class did not undergo the degree of modernization given to their contemporaries; stability problems did not allow them to handle 40 mm guns. In this mid-war view *McCall* (DD-400) has two 20 mm guns forward, two more amidships, and another two on her after-deckhouse.

41

8

The Benhams

Our fleet is a seagoing force and our tactics must be devised around battle on the high seas. Our ships must be built in keeping with those tactics.

Brockholst Livingston, 'Types and Tactics', *United States Naval Institute Proceedings*, (March 1939)

The Fiscal 1936 program also funded twelve conventional destroyers and, early in 1935, the Secretary of the Navy asked the General Board to define their characteristics. The Board found itself in a quandary. While the standard displacement of the *Farragut* class, as built, was 1,365 tons — 135 tons under the 1,500-ton Treaty limit — this margin had been completely absorbed in the *Mahan* class by added power and torpedo tubes, plus hull improvements. As long as the 1,500-ton ceiling remained in effect, there was no room left. Trials of the *Farraguts* had revealed that considerably more men were needed to man the ship under battle conditions than had been calculated originally. How were these enlarged crews to be accommodated within Treaty limits? *Mahan*'s design allowed for 150 men. Trials showed that from 193 to 217 were required in *Farragut* depending on the number allowed to handle ammunition from the magazines. The *Mahan* class would require at least ten more. The available records show no evident disposition to cheat on the London Treaty's displacement ceiling.

The Board drafted a proposed set of characteristics calling for the same 16-tube torpedo battery designed into the *Gridley* class, and a speed of 38 knots on no more than 50,000 horsepower; its draft remarked that 'great care should be exercised, in stepping up power and speed, not to over-stress these features to a point where the balance of characteristics and design will be endangered' — this last aimed at the high-pressure steam designs of the Bureau of Engineering. Four, rather than five, 5-inch dual purpose guns with four .50-caliber guns were recommended, but the Board wrote that 'the anti-aircraft features of this type have been considerably over-stressed. The full development of anti-aircraft possibilities involves greatly increased weight, especially in providing extra personnel and their accom-

modations.... Therefore anti-aircraft activities, subordinate in importance to torpedo and broadside surface gun functions, but which require much [*sic*] personnel, must be restricted.'[1]

The Bureau of Construction and Repair thought that the Board's requirements could be met within 1,500 tons at a cost of 'more than normal crowding in crews' spaces and ... no additions to the crews' galley and messing facilities and sanitary spaces.'[2] This was based on a Bureau of Navigation estimate that ten officers and 175 men would be enough to steam the ship at General Quarters with all guns and torpedo tubes manned and handling rooms and hoists furnishing 'a constant supply of ammunition', but with no relief provided for any station.[3] Rough calculations within the Bureau showed that, if the four guns were made single purpose while horsepower was reduced to 44,000 (37 knots), a ship could be built that would be 68 tons short of the Treaty limit.[4]

On 19 March 1935 the General Board forwarded its recommendation to the Secretary of the Navy noting that, since the flushdeck destroyers had been designed, demands had been raised for increased gun and torpedo power; greater radius, stability, seaworthiness, and habitability; improved fire control; heavier AA fire; and increased speed. Such improvements required considerable increases in complements, hence in weight. To accommodate crews sufficiently large to operate the weapons and machinery provided for in the design characteristics, and yet remain within the Treaty displacement limit, the characteristics themselves would have to be changed, not only in the projected 1936 ships but also in earlier 1,500-tonners. The most reasonable reductions seemed to be in horsepower and battery. The Board repeated its opinion that the cost in weight and space of the dual-purpose feature of the 5-inch battery

had been 'very considerable', and recommended a reversion to single-purpose guns.

'Centerline tubes', the Board went on, 'especially of the height of that [*sic*] in the *Mahan* class (five feet higher than in the *Farragut* class and ... nine feet above the [main] deck), appear to have the definite disadvantages of ... possibility of failure of torpedoes to clear the ship's side on ejection, and ... inconvenience in handling torpedoes. For this reason and the further reason that sixteen as against twelve torpedoes appears to be a better armament for the destroyer type, the Board favors the installation of four wing tubes, two on each broadside. This arrangement involves the sacrifice of one 5-inch gun, a cost that the Board considers reasonable.'

The engineering plant in the *Mahan* class had represented a 67-ton increase over the *Farragut* class, and the Board did not think this worth the expected two additional knots it was to provide. The General Board then repeated its call for a four-gun, 16-tube, destroyer with about 44,000 horsepower for a speed of 37 knots. Space was to be reserved for reload torpedoes, and steaming radius was to be at least 6,500 miles at 12 knots.[5]

Looking at the Board's recommendations in the light of the entire current and proposed destroyer building program, the Chief of Naval Operations, undoubtably considering the very real possibility of serious delays, cost increases and contract entanglements, recommended that the existing *Farragut* and *Mahan* class ships then building be completed according to their original designs, but detail changes shown desirable by the tests of early *Farragut* class ships, including habitability improvement, should be incorporated. As far as the 1936 program was concerned, the general scheme of hull and machinery design already drawn should be followed, and dual-purpose 5-inch guns should be included (a surface-fire single gun mount had not even been designed). Future construction was to embody the General Board's recommended characteristics 'subject to such further consideration and revision as may be prescribed by the Secretary of the Navy'. On 2 April 1935, the Secretary of the Navy approved the final characteristics for the *Benham* (DD-397) class.

The *Benham*s were built on essentially the same hull lines as the *Gridley* class, with the same 5-inch and torpedo batteries and the same gun and torpedo control systems. The Bureau of Ordnance suggested that the two after 5-inch mounts be enclosed, but Construction and Repair thought the nine tons of added topweight too much. The original concept had the two funnels of the first goldplaters, but when the uptakes of the *Gridley* and *Somers* classes were combined into a single stack, this feature was extended to the *Benham* class as well. Besides saving center-line space, this was also calculated to reduce smoke interference with the bridge. 'The change from 2 stacks to one on the [DD] 397–408', an internal Bureau of Construction and Repair memo noted, 'was a matter of Bureau initiative and everybody liked it.'[6]

The first five ships (DD-397–401) of the 1936 program were ordered from private builders. Three of them (DD-397–399) were built to the *Benham* design. The other two (DD-400–401) were ordered from Bethlehem's San Francisco yard, and the Navy approved their construction to the plans drawn up by Bethlehem for *Gridley* and *Craven* (DD-380, 382). Seven more 1936 destroyers, ordered from five navy yards on 9 September 1935, were built on *Benham* lines. Many sources lump all twelve 1936 destroyers together as *Benham*-class, but the Navy more accurately classed the two Bethlehem ships with their 1935 twins as the third and fourth ships of the *Gridley* class.[7] On 28 December 1938 President Roosevelt complained about 'the fact that destroyers DD-402 to . . . DD-408 are taking from 42 to 44 months to build. . . . We all know, of course, that Navy Yards like to maintain a steady flow of employment and when a ship comes in for overhaul or repair they take men off new construction and put them back . . . when there is a slackness of other work. That is a natural attitude, but it is absolutely contrary to the best interests of the Navy. Navy Yards doing construction should be ordered — not requested — to put as many people to work on new ships as it is possible to use at any given time — two shifts or even three shifts where they are possible. They should be ordered to keep these people steadily on the job and not take them off for other Navy work. We are, all of us, being seriously criticized and it is time to get action.'[8] The Secretary assured the President that Navy Yards had been ordered to increase the work force involved in new construction, but that the long delay in completion of the last seven *Benham*s was a matter of design changes and delays in obtaining their machinery. 'It does not', he concluded, 'appear possible to anticipate the dates of completion of Destroyers 402–408 because of the delay already experienced in manufacture and delivery of their machinery.'[9] The ships were finally placed in commission during July–November, 1939.

Trial speeds for these late-1930s destroyers were high. The *Mahan* class was credited with speeds in excess of 39 knots, the *Gridley*s with 40. The *Benham*s were listed in classified official publications as doing 40 to 40.7 knots on trials,[10] while the heavier *Somers* class was slightly slower. Contemporary published

Lang (DD-399), one of twelve *Benham* class destroyers commissioned in 1939. Designed by the New York firm of Gibbs and Cox, they had high-speed turbines and double-reduction gearing. Generally similar in configuration to the *Gridley* class, their machinery was lighter and their cruising radius greater. The same 4-gun, 16-tube battery was mounted; only eight tubes could be fired to either side, although curved fire ahead or astern could be used. Two .50-caliber machine guns are forward of the bridge, with two more on the after deckhouse. All of these 'goldplaters' of the 1930s would have been susceptible to a well-managed air attack.

sources ascribed very high speeds to the *Benham* class; the 1939 edition of Fahey's *Ships and Aircraft of the US Fleet*[11] said that '*Benham* . . . broke all records for the trial course off Rockland, Maine — considerably bettering 40 knots'. When *McCall* (DD-400) arrived at Pearl Harbor shortly after her commissioning. *The Honolulu Star-Bulletin* of 8 September 1939 headlined its story '*McCall* Navy's Fastest; Unofficially 48 mph', and went on to cite the United Press as having reported *McCall*'s trial speed at 42 knots. The ship's commanding officer was quoted as saying that 'after our trial runs the San Francisco papers called us the fastest American ship. Now, I don't know what the records are; but you wouldn't be the first to say we are the fastest, if you want to say so.' A rather nice bit of side-stepping, if anyone chose to read it that way!

A report by the Navy's Board of Inspection and Survey bears out the raw figures, but puts them in a more realistic light. *Benham* is described as turning up 40.8 knots on her preliminary trials at 50,700 horsepower. A study of the trial results showed that a small reduction in speed would allow a large reduction in horsepower; 39 knots could be achieved for 44,300 shp, while 37 knots would only require 38,500. The Board concluded that these ships could make their trial speed only in good weather; at this top speed, 'except in the very best weather, the ordnance equipment could not be used on account of spray.' In 'average' weather, speed would have to be reduced to about 30 knots to employ the ship's battery; in foul weather, speed would have to be cut still further. 'Considering the wartime service of this class of vessel,' the Board felt that 'too big a price is being paid for speed. Other important mili-

tary characteristics have been sacrificed to obtain the last few knots in speed.' The Board recommended a ten per cent cut in speed for destroyers, 'thereby reducing this military feature slightly, but not below a speed which even then is not practicable under all weather conditions, weight and space are made available for improvement in all other military characteristics.' Its unanimous conclusion was that 'a 10% reduction in speed of destroyers with the consequent possible increase in all other military features along the lines stated above would produce a vessel of distinctly greater military value.'[12] The Chief of Naval Operations took issue with this, and the Secretary of the Navy backed him up by directing that 'there should be no reduction in the present maximum speeds of destroyers'.[13] In support of this, the Bureau of Engineering wrote that the essential unreality of trials was recognized and had to be taken into account in building destroyer machinery that would be able to produce good results under service conditions, and that in the classes subsequent to the *Benham*s more realistic displacement requirements were being written into building contracts. The Bureau could 'not stress too strongly the importance of providing reasonable margins in naval machinery; it is an essential war service requirement.'[14]

This view of *Benham* (DD-397) completing at Kearny, New Jersey, on New Year's Day of 1939, illustrates the general appearance of the class.

Trippe (DD-403), another ship of the *Benham* class. The wide, glassed-in bridges, their fronts angled back to either beam, were liked by the destroyer officers. They provided good visibility and ample weather protection, unlike the Spartan open platforms of earlier American destroyers and other warships.

Maury (DD-401) and *McCall* (DD-400) were built to details drawn up by Bethlehem Steel. Flat-sided stacks, and the absence of any midship deckhouse, distinguish these ships from the *Benham* class. Some contemporary works refer to the *Benham*s as the *McCall* class. *Maury* and *McCall*, with the earlier Bethlehem-designed *Gridley* and *Craven*, were plagued by stability problems throughout their service lives.

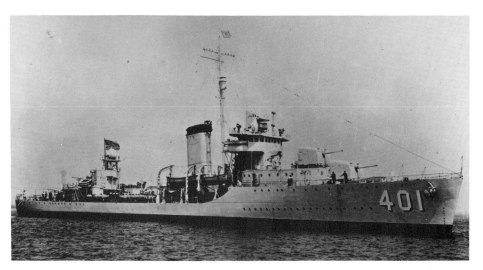

A stern view of *Ellet* (DD-398) at New York, 1939. The 1,500-ton destroyers of the 1930s give an impression, from some perspectives, of delicacy when compared with their bulkier descendants of the war years. To complete the effect of peacetime tranquility, a movie screen has been set up on *Ellet*'s fantail.

The bridge of a *Benham* class destroyer, *circa* 1941. Points of interest include the Mark 33 director with its rangefinder mounted on the face plate of the shield; tactical rangefinders still mounted to port and starboard; and shrouded .50-caliber guns, with ready-service ammunition boxes, on the deck below. (US Navy, courtesy Robert J. Cressman.)

A *Benham* class destroyer refuels from the carrier *Enterprise* (CV-6) in the Pacific, November 1941. Open-mount guns and main-deck torpedo tubes were, as can be seen here, vulnerable to frequent soaking even in moderate seas which, if it had no other effect, must have made proper maintenance a headache. (US Navy, courtesy Robert J. Cressman.)

Benham (DD-397), with *Balch* (DD-363) in the background, escorts the Doolittle strike force towards Japan, April 1942. She is already equipped with an SC air-search radar.

A variety of mottled camouflage patterns, such as this one seen on *Sterett* (DD-407), appear on many American warships in 1941–42. *Sterett* has the 4-gun 5-inch battery which became standard for most destroyer classes of the 1930s during the war; Mount 54, unlike that of *Benham* in the preceding photograph, is closed and Mount 53 wears an open-top version used in many late-third generation and early fourth-generation ships to save weight. *Sterett*'s short-range AA battery still consists of .50-caliber machine guns, and she has not yet received radar.

Lang (DD-399) on 26 October 1943. She has an improved version of the SC radar above her SG, and an FD antenna mounted low on the face of her Mark 33 director. 20 mm guns are forward and amidships, with a pair of 40 mm twins aft. *Lang*'s depth-charge tracks hold the standard 600-pound 'ash cans', but her K-guns have been provided with streamlined 300-pound Mark 9 charges with a faster sinking rate.

9

Development of the Sims Class

... the functions of the [destroyer] type ... must of necessity include: ability to attack with torpedoes, their primary weapon; screen the battle line against attack from ... destroyers, submarines, and airplanes; and offer a certain amount of support to the scouting line while, within the limitations of the type, assisting in the procurement of information.

Brockholst Livingston, 'Types and Tactics'

The *Sims* (DD-409) class, the last of the 'single-stackers', had its origin in a March 1935 request by the Chief of Naval Operations to the engineering Bureaus, asking them to take up a design for a 'new destroyer, more distinctly torpedo destroyer type' for possible construction in Fiscal 1937.[1] On 21 December 1935 a letter from CNO went to the forces afloat with an outline of the characteristics of existing destroyers, on hand or under construction, and asked for opinions. Addressees were told to keep in mind, not only the existing Treaty requirements, but what the effect might be if the naval treaties were not renewed. They were to remember that 'new destroyers are up to the treaty limit of 1500 tons; therefore, if any additional gear or equipment is recommended, a corresponding weight must be removed,' and that the 'matter of living space and habitability is a very serious one'.[2]

While the Fleet was considering its recommendations, the Bureau of Construction and Repair was drawing up preliminary designs. On 25 March 1936 it forwarded three schemes to CNO. Using the *Benham* class as its basis, BuCon aimed at strengthening the hull girder, enlarging the machinery spaces for easier maintenance, increasing crew space, reducing the silhouette, and streamlining the superstructure and gun mounts to reduce air resistance at high speeds and to cut down the eddying that had been criticized in earlier ships. This was to be done by reducing the size and the height of deckhouses, reducing fuel tankage to that necessary to attain the specified steaming radius of 6,500 miles at 12

knots, and providing a single pole mast as was already being done in the *Gridley* and later classes. The Bureau further proposed that contract trials of all new destroyers be 'based upon a displacement more nearly approaching their average displacement in service, and that trials of all new vessels be held only at that displacement.' The suggested trial displacement was to be equal to the estimated full-load weight, minus a third of the maximum fuel and reserve feed water, a reversion to the pre-Washington Treaty concept that the US Navy had called *normal* displacement.[3]

All three design schemes were based on the hull of the *Benham* class, with dual-purpose 5-inch/38s and quadruple torpedo-tube mounts. Scheme A was described as 'a refinement of DD-397-408, retaining the same armament, power and general topside arrangements.' Speed was increased by about 0.6 knot by reducing the radius to about 6,650 miles. Scheme E was a lightweight 1,400-tonner, with three 5-inch guns and a smaller maximum horsepower, its trial speed cut to an estimated 35.75 knots. Under the existing London Treaty limit, the United States still had 54,000 unused destroyer tons available, and a drop to 1,400 standard tons would permit construction of two additional ships. Scheme F carried four guns in two twin mounts, the after mount on top of the after deckhouse. Two quad centerline torpedo tube mounts were carried amidships with a third set on the stern (a feature of some pre-World War I American destroyers). The after gun mount had a theoretical arc of fire to within 7 degrees of the bow, allowing a higher volume

of ahead fire than was possible with earlier ships. This scheme could be shortened by about fifteen feet 'without sacrifice in military characteristics and with a corresponding gain in maneuverability.' Standard displacement could then be cut to 1,385 tons; 39 such ships could be built on the remaining London Treaty tonnage instead of 36 1,500-tonners.[4]

On the same day a separate letter forwarded an additional sketch, Scheme G, outlined after the previous three schemes had been completed. It resembled Scheme F on a full 1,500-ton displacement, with two single 5-inch guns forward and Scheme F's three quad tubes and deckhouse-mounted 5-inch twin aft.[5]

On 30 March 1936, Rear Admiral Pye, the director of the War Plans Division, presented his views to CNO. Basing his assumptions on the expectation that any naval war involving the United States would be fought against Japan — or *Orange* as it was called in the various war plans — Pye outlined the requirement for an offensive campaign to establish the American fleet in 'superior strength' in the Western Pacific. The threat of Japanese 'battle-cruisers' (the four fast *Kongo*-class battleships) would require the United States Navy to use its battleship force to support any island-hopping westward thrust. This would expose it to attrition from Japanese submarines, destroyers and aircraft. This was, in fact, the plan being drawn up at the time by the Japanese Naval General Staff. In the event of war with the United States, the Combined Fleet would theoretically operate in two major task forces. An Advanced Force, consisting of the four *Kongos* plus cruisers and destroyers heavily armed with the fast, long-ranged Type 93 *Long Lance* 24-inch torpedo, would attempt to reduce the numerical superiority of the American fleet by massive night attacks before the Main Body of battleships, cruisers and destroyers attempted a decisive day gunnery action.[6] The gun armament of American destroyers in such a scenario would thus assume considerable importance.

Because of its numerical inferiority, the Japanese battle line was not expected to expose itself to attrition and 'consequently, *Blue* American types carrying torpedoes, mines and bombs will, at least in the early stages of the campaign, have no opportunity to attack enemy capital ships. Torpedoes, bombs, and mines are the weapons which constitute the main hope and reliance of the *Orange* fleet, and are the greatest menace to the attainment, by the United States Fleet, of that supremacy in the Western Pacific which is essential to victory.' The first problem before an American fleet in a war with Japan would be defense against Japanese light

These photographs of *Hughes* (DD-410) and *Sims* (DD-409) illustrate the early steps taken to insure the stability of the *Sims* class. *Hughes* is shown as completed, with five 5-inch guns and three quadruple torpedo tubes arranged as in the *Mahan* class. *Sims* is seen after modification. Two waist tubes have been replaced by a single centerline quad tube; after boat stowage has been lowered and the after-deckhouse cut down. Even the foremast has been shortened as part of the effort to bring down the center of gravity.

forces, not battleship guns — not a bad prediction for 1936. Torpedoes, Pye thought, were most valuable in a fleet action to the side with the weaker battle line: 'torpedo carrying vessels . . . were first designed in an endeavor to obtain a cheap means to reduce enemy battle line strength . . .' He went on: 'The best tactical reply to the . . . torpedo boat was the torpedo boat destroyer, a larger, faster vessel with gun power adequate to destroy the torpedo boat. . . . With each successive wave of design the destroyer has grown in size until it has become necessary to sacrifice either maximum gun power or maximum torpedo bat-

tery or to increase displacement until the resulting type loses the handiness of the destroyer, presents a large target and becomes readily visible at night when reduced visibility is a desideratum, and its usefulness as a torpedo-carrying type is threatened.' No American destroyer could be successfully used in a conventional day action as long as the Japanese had enough fast capital ships 'to control the destroyer attack area'.

Pye concluded that the remaining ships of the 1,500-ton building program should have 'the maximum gun power, with a . . . gun . . . effective against . . . destroyers, submarines

Mustin (DD-413), showing the streamlined bridge introduced in the *Sims* class to cut wind resistance and reduce eddying of stack gases around the bridge. This bridge was also to be used in the later *Benson*, *Gleaves*, and *Fletcher* classes. A new Mark 37 5-inch gun director is mounted on a cylindrical structure containing the ship's fire-control station. Below this is an enlarged level which includes wheelhouse, charthouse, and captain's sea cabin on one deck. Torpedo directors are mounted on the open bridge wings. Accommodations for a division commander are below the pilot house. Below this, at forecastle-deck level are the radio room, handling room for the superfiring 5-inch gun, and quarters for captain and executive officer. Officer and chief-petty-officer quarters are on the main deck, below the forecastle (the upper row of hull ports), with crew quarters on the second deck forward and aft of the machinery spaces.

on the surface ... auxiliary cruisers and, if practicable, against bomb-carrying aircraft. A torpedo battery designed for firing on either side, sufficient torpedoes to justify the use of the type as a torpedo carrier in a major fleet action under favorable conditions, and to provide adequate salvo dispersion in short-range surprise attack ... or in night attacks against cruisers, aircraft carriers or capital ships. Depth-charge equipment should also be carried for use against submarines.' He thought five 5-inch guns adequate; this was the maximum number of weapons which could be accommodated in a 1,500-ton hull without going beyond the Treaty limit, and it might 'give some possibility of victory' even in an engagement with the 6-gun 'Special Type' destroyers of the *Fubuki*, *Ayanami*, and *Akatsuki* classes.

Pye felt that proposed reductions in gun power were ill-advised, as was the substitution of single-purpose guns for dual-purpose in future construction. Modern bombers and torpedo planes had increased their speed to an extent that fighters were no longer completely sufficient, but had to be backed up by fleet antiaircraft guns. Successful fleet operations and amphibious landings demanded an AA capability, to which destroyers could make an appropriate contribution; this would be lost if the 5-inch DP capability were discarded.

The proposed design, Pye believed, should provide for firing at least an 8-tube torpedo salvo to either beam, but at no sacrifice in gun firepower; he recommended the 12-tube configuration used in the *Mahan* class. The desired destroyer type should include no less than five guns and eight, preferably twelve tubes arranged to allow an 8-tube salvo.[7]

During the first weeks of 1936 comments and recommendations had been coming in from the fleet in response to CNO's request of 21 December 1935. All agreed on a 1,500 ton hull, some specifying additional hull stiffening. Maneuverability was important to some; light ballistic protection for engineering spaces was wanted by others. The Commanding Officer of *Hull* (DD-350) thought that 'the new destroyers handle well under all conditions, have good steaming radius, sufficient speed, armament, weight and stores capacity.' The captain of a sister ship, *Worden* (DD-352) felt that the general hull design was satisfactory, and was 'seaworthy and powerful for screening and scouting.' The captain of *Aylwin* (DD-355) praised the *Farragut* class as having 'excellent sea-keeping qualities and ... the maneuverability desired in a destroyer.' Only two officers expressed any interest in an increase in size; the others professed themselves satisfied with 1,500 nominal tons. A number of votes were received for two separate engine rooms. Everyone involved wanted a dual-purpose gun battery, most preferring four or five 5-inch/38s although a couple liked the 5-inch/25 gun and *Farragut*'s captain suggested five 4.7-inch/40-caliber DP guns firing fixed ammunition. The Commander, Battle Force, in advising five 5-inch/38s remarked that 'these boats will probably be employed in extended operations prior to delivering massed attack on enemy battle lines. This gun power will greatly assist in carrying the boats through these operations up to the time of torpedo attack and will be of value in driving home the attack through covering light forces,' again underlining the lack of light cruisers in the US Navy even

though work on the new *Brooklyn* class was underway. All the officers polled desired quadruple-mount torpedo tubes in various centerline and/or wing arrangements. Commander, Destroyer Squadron Six, felt that the 'number of guns should be sacrificed if necessary to secure adequate torpedo armament.' Although he was the only one to put it so explicitly, the batteries suggested by the other respondents indicated some differences as to the relative need for guns and torpedoes. ComDesRon Three was the only officer to suggest provision for reload torpedoes 'if practicable'. The captain of *Dewey* (DD-349) called the Mark 33 5-inch gun director 'too heavy, complicated and vulnerable' and advised that the rangekeeper be separated and located belowdecks, something that would be realized in the destroyers now under consideration.[8]

On 12 May 1936 the General Board sent its proposed characteristics to the Secretary of the Navy. On 25 March of that year a new naval limitation treaty had been signed at London, and on 18 May the Senate would vote for its ratification. This second London Treaty included a new definition for the destroyer, which was lumped together with the cruiser under the category of Light Surface Vessels. The Board concluded that, under the provisions of this new treaty, the standard displacement of a destroyer might go up to 3,000 tons. It was not, however, deemed advisable to build such ships since the greatest need at that time seemed to be for ships generally along the existing lines of development. Rather than sacrificing desirable military characteristics, the General Board judged it better to add a small amount of displacement 'to permit the construction of a destroyer sufficiently rugged and seaworthy to meet service conditions, and to overcome the defects recognized in previous designs' — such as the hull stress noted in the *Farragut* class.

49

The two views of *Russell* (DD-414) and *Sims* (DD-409) (*right and below*) and the two of *O'Brien* (DD-415) and *Walke* (DD-416) (*opposite top and bottom*) taken on 16 December 1941, give a detailed look at the early-wartime *Sims* class. All four ships have their 5-inch guns in closed mounts, Mount 53 being without a steel top to save weight. K-guns are being installed alongside *Walke*'s after-deckhouse; a Y-gun has been mounted on *O'Brien*'s fantail and seems to have been just removed from *Walke*. The dark vertical objects stowed among the depth charges on the starboard side of *O'Brien* are Y-gun arbors: steel shafts, which fitted into the Y-gun's barrel, to which a depth charge was strapped for firing. 20 mm guns have been installed on *Walke*'s after-deckhouse; *O'Brien* still has .50-caliber machine gun pedestals next to her canvas-covered searchlight, but a platform is being installed just forward of this for 20 mm guns. Of these four ships, *Russell* was the only one to survive the war. (US Navy, courtesy Robert J. Cressman collection.)

The Board proposed a 1,570-standard-ton ship with five 5-inch guns and twelve tubes, the latter arranged as in *Mahan* with one quad mount on the centerline, the other two in wing positions. A speed of 35 knots was wanted on the new displacement recommended by the Bureau of Construction and Repair; radius at 12 knots, four months out of dock, was to be at least 6,500 miles. Machinery spaces were to be divided into two firerooms and two, instead of the previous one, engine rooms. Reserve space for four reload torpedoes was included.[9] CNO concurred in the Board's specifications, and the Secretary approved them on 13 May 1936.

The twelve destroyers of the 1937 program became the *Sims* (DD-409) class. All of the ships were completed by 1940. Slightly enlarged versions of the earlier single-stackers, they mounted five guns in a 2-A-1-2 arrangement. Their rounded bridge structure produced less wind resistance and turbulence than the more angular structures of predecessor classes. These were the first destroyers to get a new gun director, the Mark 37. This improved director had only the director mechanism itself in the rotating house atop the bridge. The rangekeeper — a new model called the Computer Mark 1 — and the stable element were located in a plotting room deep in the hull. This reduction in topweight was not enough to prevent problems, and the first ships of the class were found to be topheavy. The two wing torpedo-tube mounts were quickly removed and replaced by another single centerline mount, giving the class a new armament of eight centerline tubes.

Opposite top
The *Sims* class *Hammann* (DD-412), January 1942. Note her reduced after superstructure, 20 mm AA guns, and SC-FD radar installation. The *Mahan*-like 12-tube arrangement used in the first of the *Sims* class was soon replaced, as seen here, with eight tubes on the centerline.

Opposite bottom
Mustin (DD-413) in dapple camouflage, 1942. This silhouette, high forward and flattening out abaft the stack, characterizes wartime American single-stackers. The *Sims* class were the first destroyers to use the more capable Mark 37 dual-purpose gun director, seen here with an FD radar installed.

Top
Anderson (DD-411) on 17 May 1943, with shipyard workers apparently taking their midday break below new 20 mm gun tubs forward of the wheelhouse. The antenna for a new SC-3 air-search radar is at her masthead.

Bottom
Russell (DD-414), refitting at Mare Island on 17 July 1943, has had two twin 40 mm mounts installed forward of a new raised platform which accommodates her fire-control searchlight and a 20 mm gun. Mount 54 is closed, while Mount 53 is open; variations were still seen in the configuration of the after 5-inch mounts in the single-stack destroyer classes.

Top
Morris (DD-417); compare this view with the earlier photograph of *Hammann*. Reduction of topside weight was a critical matter in all wartime destroyers, but particularly so in the '1,500-tonner' classes.

Bottom
Wainwright (DD-419), alone of the *Sims* class, had an unusual late-war AA battery. She has three 20 mm guns in the customary two-level arrangement forward, with two 40 mm twins and a fourth 20 mm gun aft. *Wainwright*'s after quadruple torpedo tube has been replaced by a platform supporting three single 40 mm guns on Army-type mounts. By the end of 1944 thirteen low-number *Benson*s and *Gleaves* had received two 40 mm singles apiece, with two more scheduled to get them. *Wainwright* and the later ships all lost these mounts during 1945.

Top
Roe (DD-418) off Guam in April 1945, in the bicolor camouflage widely used in the Pacific Fleet at the time. By late 1945 two of her sisters had their torpedo tubes removed, two more 40 mm twins installed, and their four 20 mm singles replaced by twins. This improvement would have given them a better chance to survive suicide attack during the projected invasion of the Japanese home islands; *Roe*, with two 40 mm twins and four single 20 mm guns as seen here, was in a less fortunate situation than her bigger descendants with respect to close-in AA gunnery.

Bottom
Wainwright (DD-419), operating with British units in the Atlantic in 1942. *Wainwright* survived the war to become a victim of the Bikini atom bomb tests. (From the collection of John Batchelor.)

10

The Bensons and Gleaves

**Life is the art of drawing sufficient conclusions
from insufficient premises.**

Samuel Butler

Eight destroyers were funded for the Fiscal 1938 program, and the design produced for the *Benson* (DD-421) class represented a further improvement on the *Sims* concept. Starting with the same basic hull dimensions, an added fifty tons of standard displacement were worked into hull strengthening and a new arrangement of machinery, intended to give the new ships a better chance to survive torpedo damage. Two boiler rooms and two engine rooms were arranged in alternating sequence forward to aft. 'Plumbing' was laid out so that connections from one propulsion unit to the other could be closed off, and enough redundancy in auxiliary machinery was provided to enable the ship to steam and steer on either half of the engineering plant. While this represented additional weight, the designers hoped that the new configuration would better enable the *Benson*s to live through a torpedo hit. The new 'split plant' gave these ships a new silhouette, with two stacks.

The *Benson* class was given the gun battery of the *Sims* class, with two new quintuple tubes on the centerline. Close-range AA armament as built — six .50-caliber machine guns — was better than the four guns in earlier destroyers, but still rather negligible.

The engineering installation in the new destroyers became a cause of controversy, and eventually led to a division of a group of very similar ships into two classes.

The eight destroyers of this program were ordered in 1937, four from Navy Yards and two each from Bethlehem and Bath (Maine) Iron Works. An argument arose over the question of which commercial yard was to prepare the working plans for the entire block of ships. The Bureau of Engineering wanted these drawn by Bath, whose design agent was the New York firm of Gibbs and Cox. In the end the contract for detail development of the design was given to Bethlehem. Shortly afterward, Bethlehem requested the Navy's authorization to revise the contract design to

incorporate some engineering changes in line with their own practice. As Admiral Bowen described it: '[I was] most reluctant to accept the ... proposals since I believed that they represented a definite lowering of the basic design standard which I had determined to pursue. However ... Bethlehem had a contract to design and build two destroyers ... they had no previous experience to guide them ... were definitely not in sympathy with the design policies of the Bureau of Engineering, and ... were of the opinion that ... they could produce a destroyer of equal efficiency to those which incorporated the Bureau's ideas of design. I therefore ..., with the greatest reluctance, ... accepted their proposed changes in the design of DDs 421–428.' Bowen did not intend to support this 'bastard design', but was willing to give some ships of this type a service trial in comparison with

others built in line with the Bureau's thinking.

Consideration of the 1939 program began in mid-1937, when the General Board circularized senior fleet officers for opinions. The program included eight destroyers of 'approximately 1,600 tons standard displacement'. The remaining unbuilt destroyer tonnage ceiling under the London Treaty permitted construction of 32 ships of about 1,600 tons, or about 42 ships in the neighborhood of 1,200 tons. The first 1,500-ton 'gold-platers' had now completed about two years of service, and the Board wanted opinions 'as to the ability of this type to meet successfully all the duties required of a destroyer; whether some of these duties such as anti-submarine work can be performed more efficiently by units of less tonnage and, if so, the number of each type, viz., 1500 and 1200 tons, required for work with the Fleet.'

The approved characteristics for DD-421–428, of the the 1938 program, had included five 5-inch guns, four .50-caliber AA machine guns, and three quadruple tubes (later altered to two quintuples), and 35 knots on a 1,620-standard-ton hull with split plant and two

The *Benson* class *Farenholt* (DD-491) in an unusual form of 'wave-mirror' camouflage. She does not show any search radar. Many wartime photographs had their electronics air-brushed out by the censor, but since *Farenholt*'s gun director displays an untouched FD antenna this would not seem to have happened to this view. Such things as radar were installed as supply and opportunity allowed during wartime, and many irregular combinations of weapons and sensors appear.

stacks. Preliminary studies indicated that these characteristics could be had on smaller displacements:

1,350 tons	1,200 tons
35 knots	35 knots
4 × 5-inch/38	3 × 5-inch/38
4 × .50 AA MG	4 × .50 AA MG
2 × quad tubes, centerline	2 × quad tubes, centerline

The General Board asked whether the existing trend of destroyer construction, from the 1,500-ton *Farragut*s to the 1,620-ton *Benson*s, was satisfactory; whether the 1938 *Benson* design should be repeated in the 1939 building program; and whether either the 1,350 or 1,200-ton concept might 'have sufficient field in the Fleet to warrant construction.' The Board also wanted recommendations from the Fleet as to the displacement, speed, and armament considered desirable for future destroyers.[1]

The Commander, Battle Force, thought destroyers vulnerable to aerial strafing, particularly dangerous to high-pressure steam plants. Their large silhouettes were disadvantageous in night torpedo attacks. ComBatFor suggested 'a minimum actual speed of 38 knots as that necessary for destroyers to maneuver effectively with and against battleships of speeds equal to or greater than that contemplated for battleships 55 and 56.' (These were the $27\frac{1}{2}$-knot *North Carolina* class, commissioned in 1941, but this recommendation was soon thrown out of kilter by the 33-knot *Iowa* (BB-61) class.) He liked the seakeeping qualities and offensive power designed into the *Benson* class as a basis for the 1939 design, but felt that this speed margin should be attained. The 1,200-ton concept was weakly armed, and a satisfactory design could not be achieved from it. The 1,350-ton type was not so bad, but would end up with the drawbacks of the existing 1,500–1,620-ton classes and without their offensive value. A reasonable balance had to be struck. To make up for insufficiency of numbers in wartime, it was necessary to use weaker ships to perform the duties of the stronger.[2] ComBatFor had good historical precedent for his opinion; the thread of wartime substitution runs through the American destroyer story from the Spanish-American War (when the existing torpedo boats 'carried laundry' while converted yachts scouted and patrolled) through World War I (when more yachts were commandeered, and submarine chasers were mass-produced, to make up for the lack of destroyers). History would soon repeat itself, during World War II, in large-scale subchaser and destroyer-escort programs.

Gillespie (DD-609) on 2 October 1942 in what was to be the typical configuration for wartime *Benson* and *Gleaves* class ships. Both classes were similarly modified and were tactically interchangeable; the flat-sided stacks, as seen here, of the *Benson* class and the round stacks of *Gleaves* and her sisters are the only external distinctions between the classes. *Gillespie* has four closed 5-inch mounts, with two 40 mm twins forward of Mount 53 and 20 mm guns amidships and forward. She has one 5-tube mount between her stacks, with her fire-control searchlight carried at the after end of the midship deckhouse. Others of these classes retained ten tubes and mounted their searchlights with the 40 mm guns. Such minor variations are inevitable in any large production group of ships, and rapidly multiply as ships are refitted after completion.

Commander Destroyers, Battle Force, mentioned the excessive stress in *Farragut*-class hulls, plus the lack of space in the *Mahan* class' engineering compartments. Both classes had been reported 'excessively wet amidships in even moderate seas when heavily loaded.' He thought their offensive power, speed, radius, and seakeeping 'distinct improvements' over the flushdeckers, and expected the first *Benson*s of the 1938 program to be 'satisfactory in all respects.' The *Benson* design should be repeated in 1939, but depth-charge capacity should be increased and the four .50-caliber guns of the *Benson*s should be increased to six if possible.

As to the smaller concepts, ComDesBatFor thought the 1,350-ton and 1,200-ton types all right for scouting duties or for screening battleships against submarines as well as for convoy work. Any gain in numbers which might be achieved by building such ships would not be worth the loss of homogeneity and other destroyer characteristics. Better, he thought, to build a smaller number of ships with good power, radius, and seakeeping than a larger number of more specialized — and thus restricted — types. If, at some later date, Treaty tonnage limits were removed, then smaller destroyers could be built in desired numbers without 'compromising the destroyer force with ships of inferior cruising radii [*sic*]'.

As matters then stood, ComDesBatFor wanted no smaller destroyers. His preference was for a 1,600-tonner with rugged hull and bridge, capable of 34–35 knots at full load and armed with five 5-inch, six machine guns, and twelve tubes arranged as in the original *Sims* class design (the first *Benson*s had not even been ordered, let alone built, at this

time). The AA machine guns should be located to allow the best possible arcs of fire.[3]

The Commander, Scouting Force, raised a number of questions. It was difficult, he felt, to make definite recommendations in some areas where adequate information was lacking. How good, he wondered, would the proposed 1,200-ton boats be? Would they be able to make 25 knots in a moderate sea? Could a 6-tube mount be developed, possibly carrying two layers of three tubes? If a dual-purpose 5-inch twin gun mount suitable for destroyer use were developed, would it be practicable to include an auxiliary power supply adequate to enable the gun battery to fight effectively if the ship's main electric power system should be disabled or cables severed? If light armor were to be provided for bridge, gun director, 5-inch mounts, and engineering plant, what weights were involved, and what other features would have to be limited or sacrificed? ComScoFor could see a shift in the functions of the fleet destroyer, remarking that 'the tendency in recent destroyer design has been to fit destroyers to perform cruiser functions [again, the lack of cruisers in numbers suited to current operational concepts] at the expense of performing the function . . . formerly most important for destroyers, . . . effective torpedo attacks. Consideration of the duties which our destroyers must perform in any probable campaign leads to the conclusion that the change is a proper one for the number of new destroyers now built or building. It is probable that these vessels will use their guns many times before they encounter a target for their torpedoes, and that if their gun power is inadequate their torpedoes will be useless.' He considered the new destroyers too big for day or night torpedo attack, and thought that some smaller destroyers, with heavy torpedo batteries and 'a high degree of seaworthiness' at a sacrifice of gun fire-power, should be built in the 1939 program. If studies should show that high performance could not be attained on a smaller displacement, then an improved *Benson* would be best. New destroyers had taken on so many characteristics hitherto ascribed to cruisers that ComScoFor could see a day in which destroyer attacks would be launched 'without the orthodox cruiser support heretofore considered necessary.' This would so

increase the tactical value of destroyers that fleet commanders would be reluctant to use them in such other functions as antisubmarine screens, patrol duty, amphibious landing support, and the like. The ability to produce ships in numbers was essential for the destroyer type, and ComScoFor suggested an investigation 'of the types, some . . . novel, required by *all* the phases and subsidiary operations . . . now included in the basic war plans. . . . destroyers seem to have outgrown some of the functions hitherto assigned them and perhaps there is a need for . . . smaller craft . . . beyond the requirements of the fleet for offensive torpedo launchers.' It seems particularly important that we have a proven type of small modern destroyer which could be quickly produced in large numbers when hostilities appear imminent.'[4]

The Commander Destroyers, Scouting Force (Rear Admiral Pye, last heard from in 1936 concerning the design of the *Sims* class), thought the 1,500–1,620 tonners superior to any foreign type of their approximate size although they had 'numerous defects'. He did

not think that the *Benson* design should be repeated in the 1939 program unless preparation of a new design would seriously delay construction. If the *Benson* design was continued, careful attention needed to be given to the elimination of known flaws. Smaller destroyers were not wanted; instead, a 1,800-ton, 36-knot ship should be drawn to mount at least five dual-purpose 5-inch guns, giving careful thought to the use of twin mounts. Besides .50 caliber or 1.1-inch AA machine guns, depth charges, K-guns, and as many centerline tubes should be included as the

Two photographs, taken in December 1942, give a composite look at a typical wartime *Benson* class destroyer. The forward view of *Kalk* (DD-611), with the after photograph of *Kendrick* (DD-612), illustrate their arrangement of deck details, 5-inch guns, tubes, 20 mm guns — note the guns added to the after end of each bridge wing — and 40 mm twins with directors. *Kalk*'s bridge is derived from the design drawn for the *Sims* class, and its design was used in earlier ships of the *Fletcher* class as well. Streamlined to reduce wind resistance in the interest of speed, the design was criticized for not allowing all-round visibility for the conning officer or tactical commander.

displacement would stand. Admiral Pye reiterated his thought that the most likely naval war for the United States would be a campaign against Japan and called for a 1,800-ton destroyer with five 5-inch guns, ten to twelve centerline tubes, eight AA machine guns, depth charges and ballistic protection against strafing for the engineering spaces. A new destroyer should have at least 35 knots speed and the 'latest fire and torpedo control, and distant control and power operation of the battery. In destroyer operations, to hit first is of primary importance, therefore long range and maximum efficiency of control is [sic] essential.'[5]

Reflecting the lack of unanimity among naval officers concerning the destroyer of the future, Commander Robert Carney (later Admiral, and Chief of Naval Operations) advocated dividing the Navy's remaining unused destroyer tonnage between 5-gun 1,500-tonners with twelve to sixteen tubes, good endurance and 'excellent' seaworthiness and 1,000-ton ships with three guns, eight to twelve tubes, and a low silhouette for night torpedo work. Such a program, he felt, would yield destroyers of good qualities in the numbers required for fleet screening.[6]

The President of the Naval War College, after discussions with commanding officers of new destroyers and an examination of fleet maneuvers — the annual Fleet Problems — and War College studies, felt that others were in a better position to offer advice on design details. He preferred, instead, to 'confine himself to general opinions upon matters that are important from the strategical and tactical viewpoints.' While the destroyer was capable of performing many tasks, this should not be allowed to obscure its two principal reasons for existence: torpedo attack on an enemy's heavy ships, and defense of one's own main forces against air, submarine, or torpedo attack. The destroyer had become an essential part of the fleet, and nothing should be allowed to detract from its suitability for this vital function. 'In war, the United States Fleet may be required to operate in very large theaters, at long distances from bases, and under greatly diversified sea conditions. Wherever it goes, it needs destroyers to help protect it from the aircraft and the torpedo menace, and needs destroyers for offensive action. The design requirements for American destroyers may, therefore, well be quite different from those of foreign navies whose operations are almost certain to be conducted in restricted waters. It seems apparent that the principal strategic requirements of an American destroyer are good seakeeping qualities and long cruising radius.'

Weighing the numbers-versus-individual power question, the President thought a choice difficult but finally came down in favor of a larger ship, with the longer radius and better bad-weather seakeeping ability that he had judged necessary. Since battle line speed would probably increase in the future — in fact, the 27-plus-knot battleships of the *North Carolina* (BB-55) class had just been ordered — top speeds of new destroyers should be increased from 35 knots to 38–40, even at the price of an increase in individual displacement or the sacrifice of some gun power.[7]

The President of the General Board, Admiral Thomas C. Hart, complained to CINCUS (Admiral A. J. Hepburn) that there was 'great divergence among the destroyer people as to just what our next destroyers should be.' There was extensive agreement about the desirability of ballistic deck plating over the machinery spaces for protection against air attack, but calculations had shown that if this were added, a *Somers*-size ship would be needed to carry a *Benson*-size battery. 'The present ideas of the Board', he concluded, 'are that the cost of this protection is not commensurate with its probable value and that we had best continue to rely upon our own fire against strafing attacks. My own idea is that our whole Service is very much inclined to over-estimate the dangers from machine guns carried in aircraft.'[8]

The General Board returned to its considerations. The destroyer gun-torpedo balance had been accepted as five guns to twelve tubes in the *Sims* class and reduced to five guns and ten centerline tubes in the first *Benson*s, an arrangement resulting from recommendations from the forces afloat. Centerline tubes were less susceptible to interference from heavy seas and were considered more effective than wing tubes, provided they could be installed at a height sufficient to allow torpedoes to clear the side of the ship when fired, but not so high as to cause the torpedo to be damaged on hitting the water or to run erratically.

Service opinion of the 5-inch/38-caliber gun had deemed it satisfactory. Its remote director-control feature, though expensive and requiring a good bit of maintenance, was considered justified. The close-in AA defense picture was not so good. The fleet was almost unanimous in a desire for more AA machine guns, and the Board thought a study of the relative merits of the .50-caliber gun and the 1.1-inch automatic shell gun, with director control, would produce valuable results. If a heavy battery of close-in AA guns could not be incorporated into a design of *Benson* dimensions, the Board suggested 'that very definite consideration be given to the reduction of one 5″ gun and the substitution there-for of the maximum possible number of 1.1″ guns.'

'In the general design of these destroyers,' the Board remarked, 'their estimated employment during a war with Orange [Japan] has always been kept to the forefront. It is unquestioned that Orange would employ attrition tactics. The design of their light forces plainly indicate this. For the protection of the major units of the Battle Fleet, preference therefore must be given to the gun rather than to the torpedo and these ships undoubtedly represent a new class and cannot be measured with previous conceptions for a pure destroyer. Whether or not they will ever be required or find opportunity to use torpedoes in a general engagement is questioned but, even so, the torpedo battery carried is considered ample for such purpose.' Protracted operations in distant waters made replenishment of ammunition vital; though only a limited amount of gun ammunition could be carried, 'it should be practicable on mobilization to take aboard some reload torpedoes.' New destroyers should be able to make 25 knots in a moderate sea; added weight should be assigned to hull strengthening, as necessary, even if this meant a reduction in offensive qualities.[9]

Characteristics for the eight destroyers of the 1939 program were submitted by the General Board on 11 December 1937. Externally, they were to be 'repeat *Benson*s' with two more .50-caliber guns for a total of six, and two centerline quintuple tubes. Strafing protection was to be applied to the bridge and 5-inch gun director; though such protection for the engineering spaces was desirable, the weight could not be provided for it without an increase in size.

The General Board considered these changes a 'great improvement', and recommended that they be retroactively approved for the eight original *Benson*s. The Bureau of Construction and Repair discussed the matter with Bethlehem, which was drawing the detail plans, and agreed to incorporate the changes. In the meanwhile, the Bureau of Engineering had decided to include a high-speed 850-degree steam plant in the 1939 destroyers. The revision in the characteristics for the 1938 ships meant a two-month delay in their construction and the Bureau of Engineering took advantage of this to include the new machinery in the two 1938 ships being built by Bath Iron Works. This generation of destroyers now began to fall into differing groups. Six ships of the 1938 program (DD-421–422, 425–428) were built according to Bethlehem's machinery specifications; two Bath ships (DD-423 and -424) received the high temperature system favored by the Bureau of

Engineering. The eight ships of the 1939 program were built to the Bureau's specifications, and eight more (DD-437–444) of the same type were approved by the Secretary of the Navy on 19 December 1938 under the Fiscal 1940 program.

Right
Benson (DD-421) in an early-wartime 5-gun, 5-tube configuration, Mounts 53 and 54 in canvas-covered, open-topped shields.

Bottom
Benson in 1944. She retains her original ten tubes, and is painted in the 'dazzle' finish discarded by the Pacific Fleet early in 1945 as providing a more conspicuous target for *kamikaze* pilots.

11

Buildup: 1941

We must become intolerant of delay. We must tear our way through red tape. We must pillory bureaucrats who stupidly sacrifice time in the pursuit of an impossible perfection.

Secretary of the Navy Frank Knox, 1940

The destroyer building program for 1941 was to consist of ships of the new *Fletcher* class (the background of which will be discussed in the following chapter). However, as the pace of war accelerated in Europe and the Far East, the General Board recommended that twelve more of the 1938–40 pattern ships be included in the 1941 program to keep up the pace of construction while the plans for new-departure *Fletchers* were being completed. The Secretary of the Navy concurred in this reasoning, and approved their construction on 23 May 1940.[1] These twelve ships were contracted for during the summer of 1940 (DD-453–464). Another fifteen (DD-483–497) were ordered in September, with 41 more (DD-598–628, 632–641) following in December, and a final four ships (DD-645–648) completing the schedule in February 1941.

Later-construction ships, beginning with *Bristol* (DD-453), were armed with four 5-inch guns instead of five. The various combinations of armaments, building programs, and engineering plants led to some confusion in class designations during the war years. The Bethlehem-developed 1938 design was known as the *Benson* (DD-421) class. The high-temperature ships of the 1939 program were first called the *Livermore* (DD-429) class. Since DD-423–424 had been completed to that standard, the high-temperature ships eventually came to be referred to as the *Gleaves* (DD-423) class. The early 4-gun ships were called the *Bristol* (DD-453) class at first, but as time went on the 5-gun ships lost one of their 5-inch guns to improve stability and make room for AA guns, and this distinction became meaningless. The final breakdown fell into the *Benson* and *Gleaves* classes; by mid-war both were essentially alike in armament and operated together.

As the war went on, the need for electronics and close-in AA guns led to the removal of the fifth 5-inch gun and, later, of one torpedo-tube mount. By 1945 the 'basic' battery for these ships consisted of four 5-inch guns, five torpedo tubes, two twin 40 mm AA gun mounts, seven or eight 20 mm guns, two depth-charge tracks, and four to six K-guns. In mid-1945, as part of the extensive destroyer AA rearmament program called forth by the planned invasion of Japan, some ships had their remaining tubes removed and a pair of 40 mm quadruples installed amidships.

As in the *Fletcher* class, wartime experience dictated a redesign of bridges in later ships of this type. All of the 1,620-ton *Benson* class were built with a bridge similar in form to that of the *Sims* class. *Gleaves* class ships ordered through the summer of 1940 also had this configuration, along with Navy Yard-built ships ordered later in 1940. Later-production vessels of this class had a redesigned bridge with an open walkway across front and sides, and the heavy weight of the Mark 37 gun director lowered.

As work got underway on the post-Pearl Harbor Maximum Effort building program, the Bureau of Ships suggested that additional ships of a 'modified *Gleaves*' type be included in the Fiscal 1943 program to keep destroyers coming in quantity until the building plans for the *Allen M. Sumner* (DD-692) class were completed and shipyards could begin work on them. The Bureau proposed military characteristics for 'repeat' construction of *Gleaves* and *Fletcher* class ships along their existing lines.[2] On 18 April 1942 the General Board submitted characteristics for an improved *Gleaves*, which it described as a 1,740-ton 'medium destroyer'.[3] This 4-gun, 5-tube ship was to have two 40 mm twins, four 20 mm guns, two depth-charge tracks and six K-guns, with at least 35 knots trial speed and splinter protection for ship and gun control, 5-inch and 40 mm. COMINCH, Admiral Ernest J. King, took a jaundiced view, holding that since a combination of larger destroyers and destroyer escorts (DE) was now under construction and even larger destroyers had been proposed for the future, the continuation of the *Gleaves* concept was 'unacceptable from both the material and the production standpoint', and recommended that no such ships be built. On 11 May 1942 the Secretary of the Navy concurred with King's View and rejected the 1,740-ton destroyer.[4]

By the eve of the Korean War, in 1950, three *Gleaves* and two *Benson* class destroyers were serving as Naval Reserve training ships. Twelve *Gleaves* class ships, converted to *Ellyson* (DMS-19) class fast minesweepers, were still active. Soon after the end of that conflict all of the *Bensons* and *Gleaves* had entered the inactive fleet. Some were transferred to foreign navies, while the rest gradually went to the scrapyards or were expended as ordnance targets.

During 1954 a study of destroyer types was undertaken within the Office of the Chief of Naval Operations. This suggested that obsolescent *Benson/Gleaves* and *Fletcher* class destroyers might advantageously be converted to corvettes and used as specialized antisubmarine vessels with hunter-killer teams or as convoy escorts. Configurations were discussed through the summer and fall of 1954, and on 26 November of that year the Chief of Naval Operations approved characteristics for a *Benson/Gleaves* corvette (DDC) conversion. The modified ships were to have the two boilers from their forward fireroom replaced by enlarged fuel tankage for a 4,200-mile radius at 20 knots. Up-to-date radio, radar, sonar, and countermeasures installations were to be provided. One of the ship's four 5-inch guns was to be replaced by a Weapon *Able* ahead-throwing depth-charge projector (as in the *Fletcher* class DDE conversion). A simple launching system for Mark 32 antisubmarine torpedoes and one depth-charge track, plus two twin 20 mm mounts, made up the rest of the corvette's battery. This rearrangement was calculated to produce an antisubmarine ship with 'excellent submarine detection and kill capacity, with good seakeeping qualities and with a sustained speed of about 26 knots', available in numbers in the event of war.[5] Though this plan was, at least, still under consideration for some time afterward, it never came to fruition and antisubmarine conversion efforts were directed to the *Fletcher* and later classes.

The enlarged destroyers of the *Benson* (DD-421) and *Gleaves* (DD-423) classes served usefully in the Atlantic and Mediterranean during the war years. Both classes generally paralleled each other in original appearance and in later modifications. The new *Gleaves* class *Monssen* (DD-436) shows the silhouette of the early members of these classes with five 5-inch/38s (three closed, two open) and two quintuple tubes. Close-in AA fire-power, two .50-calibers forward of the bridge and two more on the after searchlight tower, with another two to port and starboard of the second stack, is typically negligible.

Gleaves (DD-423) runs speed trials; high after superstructures were soon sacrificed in the interest of stability and AA defense. The *Benson* and *Gleaves* classes had much the same hull as *Sims*; *Gleaves'* high-pressure, high-temperature steam plant was judged superior to the older-pattern installation in *Benson*.

Bristol (DD-453) as completed, seen here on 21 October 1941. This production block of ships was finished without the fifth 5-inch gun of the earlier models, and some contemporary sources mentioned them separately as a '*Bristol* class' on this account.

Meredith (DD-434) in dapple finish on 23 June 1942. Her fifth gun is gone, as is her after searchlight tower, and she has a combination of 20 mm and .50-caliber AA guns.

Five-inch cartridge cases litter the deck of *Hobson* (DD-464), one of the *Gleaves* class, after the bombardment of Utah Beach on D-Day, 6 June 1944. *Hobson* provided shore bombardment for thirteen straight hours.

Bottom left
An excellent three-quarter stern view of the *Benson* class *Eberle*. This ship operated in the Atlantic and Mediterranean throughout most of World War II. Among other credits, she fended off a German *Schnellbooten* attack, sinking three of the torpedo boats in the process. After a time in reserve, she eventually returned to her old haunts after being transferred to the Greek Navy as *Niki*.

Bottom right
The reader may notice something odd about this photograph. While this *Gleaves* class ship appears to be making high speed, there is no wake in the background. Acceptance trials were quite thorough for such ships and included an exercise termed 'backing down full', which is to say going from full ahead to full astern.

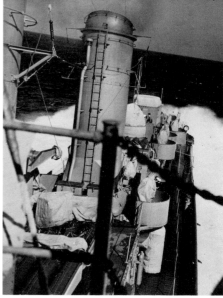

Gwin (DD-433) in February 1943, a typical wartime
'ten-tube' ship of the *Gleaves* class. Thinner stacks and a
2-A-2 arrangement of 5-inch guns further distinguish
these 'broken-deckers' from the flushdecked *Fletcher*
class. *Gwin*'s Mount 53 is open; her 40 mm twins have
Mark 49 directors, a design developed to control AA
guns but seen in destroyers only to a limited extent after
it proved unsatisfactory. Those Mark 49s that did go to
sea were eventually replaced by the Mark 51.

Herndon (DD-638) at New York, 10 October 1943. She is
a 5-tube *Gleaves*, in bicolor 'horizon' finish. Instead of a
search antenna at her masthead, she has an HF/DF
antenna with an SG just above the yardarm; this
combination indicates assignment to North Atlantic
convoy work, where the submarine rather than the
aircraft was the threat. *Herndon* has had lightweight,
ahead-throwing *Mousetrap* antisubmarine rocket
launchers mounted on her forecastle; *Turner* (DD-648) is
also known to have had this weapon at the time.

Left and opposite top
McCalla (DD-488) at Mare Island, 5 January 1944. A
good look at a 5-tube *Gleaves* class ship can be had
through the overlay of shipyard rubbish. *McCalla* has
evidently just had her 40 mm twins installed; wartime
modifications took place in typically piecemeal fashion,
and various rigs usually co-existed within any class.

Baldwin (DD-624) in disruptive (pattern) camouflage, 1944. She has the redesigned bridge seen in later *Gleaves* and *Fletcher* class destroyers; this new structure allowed open visibility forward and, with its lowered Mark 37 director, contributed to stability. *Baldwin* has an SA air-search radar with her SG; the FD radar, by now redesignated Mark 4, on her gun director, is supplemented by a new Mark 22 — the small banana-shaped antenna alongside the main antenna — to provide low-angle coverage.

Nicholson (DD-442) in 1945. Like *Benson* in the photograph on page 60, she has ten tubes and a canvas-topped Mount 53. The Mark 12 radar mounted on *Nicholson*'s director, supplemented by a Mark 22, is an improved dual-purpose equipment developed during the war to replace the Mark 4.

Top
A late-war view of *Shubrick* (DD-639), with four closed
gun mounts and five tubes. Compare this *Gleaves* class
ship with the photograph of the *Benson* class *Gillespie* on
page 57.

Center
Nelson (DD-623) in November 1945, with a lightweight
Mark 28 radar antenna on her 5-inch director. Like some
others of her class she has had her torpedo tubes
removed. Two 40 mm quads have been installed aft in
place of her original two twin mounts; the latter have
been moved to new outboard tubs between the stacks. A
twin 20 mm mount can be seen forward of the bridge.

Ellyson (DD-454) on 13 October 1954, ready for transfer
to Japan. Ending the war as a high-speed minesweeper
(DMS-19), she has been reconfigured as a destroyer and
given the quad-40 mm installation as seen in *Nelson*,
though without the midship twin mounts used in the 1945
AA improvement.

An aerial view of the 'business end' of a *Gleaves* class ship converted to a high-speed minesweeper (DMS). Mount 54 has been replaced by a large minesweeping winch with a drum for the heavy cable used for sweeping magnetic mines. Sweep wires are led out through the chock at the extreme stern; depth-charge tracks have been moved forward and offset to the sides. This DMS has the same 1945 quad-40 mm installation seen in *Ellyson*. Twelve *Gleaves* class received this conversion at the end of 1944 and performed fast assault sweeping at Okinawa. They would have had the same risky share in the landings on the Japanese home islands.

A 1950s photograph of *Thompson* (DMS-38) (ex-DD-627). Originally built as a 'low-bridge' *Gleaves* class destroyer, *Thompson* was subsequently modified for her minesweeping role. Some of these ships served through the Korean War, the last ships of their class to see active duty.

12

Antiaircraft Defense

The history of warfare from antiquity ... records innumerable attempts to secure by some new contrivance an immediate tactical advantage, perhaps a decisive one. In such inventions the essential purpose is to obtain one's end before the adversary can bring counter-measures to bear. It is the time interval that counts.

Bernard Brodie, *Sea Power in the Machine Age* (Princeton, 1941)

It may, at first, seem a bit odd to omit any discussion of antisubmarine warfare or torpedo developments in an outline of destroyer development. These areas, though, are relatively well-known and information on them is fairly findable. The same cannot be said for the air-defense function which, even before Pearl Harbor, was a major concern of the destroyer Navy and which gained in importance as the war progressed. A summary of destroyer antiaircraft developments may not, therefore, be amiss.

The dual-purpose 5-inch batteries of third- and fourth-generation American destroyers gave them at least some measure of air-defense capability, although, using optical range-finders and mechanical time fuzes, this was less effective than it was to become after the introduction of fire-control radar and the proximity fuze. Short-range antiaircraft defense was another matter. As we have seen, the original standard close-in AA armament for 1,500-tonners consisted of four .50-caliber machine guns; the 1,850-ton 'leaders', to compensate for their single-purpose 5-inch batteries, had two quadruple 1.1-inch mounts with two .50-caliber guns. The first ships of the *Benson* and *Gleaves* classes, ordered under the Fiscal 1938–39 programs, were designed to have six .50-caliber guns, while the *Fletcher* class' design called for one 1.1-inch quadruple mount and four .50's.

This was hardly a formidable battery by any standard, especially since gunnery exercises of the period did nothing to build fleet confidence in the machine gun as an antiaircraft weapon. Battleships, firing at 'low and slow' targets, scored few or no hits; destroyer gunners could hardly be expected to do any better or even as well. As early as 1936 the Commander in Chief, US Fleet called attention to the problem. The existing 5-inch/25

and 5-inch/38 guns were, he thought, effective against horizontal attack and should provide reasonable protection from it. 'Light craft', however, he continued, 'are particularly vulnerable to dive bombing and strafing attacks and will undoubtedly be subjected to this form of attack at every opportunity.' The existing machine gun was inadequate. To do an effective job of stopping an attack it had to hit the aircraft's vitals, and iron sights and the light .50-caliber slug were not up to the task. CINCUS thought that the 1.1-inch AA mount, then being introduced, might prove helpful but felt that a larger-caliber AA machine gun, firing explosive ammunition, should be 'pushed ahead with all speed possible.'[1]

The quadruple 1.1-inch automatic gun mount was introduced to the fleet with the *Porter* and *Somers* classes, but these few mounts were the only close-in guns heavier than .50-caliber in the destroyer force when the European war began in 1939. Air-defense received increasing attention as the lessons of this new war were absorbed; in the spring of 1940 the Secretary of the Navy ordered (then) Rear Admiral Ernest J. King to study the subject of fleet protection against aircraft. CNO, writing to the Secretary on 7 May 1940, asked that the General Board study the best means for defense of existing and building ships and make recommendations for changes in ships and for areas where study and experiment might bear fruit.[2] Two days later the Secretary directed the Board to begin a 'comprehensive study' of the problem.

On 12 June the General Board forwarded a memorandum to CNO. This summarized fleet AA firing of 1939–40 and concluded that 'the firing is generally ineffective, that a large amount of ammunition is expended in obtaining only occasional effective hits, and

that anti-aircraft gunnery — as at present developed — does not provide reasonable security against air attack.' The Board noted that the pace of weapon development had been 'unduly slow', and that there had been 'an absence of coordinated effort toward attainment of the required objectives.' The fleet, it went on, was 'poorly equipped to defend itself against aircraft', and recommended that a board of experienced officers and civilian specialists be set up under CNO to study and implement measures to improve AA defense.[3]

On 9 August 1940 CNO formally designated Admiral King and the officers assisting him as the Navy Department Anti-Aircraft Board to carry out such a continuing study. The General Board had, in the meanwhile, proceeded with its own study in accordance with the Secretary's earlier request and, on 13 August, submitted its report. After discussing active and passive forms of AA defense — gunfire on the one hand; hull protection, compartmentation, speed, and maneuverability on the other — available to naval ships to supplement the protection of the fleet's shipboard fighting planes, the Board pointed to the projected *Atlanta* class of light cruisers 'and *all* new destroyers' as particularly suited to fleet AA screen work. (The *Atlanta* class, the US Navy's equivalents of the Royal Navy's *Dido* class, were small (541 feet, 7,500 tons fully loaded) cruisers armed with dual-purpose 5-inch/38-caliber main batteries.) Existing close-in AA guns were short-ranged and effective only for a ship's own protection, but the 5-inch/38 had the range and power required to supplement the defensive fire of heavy ships. 'The use of destroyers in multiple, as normally in company with battleships and carriers, thus affords additional means of active anti-aircraft defense.' The Board concluded that the most effective AA defense of the fleet must be primarily premised on the combination of active and passive defense capabilities that could be provided by the ships themselves, with 'early and directional detection' of aerial attackers and the installation of both long- and short-range AA guns with adequate control systems and an ammunition capacity sufficient for sustained fire. In forwarding the General Board's report of 12 June to CNO the Board's chairman, Rear Admiral Walton Sexton, had noted that 'it must be borne in mind that anti-aircraft ammunition on board ship is strictly limited, and the fire of this ammunition must be extremely effective.' Existing ships, as well as future construction, needed to be provided with improved means of AA defense, and a continuing program of research and development was necessary to keep the fleet's air-defense program up-to-date once it was begun.[4] The report of the Anti-Aircraft Defense Board, signed on 26 December 1940, also viewed the situation with alarm, telling CNO that 'the lack of adequate close-range antiaircraft gun defense of existing ships of the Fleet constitutes the most serious weakness in the readiness of the Fleet for war.'[5]

Information on European-theater destroyer operations available by the summer of 1940 had indicated that current destroyers did not have sufficient ballistic protection or short-range automatic weapons to defend themselves against low-level air attack. The Bureau of Ordnance called on the operating destroyer forces for recommendations and, on 3 November 1940, Commander Destroyers, Battle Force, forwarded the results of a number of studies. Intelligence reports from abroad had repeatedly stressed the need for large numbers of AA machine guns which, though they might not down an attacker, would disrupt his approach enough to prevent him from scoring a hit. ComDesBatFor believed that, if additional machine guns were available, they should be so arranged that at least six guns could fire to any bearing. New weapons were needed. Destroyer AA practices had 'consistently been unsatisfactory', and better material was needed if better results were to be had. An efficient director was essential if the 1.1-inch gun was to realize its potential, and the .50-caliber machine gun would not be effective until larger numbers of them became available (ComDesBatFor was, presumably, hoping to offset individual inaccuracy with larger numbers of guns).[6]

Commander, Battle Force, concurred and wanted the existing situation remedied quickly. At this time 'certain 20 and 40 mm guns of foreign design' were under consideration, and these should be substituted for the .50-caliber gun if they should prove superior.[7] The Commander in Chief, United States Fleet (CINCUS), thought some of these recommendations extreme; they went, he felt, beyond practical questions of weight, magazine capacity, and personnel as well as what he termed 'the commensurateness of the armament to the value and probable employment of the ship.' Eight .50-caliber guns, he thought, so arranged that four guns could fire forward or aft, was an acceptable minimum close-in armament for a destroyer. Any further improvement in ship armaments would have to depend on the development of multiple gun mounts.

CINCUS did agree that existing AA armament needed improvement; 'it is a matter of common knowledge', he said, 'that most of our ships are inadequately armed against close air attack.' The 5-inch/38 was not agile enough

to cope with low-flying planes; the .50-caliber machine gun was not powerful enough, nor did it have enough range. The 1.1-inch gun, he thought, made a 'satisfactory intermediate battery' between the 5-inch gun and the machine gun, but he doubted if it was desirable to equip destroyers with three calibers of guns. 'The 20 mm machine gun offers possibilities towards bridging the gap between the .50 caliber machine gun and the 5 inch gun, and hence of obviating the necessity, at least on smaller types, of providing an intermediate battery.'[8]

Early in 1941 the Anti-Aircraft Defense Board pronounced the present short-range batteries of current destroyers inadequate. The vulnerability of the destroyer to low-level attack made the type of much less value for fleet screening and convoy work than was possible or acceptable. The Board was aware, as ComDesBatFor had not been, that work was underway to provide improved AA guns, and recommended that additional .50-caliber and 1.1-inch guns be installed in destroyers 'without delay', to be replaced by 20-millimeter and 40-millimeter guns 'as fast as these weapons become available'.[9] After going to CNO and the Secretary of the Navy, this report then went to the General Board for consideration in its continuing study of AA defense.

The new weapons mentioned by the Anti-Aircraft Defense Board had been under consideration for some time, though they were still far from ready for the fleet. Examination of the Bofors 40 mm gun began in the fall of 1939; after negotiations with the manufacturer a specimen gun was tested in September 1940. The Bofors was pronounced superior to other American and foreign types, and a contract was signed in June 1941, to permit American manufacture. Much work was still needed; the Swedish guns were painstakingly-handicrafted weapons using manually-operated single or twin mounts. Power-operated twin and quadruple mounts were designed for American naval use (some adaptations of the single hand-operated US Army mount were also procured for the Navy). Though the inevitable problems were plentiful, production lines were eventually able to turn 40 mm AA gun mounts out in great quantities. Twins and quads, as well as some singles, came to form part of the AA battery of the modern American destroyer (except, as noted, in the case of four ships of the *Gridley* class, whose stability situation did not permit them to use the 40 mm twin mount), and the impact-fuzed 40 mm explosive round proved itself highly effective not only against aircraft but against targets ashore as well.

Associated with the 40 mm gun was the Gun Director Mark 51, a simple but effective device consisting of a lead-computing Gun Sight Mark 14 mounted on a pedestal. Installed a short distance from the guns which it controlled, the Mark 51 allowed more accurate control of AA fire and alleviated the problems of vibration and powder-gas distortion of visibility associated with local control of the 1.1-inch quadruple mount. Toward the end of the war some 40 mm mounts came to be controlled by a new, radar-equipped, Gun Fire Control System (GFCS) Mark 63 which was capable of 'blind' firing.

Like the 40 mm gun, the 20 mm AA gun of World War II was not an American invention. Developed by Oerlikon in Switzerland, the gun was tested and adopted for British use. A combination of firing tests and British urging led the US Navy to select the gun for its own service, and manufacture began in the United States in the summer of 1941. The first 20 mm gun was delivered to the Navy in July of that year,[10] and a small number of guns was on hand by Pearl Harbor. As with the 40 mm Bofors, production was stepped up in spite of difficulties. Peak production was achieved by the second half of 1943, when more than 25,000 guns were delivered. American destroyers used 20 mm single mounts throughout the war years, these being replaced or supplemented in some ships by twin mounts in 1945. The pedestal-mounted, free-swinging, 20 mm automatic gun dispensed its services from 60-round drum magazines at a cyclic rate of 450 rounds per minute and, with its explosive projectile and quick reaction time, formed a valuable part of the destroyer's close-in battery. Even in 1945, with many advocating replacement of these guns by the heavier Bofors, the 20 mm gun's ability to get into action in a hurry continued to be valued and the lighter gun continued to share in the fight against the *kamikaze*; its ability to operate without power also counted in its favor.

The original control system for the 20 mm gun consisted of a ring sight with which it was theoretically possible for an experienced gunner to lead a rapidly-moving target. Before Pearl Harbor, however, the Bureau of Ordnance learned of work being done by the Sperry Gyroscope Company in pursuit of a principle developed by Dr Charles Draper of the Massachusetts Institute of Technology. As developed, Draper's device used gyroscopes to measure rates of movement in given directions; two gyros were kept spinning by compressed air, one gyro measuring lead in train while the other did so in elevation. The sight worked in such a way that the line of sight was offset by the required amount of lead; a sightsetter manually set target range into the sight, and the gunner held the sight reticle directly on the target. An experimental sight was tested in mid-1941, and contracts were soon placed for the device as the Gun Sight Mark 14. The sight was in fleet service by the fall of 1942 and soon demonstrated its value, though it was difficult to persuade gunners that they should trust the sight and not attempt to lead by eye. Mounted on a pedestal, the Mark 14 also came into use in 1942 as an element of the Gun Director Mark 51 for service with 40 mm guns. The Mark 51 was modified to control 3-inch and 5-inch guns as well, though it was not suited for surface fire. Some Mark 51s were replaced, during the war's final months, by the more sophisticated GFCS Mark 63. An improved version of the Mark 51 was built around a new Gun Sight Mark 15; this new director could handle guns, from 40 mm to 5-inch, with greater range and improved accuracy. Introduced in 1944 as the Gun Director Mark 52, this new device was installed in many destroyer escorts as their main-battery director.[11]

To return, however, to the prewar period, a comprehensive plan for improving warships' AA defenses had been approved by the Secretary of the Navy on 1 June 1940; a supplemental defense appropriation act for Fiscal Year 1941, signed into law on 26 June 1940, included $24,360,000 for alteration and conversion of naval vessels, 'including the provision of antiaircraft defense', for which a third of this money was earmarked. The Navy plan was predicated on increasing the number of guns to augment the volume of fire available for defense against dive bombers and other low-altitude attackers, and on providing suitable bulwarks and shelters to protect topside personnel against strafing and fragmentation. Emphasis was placed, during 1940, on improvement of AA gunnery in battleships, carriers, and cruisers and it was in response to that need that the 1940 appropriation was passed. Further study followed, and early in 1941 another bill was proposed and rapidly passed. This new Act provided three hundred million dollars — *1941* dollars — to improve the AA batteries of warships and auxiliaries.

Two days before this bill was signed into law by President Roosevelt, CNO suggested that the General Board give early consideration to increasing the antiaircraft armaments of destroyers. Many recommendations had been received from the fleet and from the technical Bureaus, proposing to remove such items as topmasts and crows' nests as well as some boats and bulwarks, accessory machinery, and even bulkhead sheathing in living quarters. All concerned, from the forces afloat to the politicians, were now taking the AA

question seriously indeed, but CNO warned that more weight removal and relocation was going to be needed to compensate for further added armament as well as the new radar.[12]

The General Board forwarded its recommendations to the Secretary on 14 February. Its study had not yet proceeded far enough to permit final recommendations for all classes of destroyers, but interim batteries could now be proposed for accomplishment in forthcoming overhauls. BuOrd had pronounced the twin 40 mm mount 'greatly superior' to the quadruple 1.1-inch, and one 20 mm Oerlikon was considered better than 'several' .50-caliber machine guns. The Board felt that the new guns should be substituted for the old in all projected destroyer installations, though the 1.1-inch could be used in the meanwhile until enough 40 mm mounts became available. From the standpoint of weight and stability, a 'one-point-one' could replace a single 5-inch/38 gun without compensation and, to effect an emergency improvement in short-range fire-power, the Board recommended that all ships with five 5-inch guns from the *Farraguts* through the *Benson* and *Gleaves* classes have one gun replaced by a 1.1-inch quad mount with a director.[13]

The War Plans Division of OPNAV advised that, since 40 mm mounts would not be available for destroyers until, at least, 1942, that 5-gun *Benson*s and *Gleaves* built or building, should not be altered until the new AA guns were ready for installation.[14] CNO agreed, noting that directors would also not be available in quantity until early 1942 and, even then, were slated for initial installation in bigger warships before being allocated to destroyers. Until directors could be

One of the 5-inch/38 open-mount guns of *Shaw* (DD-373), manned and ready. This semiautomatic, power-operated dual-purpose gun represented a major improvement in destroyer gunnery when it was introduced with the *Farragut* class in 1934. Firing a 54-pound projectile at a muzzle velocity of 2,600 ft/sec, it had a maximum horizontal range of 18,000 yards and a vertical range of 37,300 feet. Effective shooting range was determined by the fire-control equipment used; 1944 gunnery doctrine called 10,000 yards the maximum slant range for good antiaircraft work, with 12,000 yards the top range for firing on low-flying torpedo planes. Instructions for Navy armed-guard crews on merchant ships held that accurate shooting under local (mount) control could be done up to 3,750 yards. The nominal rate of fire with the 5-inch/38 was 15 rounds per minute but, with good crews, rates of 25 rounds and more were reported. To get the best out of their gun, crews like this had to be drilled to a high degree of coordination.

provided with the guns, he considered, the 40 mm mounts should not be installed.[15]

The Bureau of Ordnance asked, a few weeks later, that characteristics for all new and existing ships be revised as quickly as possible to substitute 40 mm and 20 mm guns for the older weapons. These should be installed wherever possible, the Bureau thought, and foundations for them should be built into new ships even where temporary arrangements of .50-caliber and 1.1-inch guns were being used due to lack of the new guns. BuOrd recommended a general AA installation policy to the effect that all arcs of fire should be covered by 40 mm guns (the Bureau preferred to install these to the exclusion of 20 mm or smaller weapons where this could be done), and that a maximum battery of two 40 mm twins, backed up by 20 mm singles, was satisfactory for destroyers.[16]

The process of tophamper reduction and improvement of short-range AA batteries, begun before Pearl Harbor, was still continuing apace when V-J Day ended the war. It

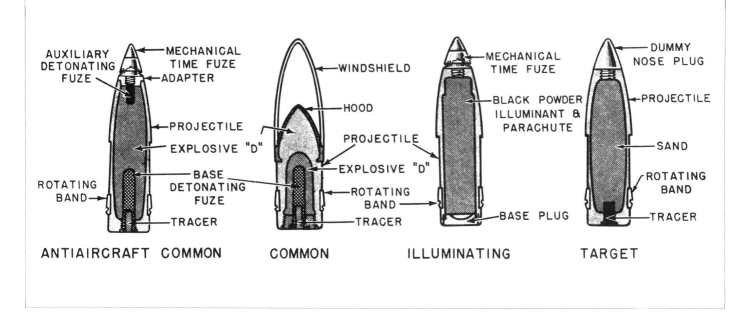

| AUXILIARY DETONATING FUZE — MECHANICAL TIME FUZE — ADAPTER — PROJECTILE — EXPLOSIVE "D" — BASE DETONATING FUZE — ROTATING BAND — TRACER | WINDSHIELD — HOOD — PROJECTILE — EXPLOSIVE "D" — ROTATING BAND — TRACER | MECHANICAL TIME FUZE — BLACK POWDER ILLUMINANT & PARACHUTE — BASE PLUG | DUMMY NOSE PLUG — PROJECTILE — SAND — ROTATING BAND — TRACER |
| ANTIAIRCRAFT COMMON | COMMON | ILLUMINATING | TARGET |

The 5-inch/38 gun fired semi-fixed (separate-loading) ammunition. While fixed (single-loading) ammunition meant a slightly higher rate of fire, this had to be sacrificed when destroyer gun calibers went from 4 to 5 inches. 'Common' projectiles, a general-purpose round designed principally for use against lightly-protected ships, as well as illuminating projectiles ('star shells') and inert target rounds were originally provided. The AA Common projectile, with thinner walls and a heavier bursting charge for better blast and fragmentation, was developed during World War II. This shell took a mechanical time fuze for AA use, and was later used with proximity fuzes. Another wartime addition was the white-phosphorus shell, used both for laying smoke and for its antipersonnel effect.

was begun by reducing such things as non-essential superstructure and masts, and by removing most ships' boats and even, in many ships, an anchor. Where possible, such items as fire-control searchlights, which had to be retained, were lowered. The 5-gun *Farragut*, *Mahan*, *Dunlap*, *Sims*, and *Gleaves* classes eventually gave up one gun. The bigger *Porter* and *Somers* classes, with their four twin single-purpose 5-inch mounts, kept all four until well into the war years but had other top-weight reduced or lowered and, eventually, landed one twin gun mount to make room for AA guns before beginning a piecemeal modernization. The later fourth-generation *Fletcher*, *Allen M. Sumner*, and *Gearing* classes were big enough to handle heavier AA batteries and radar without the kind of alterations required in the earlier classes, though torpedo tubes had to be sacrificed in 1945 to allow installation of improved 40 mm batteries and control systems.

Earlier wartime additions to light AA batteries in destroyers were relatively modest when compared to the large arrays being mounted in bigger warships but, within the

size limitation of the destroyer type, they were a decided improvement.

The *Farragut* class first received 20 mm guns to replace their .50-caliber machine guns during the winter of 1941–42, getting four 20 mm singles in lieu of their four 'fifties'. By 1943 a pair of twin 40 mm mounts, with directors, was replacing the amidships 5-inch gun. The short-range batteries of the *Porter* and *Somers* classes were being criticized before the European war was very old. By the spring of 1940 the AA modernization of these classes was being discussed; suggestions for their improvement were made.[17]

The War Plans Division considered alteration of the 5-inch batteries in the 'leaders' from single- to dual-purpose the most important alteration possible for them. A gun-for-gun conversion would go beyond the limits of stability, but War Plans thought that 'the desirability of proper protection against aircraft is, however, so important that it is recommended a study be made as to the maximum number of 5''/38 caliber double purpose guns that could be mounted in the 1850-ton destroyers.'[18]

The Bureau of Ordnance thought that this would cause production problems. The existing gun mounts in these classes were not suitable for conversion to dual-purpose, and new mounts would have to be manufactured. One new twin mount, with the same light weather shield as the existing mount, would weigh about 93,500 pounds as compared to the 76,840 of the existing ones. Whether these could be gotten into the 1,850-ton hull would depend on the results of stability and displacement studies being made by BuShips. Production facilities for ordnance were limited

and demands were severe; manufacture of new gun mounts for the thirteen *Porters* and *Somers* would cut into the supply of guns for new construction. The Bureau estimated that no space would be available belowdecks in these ships for a plotting room to contain the separate computer and stable element associated with the current-production Mark 37 gun director. If these classes received dual-purpose batteries, though, they would require a fire-control system for them. The only dual-purpose director in existence which did not require a plotting room was the Mark 33, all the elements of which were contained in the abovedecks director housing. This, however, was now out of production; a special order for a 'repeat' lot of Mark 33s would require a three-year wait from order to delivery — the Bureau did not explain why it would take three years to produce thirteen gun directors — and would mean further interference in current production programs.[19]

The General Board felt that modernization of the 1,850-tonners could wait until the desired changes could be made without deranging the expanded shipbuilding program then underway. Since all new destroyers, other than these two classes, had 5-inch dual-purpose guns the 'leaders' could be used in 'employment suited to their armament' for the time being. When the building program permitted, the large destroyers could then be altered. The Board judged that the ships could handle two twin dual-purpose mounts in the 'low' positions, with two single mounts in superfiring positions, not too far an estimate from what was ultimately to be built into the two classes. Stability would be maintained by removing the after director

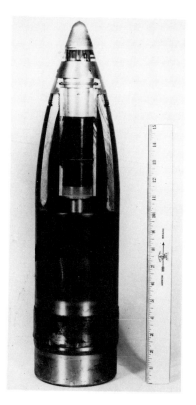

from the *Porter*s and the after quadruple torpedo tube from *Somers* class ships.[20]

An informal inquiry now went from the General Board to BuShips, asking if it would be feasible to install an additional 1.1-inch quadruple AA mount in the 1,850-ton ships. The Bureau sketched a plan calling for removal of the topweights suggested by the Board and the installation of the third 1.1-inch mount in a superfiring position forward of the existing after AA mount. The proposed addition would not impair stability, but would require a considerable amount of shipyard work 'and would at present divert technical and mechanical personnel at Navy Yards.'[21] On 3 September 1941 the General Board, on BuShips' recommendation, suggested that the leaders be given three 40 mm twins and six 20 mm guns. This was approved by the Secretary of the Navy on the 17th; this proposal involved cutting down after superstructure and removing the present two 1.1-inch mounts and two .50-caliber machine guns, but until the new guns became available the structural work could be done. The forward 1.1-inch mount could remain in place, the after one being moved to one of the new 40 mm foundations and .50-caliber guns mounted in the new locations provided for 20 mm guns.[22]

Desiderata for the *Porter*s and the *Somers* continued to be rethought. On 12 November 1941 CNO approved three 40 mm twins and two 20 mm guns for the *Somers* class. The first months of war in the Pacific brought new

AA lessons, and on 30 June 1942 CNO gave his approval to arming Pacific-area *Porter*s with two 1.1-inch quads and five 20 mm guns.[23] Further advice came from destroyer force commanders and, on 19 December 1942, a new interim specification was approved for the *Porter* class. This entailed removal of the superfiring 5-inch mount aft, and installation of a quadruple 40 mm mount, three 40 mm twins, and six 20 mm Oerlikons. An ultimate battery, based on the dual-purpose 5-inch gun mount, was under consideration.[24]

The technical Bureaus quickly brought up their recommendations for an ultimate armament for the *Porter* class. As approved by CINCUS on 28 December 1942, this called for five 5-inch dual-purpose guns (two twin mounts, one single); one 40 mm quad; two 40 mm twins; and six 20 mm guns. A similar battery, but with a third 40 mm twin in lieu of the quadruple mount, was approved for the *Somers* class shortly afterwards.[25] This projected armament, the result of detailed Bureau studies and reflecting the opinion of the forces afloat, dropped one of the 5-inch singles previously approved for the leaders, substituting four more 20 mm guns for a better close-in battery. These guns, with eight tubes, two depth-charge tracks, and four K-guns, were considered all that these ships could carry. Internal rearrangement to provide space for a plotting room so that the Mark 37 director could be installed was considered the only realistic course; the gain

in accuracy available with the Mark 37 was a worthwhile bonus.[26]

During 1944–45 this modernization program was carried out on four *Porter*s and a fifth was in hand when the war ended. *McDougal* (DD-358) and *Winslow* (DD-359), after modernization, were assigned to the Operational Development Force, a special unit set up in 1945 to develop anti-*kamikaze* measures and were configured like the radar-picket *Gearing*s. *McDougal*'s experimental service was brief, but *Winslow* was not placed out of commission until 1950, the last of the London Treaty destroyers to leave active service.

As the illustrations of wartime *Porter* and *Somers* class ships in this volume will briefly indicate, actual AA modifications depended on the usual operational and logistic vagaries. After the opening months of the war, neither class was used in a first-line striking-force role. Antiaircraft deficiencies made them more of a liability than an asset in areas where heavy air attack might be expected, and after Midway those 1,850-tonners serving in the Pacific were assigned to convoy, patrol, and bombardment duty. By the fall of 1944 all of these ships were in the Atlantic. Upperworks began to be cut down in 1941; .50-caliber and 20 mm guns were added, as were 40 mm twins when available. By the end of 1944 the superfiring after 5-inch twin mount had been removed from all the *Somers* and all but one of the *Porter*s. Six-gun *Porter*s had three 40 mm twins and one quad, with six or eight 20 mm guns. Two of this class had been modernized,

with new superstructures and 5-inch dual-purpose guns with Mark 37 directors; the new DP 5-inch battery was backed up by two 40 mm twins, one quad, and six 20 mm guns. All of these *Porter*s still retained their eight tubes. Four *Porter*s had been given AA modernizations by August 1945; one more was undergoing such a conversion, but this was dropped after V-J Day. Two *Porter*s ended the war with three of their original four single-purpose gun mounts.

The *Somers* class, as we have noted, had less of a stability reserve than did the *Porter*s. Their AA alterations generally tended to follow the same general pattern of the *Porter* class, but they could handle less topside weight and received correspondingly fewer light AA guns, even after their third quadruple torpedo tube had been removed. By December 1944, all of the class had lost one 5-inch gun mount; instead of the two twin and one quadruple 40 mm mounts given to the *Porter*s, the *Somers* class ships received three twins with six or eight 20 mm guns. One ship, *Davis* (DD-395), had been given a dual-purpose 5-inch battery, but still with two 40 mm barrels fewer than her *Porter* class counterparts (three 40 mm twins). One more of this class was modernized by August 1945, and *Somers* herself had just entered a shipyard for conversion.

The armament of the *Mahan* and *Dunlap* classes had been criticized before Pearl Harbor. Commander Destroyers, Battle Force, keeping weight and space limitations in mind,

recommended removal of their fifth 5-inch gun and installation of two 40 mm twins and six 20 mm guns. All tubes were to be retained since Battle Force ships were 'offensive vessels; they should be designed primarily to operate with the fleet, and should be fitted with offensive rather than protective armament.'[27]

CNO approved two twin 40 mm mounts and two 20 mm guns as the AA battery for the *Mahan* class but, early in 1942, prescribed eight 20 mm guns as an interim battery.[28] In actual practice, *Mahan*s of early 1942 had four 20 mm guns (two had six) or their original four .50-caliber machine guns; three ships of the class had lost their fifth 5-inch gun, but had not yet received 40 mm guns.[29] The rest of the class gradually removed their fifth guns, replacing them at first with 20 mm guns until the 40 mm mounts and directors became available. By the end of the war two 40 mm twins and five 20 mm guns (six in the rebuilt *Cassin* and *Downes*, sunk at Pearl Harbor and reconstructed) was still the standard battery for *Mahan* class ships as well as for the *Dunlap*s. Two *Mahan*s had received 1945 AA improvements, as will be noted later.

The *Gridley* class, as has been seen, had stability problems which precluded installation of 40 mm guns. They, alone among American destroyers, finished the war with eight 20 mm guns as their sole close-in battery. To handle even this safely, eight of the ships' sixteen torpedo tubes had to be removed. The outwardly-similar *Bagley* class

kept their original torpedo battery. Beginning the war with .50-caliber AA guns, they began to receive 20 mm guns early in 1942. Before the year was out some *Bagley*s had a twin 40 mm mount installed on the after-deck-house and kept this arrangement, backed up by six or seven 20 mm guns (two or three forward, four amidships) to the end of the war.

The *Benham* and *Sims* classes underwent roughly similar treatment with respect to AA augmentation. Beginning in 1941 the *Benham* class began to lose eight of their sixteen tubes to make room for K-guns and depth-charge track extensions, as well as three more .50-caliber machine guns (for a total of seven). The *Sims* class only had eight tubes to begin with, so their fifth 5-inch gun made way for four more .50-caliber guns, with added antisubmarine equipment. By the middle of 1942 some *Benham*s and all but one *Sims* had 20 mm AA guns, and by late 1943 the prescribed battery for the *Benham* class consisted of four 5-inch and six 20 mm guns (two each forward, amidships, and aft), with eight tubes. The heavier *Sims* class had received two 40 mm twins aft, with three 20 mm guns forward and a single 20 mm gun on the after-deckhouse. The *Benham*s exchanged the two after 20 mm guns for a pair of 40 mm twins during 1944, and two of the class received an AA modification during 1945. *Sims* class ships retained their 1943 configuration to the end of the war, with three of the class being included in the 1945 anti-*kamikaze* refit.

The original *Benson/Gleaves* design called for five 5-inch guns, ten torpedo tubes, and six .50-caliber machine guns. As in the earlier classes, this was soon overtaken by events. By mid-1941 ships were being completed with four 5-inch guns, ten tubes, and heavier AA and antisubmarine armaments. Four-gun ships received twelve .50-caliber guns, while earlier 5-gun ships lost one quintuple torpedo tube for a Y-gun, depth-charge track extensions, and four more .50-caliber machine guns. By August of 1941 the prescribed battery for ships nearing completion was four 5-inch, two 40 mm twins, and four 20 mm guns. This, of course, was the *desideratum*; what was actually installed for the time being was what was available. Foundations and platforms were installed where possible to facilitate later rearmament; some *Benson*s and *Gleaves* were given a 1.1-inch quadruple mount on their after gun platform, which they shared with a single 20 mm gun when Oerlikons became available. Into 1942 these two classes displayed various combinations of AA guns and closed, open, and open-top 5-inch gun mounts. By mid-1942 5-gun *Benson*s and *Gleaves* had five tubes and combinations of 20 mm and .50-caliber guns. Four-gun ships might have five tubes, with a 1.1-inch quad and five or six 20 mm guns; five ships of this type had 20 mm or .50-caliber guns only. Other 4-gun ships had ten tubes, without heavy AA guns, and mounted Brownings, Oerlikons, or both. By 1943 the standard armament for these classes had been worked out (though not always installed) as four 5-inch guns; three 20 mm guns forward; two 20 mm on the after end of the bridge wings, a novel arrangement in American destroyers; two more alongside the after stack; and two 40 mm twins on the after-deckhouse. A fire-control searchlight was installed on the centerline abaft the stacks; some of these classes retained ten torpedo tubes, and the searchlight was located on the after-deckhouse with the 40 mm guns to make room for this.

During 1944 a number of *Benson*s and *Gleaves* had had a pair of Army-type single 40 mm guns installed, as had also been done with the *Sims* class *Wainwright* (DD-419), which had received three of these mounts. By the end of this year thirteen early ('low-

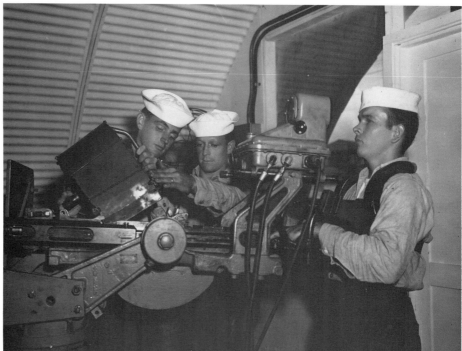

number') ships had received this 40 mm augmentation, and two more had it authorized. The single 40 mm guns were removed during 1945; by August of that year seven of the early-production ships still had their original ten tubes, with two 40 mm twins and four 20 mm guns. Twenty-three more had five tubes with seven 20 mm and two 40 mm twins. Twenty-seven of these classes had received 1945 AA improvements, as did seven of the converted *Gleaves* class high-speed minesweepers (DMS). Wartime alterations to

The 20 mm Oerlikon-designed automatic shell-firing gun was an effective and universally-used shipboard AA weapon. Explosive ammunition and free-swinging operation made it a good quick-reaction defense against surprise attack. Fixed ring sights were replaced, on most guns, by Mark 14 lead-computing sights which improved accuracy, and seem to have slightly increased effective shooting range. Late-war gunnery doctrine prescribed opening fire at 1,500 to 1,600 yards.

Opposite
Twin and quadruple Bofors 40 mm AA mounts became a powerful addition to destroyer AA batteries. They were usually controlled by Mark 51 directors, with local control by ii on sight available as a backup. The 40 mm gun was considered effective up to 2,000 yards.

had been authorized in the *Porter, Somers, Bagley, Benham,* and *Sims* classes; the larger 'leaders' were also to lose half of their depth-charge installations. Two new 40 mm quads were to be mounted amidships in the *Porters* and *Somers*. The *Bagleys* were to have two quads and two twins in place of their 40 mm twin and lose part of the antisubmarine armament. The two twin 40 mm in the *Benhams* and *Sims* were to be increased to four.[31]

The *Mahan* class seems to have had fewer difficulties with stability than some of its contemporaries, and the hull design drawn by Gibbs and Cox apparently had enough strength to handle wartime loads. In January 1945, removal of their two quadruple 'wing' torpedo tubes had been authorized to permit substitution of two 40 mm quads for their existing twin mounts. In June removal of the third, centerline, tube was authorized to make way for two 40 mm twins, these to go abreast the after stack.

All of the destroyers receiving these AA modifications were to have directors installed with their new 40 mm mounts; these Mark 51s were to be replaced, as possible, by new blind-firing GFCS Mark 63 installations with radar. 20 mm guns were to be removed where further weight compensation was necessary. The first ships of the third destroyer generation, the five surviving units of the *Farragut* class did not enter into this consideration and no AA improvement plan is mentioned as being considered for them.

By the end of the war in the Pacific, none of the *Farragut* class had had their AA batteries modified. These more 'thinly-built' ships could handle their assigned wartime armament, but nothing more. Two *Porters* had lost their torpedo tubes in favor of two 40 mm twins and three quads, supplemented by two twin 20 mm mounts; a third ship was under conversion when V-J Day put an end to the process. Two *Somers* class ships had two quads and three twins, and *Somers* herself had her modification halted by the war's end. One of the *Mahan* class had her two 40 mm twins replaced by quads when her tubes were removed; a second ship got the planned arrangement of two twins and two quads, with four twin 20 mm mounts. The *Gridley* class lacked the stability reserve to handle any 40 mm guns at all, and the *Bagley* class also escaped the AA improvement process; all of this class finished the war with one twin 40 mm mount. Two *Benhams* had their remaining eight tubes suppressed for a final armament of four 40 mm twins with four twin Oerlikons. Three of the *Sims* class ended up with four 40 mm twins, four 20 mm (one had two singles with two twins), and no tubes.

Of the 57 active ships of the *Benson* and

the AA batteries of the *Fletcher, Allen M. Sumner,* and *Gearing* classes will be outlined in the histories of those classes and need not be discussed here.

The opening of large-scale *kamikaze* operations off Okinawa brought a general reappraisal of destroyer AA defenses. Early in May 1945, COMINCH approved removal of one 5-tube torpedo mount from the *Fletchers, Allen M. Sumners,* and *Gearings*. In the 2,200-tonners this would permit installation of another 40 mm quadruple gun mount aft to supplement the two already there; in the *Fletcher* class it allowed substitution of two 40 mm quads for the two twins mounted amidships. Most *Benson* and *Gleaves* class ships now had one quintuple tube remaining; if this was removed, two 40 mm quads could be installed in addition to the existing two 40 mm twins. To the extent that production and installation capabilities allowed, 20 mm single mounts were to be replaced by new Mark 24 twin gun mounts.[30]

By mid-June removal of all torpedo tubes

Gleaves classes, 27 received AA improvements by August 1945. All of these ended the war with four 5-inch guns, two 40 mm twins with two quads, and a combination of two 20 mm singles and two twins. The sole exception to this was *McClanahan* (DD-615), which received four 40 mm twins in lieu of the twin-quad combination. Seven out of 23 *Gleaves* class high-speed minesweeper (DMS) conversions had their two 40 mm twins replaced by quads; most of the minesweepers had three 5-inch guns, the fourth having been replaced by sweep gear, but six had kept their 4-gun battery through conversion.

Primary emphasis, in the actual allocation of resources, was given to the Pacific Fleet's first-line strength: the destroyers of the *Fletcher*, *Allen M. Sumner*, and *Gearing* classes, although, as seen, the former mainstays of the Altantic Fleet — the *Benson*s and *Gleaves* — also received a large measure of attention. By the end of the Pacific war 50 *Fletcher*s out of 149 — one ship in three — had had their tubes replaced by 40 mm quads with Mark 51 directors or with the GFCS Mark 63, the latter system equipped with Mark 28 or Mark 34 rangefinding radar for blind firing. Most of these had six 20 mm twins in place of seven 20 mm singles. All but a few of the unmodified ships had the combination of five 40 mm twins, with seven 20 mm singles, that had characterized the class for the preceding months. Fifteen *Allen M. Sumner*s and fifteen *Gearing*s finished the war with three 40 mm quads, two twins, and five tubes; 21 radar-picket *Gearing*s had three quads by the fall of 1945, with all tubes removed. The 'authorized ultimate' battery configuration for these classes envisioned a return to the pre-*kamikaze* status quo, with torpedo tubes restored and quadruple 40 mm mounts removed, but, in point of fact, this reconfiguration did not take place. There were still plenty of torpedo tubes in the fleet after 1945, and the potential enemy — the Soviet Union — lacked a large surface fleet, but had respectable numbers of aircraft and submarines. Postwar development efforts were bent in the direction of improving destroyer antiair and antisubmarine capabilities, and restoration of full torpedo armaments to existing ships seems to have rather quickly faded from sight.

Before World War II radar was unknown; an enemy had to be located visually, and the Mark I Eyeball was the supreme reconnaissance tool. Tactical doctrine called for elaborate systems of air patrols and surface scouts; search patterns were mathematically calculated. Radar made it possible to detect an enemy's presence before he could be seen, and also lifted the protective curtains of night and foul weather. A supplementary development, Identification Friend or Foe (IFF), added an interrogator to a ship's radar which emitted a signal that triggered a coded response from friendly aircraft or ships and positively identified them even though they could not be seen.

The first shipboard experiments with radar were carried out in the flushdecker *Leary* (DD-158) in 1937. A prototype search radar, Type XAF, was tested in the battleship *New York* (BB-34) in 1939. It worked well, and the production CXAM was introduced to the fleet in 1941, quickly followed by the CXAM-1. These first radars were suitable for heavy warships; work followed on lighter units, suitable for destroyers and other smaller ships. A prototype SC radar was tried out in another flushdecker, *Semmes* (DD-189), during 1941; by early 1942 some destroyers were receiving production units. Gunnery radars also began to appear in 1942 for use with Mark 33 and Mark 37 directors. The FD (later redesignated Mark 4) and the later Mark 12 radars were dual-purpose equipments; neither could do an adequate job of detecting and tracking low-flying planes, so a supplementary unit, the Mark 22, was added to the earlier radars to cover this area. The new Mark 25 radar had appeared by the time the war ended, and replaced earlier equipments during the postwar years. The smaller Mark 28 and Mark 34 radars were developed for use with blind-firing AA gun fire-control systems, and the lightweight Mark 28 was installed in the 5-inch directors of many smaller destroyers by 1945 to save topside weight, another indication of how seriously the destroyer stability problem was taken. The single-purpose Mark 35 gun directors of the *Porter* and *Somers* class 'leaders' were given the FC (Mark 3) radar, originally developed for use with battleship and cruiser guns. Modernized *Porter*s and *Somers* had Mark 37 dual-purpose directors fitted, and these were equipped with the Mark 12/22 combination.

Sea-air operations, often at night or in such restricted waters as those around the Solomons, complicated information handling in destroyers. Incoming information could no longer be received and assimilated on the bridge as before. An improved system was needed to handle it, and the Bureaus of Ships and Aeronautics, with the Chief of Naval Operations, recommended establishment of a *radar plot* to be 'the brains of the organization which protects the fleet or ships from air attack.' The Secretary of the Navy approved, and a radar plot was installed in the then-new carrier *Hornet* (CV-8) for tactical situation plotting and fighter direction. During 1941 the earliest doctrines were drawn up.

Working radar doctrines came into general use after Pearl Harbor, as something that had only been discussed and speculated upon before the war now became reality. These principles of radar employment were carefully studied and revised as needed; in fact, the entire war constituted a continuing learning process as the fleet learned not only how to install the new gadget and keep it running, but also how to interpret and use the information that it provided. Radio vocabularies and information-plotting methods were standardized to facilitate accurate, orderly tallying and communication of information.

Early radars used what was called an A-scope presentation, in which the screen of a cathode-ray tube presented a horizontal line with vertical pips representing the targets. The British-developed Plan Position Indicator (PPI) scope was introduced with some search radars in 1942. This scope presented a geographical picture, with the originating ship or plane in the center of the circular screen and detected targets appearing on the screen as 'pips' of light in their correct distance and bearing from the center. This was of real value, both for tactics and for navigation. Not only could the surroundings be seen in their true relation, but the positions and movements of friendly or enemy forces could be plotted and tracked. A late-war refinement of this was a device that would identify and 'flag' moving targets.

To make proper and timely use of the increasing amount of information received from radar, radio, sonar, and lookout, tactical orders required each ship to establish a Combat Information Center (CIC). This was a space — in destroyers, in or just below the bridge superstructure — equipped with radios and radar receivers, a gyrocompass repeater and pitometer log indicator, and boards on which the tactical situation could be plotted and kept up-to-date. Its primary function was to keep the ship's commanding officer — and the unit commander, if one was embarked — informed on the identity and activities of friendly and hostile forces in the immediate area. The CIC was also made responsible for target indication to the gun and torpedo batteries; control of aircraft and small craft in the area, a function developed during the fighting in the Solomons; and navigation, when operating near land as in amphibious landings or shore-bombardment missions, or during operations in such restricted-water areas as the Solomons. The relative importance of secondary CIC functions varied with the situation, but the primary task was of universal, continuing importance whatever the situation or mission. This new organization came to be of such general usefulness that the wartime CIC's

highly-sophisticated descendants are an essential part of all modern naval operations. As the war went on the CIC became much more than a radar plotting center. By 1944 COMINCH could note that 'experience has shown that it has become the center of operations for the tactical handling of the ship and Fleet units.'[32]

During the latter portion of the war destroyer CIC functions were expanded to take in fighter direction, using VHF radio-telephone to communicate with assigned aircraft. Some ships had special radios installed for this purpose. The so-called 'Okinawa pickets', the *Gearing* class destroyers fitted with SP height-finding radars and expanded communication and control facilities, would have been an effective addition to the fleet's air-defense capability had the projected invasion of the Japanese home islands become necessary to undertake.

The radar-picket destroyer concept was tried during the approach of the invasion force toward the Gilberts in November 1943, when the fighter-director destroyer *Kimberly* (DD-521) was stationed fifteen miles ahead of the van of the invasion force and given radar-guard duty. During the Kwajalein operation, in January 1944, a radar screen of destroyers was stationed ten miles outside the antisubmarine sonar screen. During the approach to the Marianas in June of the same year, cruising instructions placed radar pickets on night station ten miles from the fleet center for early detection of air or surface attack. During the landings destroyers were stationed in the direction of likely enemy approach, charged with giving radar warning if necessary and directing fighter planes. During the first carrier task force strikes against Japan in February and March 1945, a picket line of destroyers, controlling their own Combat Air Patrol (CAP) of carrier fighters, was stationed forty miles from the carrier force in the direction of Japan. Carrier-force instructions, issued in April 1945, made employment of radar-picket destroyers and picket lines a standard procedure during strike operations.

The radar-picket destroyer, still simply a fleet destroyer assigned to special duty, came into its own during the long Okinawa campaign. Suicide attacks began as early as October 1944, during the invasion of the central Philippines. The *kamikaze* offensive placed severe burdens on fighter direction and AA gunnery alike; incoming raids now not only had to be broken up, but stopped.

The proximity fuze, called 'the most important AA development of the war', was proposed by the Navy in 1940 and was in production by 1942. Tested in firing in Chesapeake Bay, it claimed its first kill on 5 January 1943 when a 5-inch/38 VT-fuzed projectile from the light cruiser *Helena* (CL–50) splashed an attacking Japanese dive bomber. Previous AA fuzes were either of the impact type, which had to hit an aircraft to detonate, or mechanical time fuzes, clockwork mechanisms set to explode so many seconds after firing. The chances of scoring a hit on an aircraft were infinitesimal, and the time fuze had to be set very precisely to explode within lethal range of an attacking 'plane. This was beyond the capability of existing fire-control systems under many circumstances; the slightest error in prediction or fuze setting, or excessive 'dead time' between setting and firing, would send a time-fuzed shell wide of its target.

The proximity fuze, for security reasons, was referred to as the 'variable-time' (VT) fuze and the VT fuze it remained even after its existence was known. The VT fuze was, essentially, a miniature radio transceiver with its own power supply. After firing the fuze's transmitter emitted high-frequency radio waves. When it came within effective range of a target these waves were reflected and picked up by the receiver, activating an electronic switch to release energy from a charged condenser to fire an electric detonator. Flaws had to be ironed out as the war went on. Improved fuzes attained high reliability and greater sensitivity, and the VT-fuzed 5-inch/38 AA projectile became an effective anti-*kamikaze* weapon. Postwar analysis showed VT-fuzed shells to be about three times as effective as their mechanical-time-fuzed counterparts.

The general wartime trend in American naval AA armament called for heavier guns with higher velocities, greater range and destructiveness, and higher rates of fire. The prevailing policy was to install as many guns as space, weight, and personnel limits would allow. Destroyers took part in the air-defense of the fast carrier task force as well as that of convoys and other forces.

Tactical doctrine prescribed a number of antiaircraft dispositions for carrier forces. The carrier task force was divided into task groups, organized around four or five carriers. Screening battleships — the modern fast battleship was a very effective antiaircraft gunnery vessel — cruisers, and destroyers were stationed in circular fashion around the carriers to provide sonar, radar, and gun protection. Doctrine called for screening gun ships to open fire at 12,000 yards or more, using a high percentage of VT fuzes. Destroyers also served as links between task groups, and also as radar pickets. During the offensive operations of the war's final years destroyer divisions, and sometimes squadrons, were assigned picket duty in the direction of possible attack to extend the task force's radar range. Outlying destroyers took incoming raids under fire and directed fighter defense as well as coordinating returning air strike traffic to insure that enemy 'planes did not tag along with the homing carrier aircraft. Early in 1945 carrier task groups developed antiaircraft coordination plans to provide concentrated long-range 5-inch gunfire and to guard against undetected attacks. The area around each task group was divided into four sectors; a task-group AA coordinator received and evaluated incoming information — another use for the Combat Information Center — and alerted the appropriate air-defense sector of the group.

Radar, teamed with gun directors and the proximity fuze, gave destroyers the ability to detect and engage the enemy more effectively at greater ranges. This photograph taken on 2 July 1945, gives a close-up look at the SC-3 and SG search antennae of *Coghlan* (DD-606). She has had a lightweight Mark 28 gunnery radar installed on her Mark 37 director, a reminder that stability was still a delicate question to the destroyer navy.

Other forces, such as amphibious forces and convoys, could not mount so active an air defense. Such forces were slower and less amply provided with weapons, fire-control equipment, and radar and often, by the nature of their mission, had to operate near land. Surprise attack, using land masses as cover against radar, was a problem. Forces of this type also set up systems of destroyer picket stations to extend their radar coverage and engage approaching raids. The Okinawa campaign is a conspicuous example of this type of operation, where the invasion force and its supporting shipping had to remain in a specific geographical area and lacked the speed and freedom of action of the carrier striking force.

The basic AA tactic of all warships was similar. Coming under attack, a threatened ship turned up its best speed and turned to place the enemy on its beam and unmask as much of its firepower as possible. Fire was opened at long range using VT fuzes; lighter guns opened up outside of effective hitting range to make sure that, by the time the attacker reached lethal distance, all guns would be on target and firing. Heavy fire was kept up until the enemy went down or drew out of range. Many ships, toward the war's end, put their 5-inch guns under control of Mark 51 AA directors for quicker response to surprise attacks. If a raid was picked up at more conventional long ranges, control could be shifted to the main Mark 37 director and fire opened in the normal manner.

Efforts were made to speed up reaction times in air-defense. Early detection was stressed, with rapid and effective coordination between CIC and gunnery; sector control of AA batteries simplified overall control of fire; ships were trained to open fire without wait-

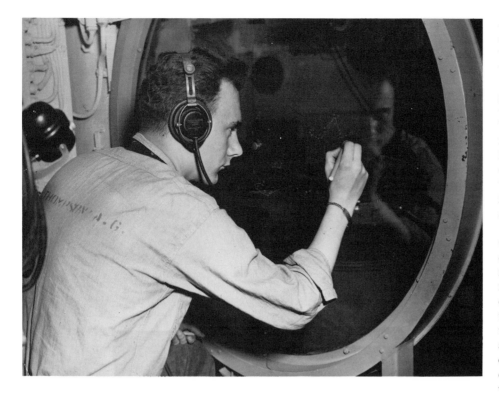

The Combat Information Center (CIC) made it possible for radar to attain its full combat effectiveness. Here a man plots information on a contact being tracked. He has been trained to do this in reverse on the back of the transparent plastic plotting board; evaluators, on the other side, can see what is being plotted without interference. Situation information from all sources was fed into CIC where it was tallied and evaluated; a captain or unit commander was thus kept up to date on what was happening without having to try to gather and assimilate large amounts of information in his head, something that might have served in a more leisurely time but simply did not work in a rapidly-moving three-dimensional war. Early destroyer CICs had to be improvised in ships which were not designed to accommodate them. CIC installations were eventually standardized although, as is inevitable during wartime, fact usually lagged behind principle. The *Allen M. Sumner* and *Gearing* classes were the first American destroyers designed from the start to accommodate radar.

ing for plot to come up with a finished gun-order solution to the fire-control problem. The 5-inch mounts stood manned and ready, with a projectile in the loading tray; when the order to fire came, a cartridge case was quickly dropped in place and the load was rammed and ready to fire. Slewing sights, in the gun-mount officer's cockpit, were originally designed as a means of bringing the gun into the area of a target so that more precise sights could take over; by the end of the war these slewing sights were being used for rapid-reaction 5-inch gun control against suicide aircraft.

Kamikaze aircraft were first used during the operations in the central Philippines in October 1944. Suicide operations increased into the end of January 1945, when they tapered

off before resuming late in March during the preparations for the landing on Okinawa. The massed *kikusui* offensive, which began in April, placed increased stress on the fleet's air-defense system. Suicide tactics were three or four times as effective in scoring hits on ships than conventional attacks, and this made heavier AA defense capabilities essential. It was not enough simply to derange the aim of a bomber or torpedo-plane pilot; the 'plane had to be smashed out of the air and physically prevented from coming within diving range. Suicide attacks off Okinawa were heavier than in the Philippines but, in *proportion*, fewer attackers achieved hits thanks to improved air defenses. Performance was hardly perfect; many ships, including radar-picket destroyers, were sunk or damaged. Yet, the contribution of the picket ships to the success of the hard-fought battle for Okinawa was such that the Commander, Fifth Fleet — Admiral Raymond A. Spruance — could write that: 'The effectiveness of radar pickets in protecting an amphibious operation against enemy air attacks was demonstrated. They provided air warning service, shot down many planes by AA fire and, by controlling their own CAP's,[33] contributed to the destruction of many more.'[34]

During the final stages of the Pacific War, operational experience indicated that a single destroyer could successfully track not more than two raids at one time. At least four 5-inch guns were needed to provide enough

AA fire to give the ship a fair chance of defeating an incoming suicider. This meant that a destroyer attacked simultaneously by two 'planes faced two unsatisfactory choices. She could divide her battery and try to engage both at once, with a less than-optimum volume of fire, or she could turn her entire battery on one attacker in the hope of defeating him in time to turn on the second before he could close. Neither method was thought effective, and COMINCH concluded that 'one destroyer cannot be expected to defend itself successfully against more than one attacking enemy aircraft at a time.'[35]

Experience gained on the picket line at Okinawa led COMINCH to the further conclusion that 'destroyers are operated very much like fighter planes. A fighter team is formed and trained as a unit. Its success is determined by its ability as a unit rather than the ability of the individual components of the unit. Destroyers have many of the capabilities and limitations of fighter aircraft. If the tactical situation permits, they deserve the increased defensive power available to them when they are operating as a division under the command of their division commander.'[36]

To insure good air-defense coordination, it was concluded that destroyers should be operated with their own divisions and not intermixed at random as had often been done. To improve picket-station firepower, at least one destroyer division should be assigned to each station. The Fast Carrier Force's experience with destroyers indicated that ships employed as divisions or squadrons under their own commanders did a better job of detection and fighter direction and would be better able to put up a strong, coordinated gunfire defense. Okinawa experience also showed that destroyers, coming under air attack, should not resort to violent evasive maneuvers since this deranged the accuracy of their AA fire. Bigger warships, on the other hand, did not pitch and roll like destroyers and could maneuver without lessening the effect of their gunfire.

The expanded detection and direction capabilities incorporated in the radar-picket *Gearings* as the war ended, together with increased 40 mm AA batteries, and new radar-equipped AA fire-control systems would have made destroyers more effective antiaircraft ships had the projected invasion of Japan been necessary. Cross-connection between 5-inch and 40 mm directors would have permitted more effective divided fire, and new IFF equipment — the Mark 32 radar — was being combined with ships' 5-inch fire-control radars to permit destroyers to identify incoming bogies more positively and rapidly.[37]

13

The Fletchers

Our plans for the future should be guided by conservatism and by calmness and if we are sure that, individually, our items of equipment and ... our personnel can bear comparison with those of other nations, the outcome of the battles we may fight is fairly certain.

Brockholst Livingston, 'Types and Tactics'

Consideration of the 1941 destroyer program began when, four weeks after war had broken out in Europe, the General Board sent tabulated characteristics for the *Benson* and *Gleaves* class ships of the 1938–40 programs to the Chief of Naval Operations and to the technical Bureaus in preparation for hearings. The Board asked all concerned to think in terms of keeping displacement, and thus size, to 'the practicable minimum in order that they may present minimum targets and that the ratio of cost to number may be as great as possible.' This, it was pointed out, would be impossible unless everyone took due account of all the weights which went to make up the full-load displacement; something more than strict parochialism was needed if a satisfactory ship was to be developed. The General Board noted that 'markedly greater' machinery weights in the earlier ships had impaired their stability at light loads; their full-load displacement, nearly 700 tons above standard, had increased their full-load drafts by three feet.[1]

The General Board circulated a list of questions a few days later, asking if, 'since destroyers are primarily torpedo vessels — for use chiefly against enemy battle lines — do not the latest type destroyers carry too few torpedoes?' and whether unarmored destroyers had not grown so big 'as to present targets unfavorable for survival in torpedo attack?' To what extent had the development of destroyer gun armament, for defense of the battle line against enemy destroyer attack, contributed to this growth in size? Did current destroyers have an adequate antisubmarine capability? What should their designed speed be — 36 knots was suggested — and what was a realistic basis for calculating their trial displacement? Should not the relation between unit cost and numbers of ships to be built be taken into consideration, even though 'present con-

ditions are apparently not restrictive as to cost'? Finally — and quite fundamentally — 'is it not the case that the present-day use of destroyers embraces so many and so varied employments that there is warranted a marked change in the conception of them as torpedo vessels and recognition of the fact that their utility is premised on several functions of which being a torpedo vessel is only one?'[2]

The chief of OPNAV's War Plans Division agreed that the importance of antiair and antisubmarine defense had so changed the function of the destroyer that its design could not be closely shaped around its torpedo-attack mission. Though torpedo work was still important, protection of the major units of the battle force was also vital. The destroyer was the most suitable ship to serve these two purposes, and both had to be taken into account. For the new design, the 10-tube torpedo battery of the *Benson* and *Gleaves* classes was enough. Size should not be reduced simply 'to secure a doubtful improvement in vulnerability in the torpedo attack.' A 5-knot margin of speed over the new fast carriers and battleships — about 38 knots — was recommended, both for screening duty and to offset the 'tin can's' vulnerability in battle. War Plans suggested a 1,650 to 1,800-ton ship with four or five 5-inch guns, ten tubes, increased depth-charge capacity, 38 knots, and a radius of about 6,000 miles.[3]

Mid-October hearings before the General Board produced support for five guns, at least ten torpedoes, and at least 36 knots. Size, the conferees felt, should not be reduced at the expense of what they considered essential military characteristics. Admiral Furlong, Chief of the Bureau of Ordnance, remarked that he felt that 'you should build as good a

destroyer as you can get while you have the money, fewer numbers and better ships, and when Congress shuts down on us we can change the characteristics and get more ships.' The hearings made it clear that prevailing service opinion called for an adequate balance between torpedoes, guns, and antisubmarine ordnance.[4]

The Chief of Naval Operations, Admiral Harold Stark, sent his 'personal opinions' to the General Board on 18 October. He agreed with the Board's suggested 36 knots, and did not want size or displacement reduced; twelve torpedo tubes were desirable, and more depth charges should be allowed. He did not think that individual-ship costs were critical: 'the best possible vessel should be designed without consideration of this relationship.' He answered the Board's final query in its own words: the '... utility of present day destroyers is premised on several functions of which being a torpedo boat is only one and ... this should be given consideration in ... the final design of these vessels.'[5]

The General Board issued tentative characteristics for the 1941 destroyers on 17 October 1939. These included, as a minimum, four 5-inch guns with four .50-caliber AA machine guns; ten centerline torpedo tubes with stowage for four reload torpedoes; two depth-charge tracks with two side-throwing launchers; 36 knots trial speed; and steaming radius calculated for 15 knots, four months out of dock. The technical Bureaus were asked to incorporate these *minima* into three sketch designs, the first based on the 5-gun *Gleaves* class ships of the 1940 program with increased depth-charge stowage and the second a 4-gun modification of this with reload torpedoes in place of the fifth 5-inch gun. The third concept was to include several combinations of single and twin 5-inch mounts.[6] By 10 November the Bureaus of Construction and Repair and of Engineering had sketched six schemes, basically developments of the *Sims* and *Benson/Gleaves* classes but with hull and machinery weights reduced or lowered as much as possible for stability. Four or five guns were arranged in combinations of twins, singles, or both, and ten tubes with four spare torpedoes were provided. All six studies, based on the *Gleaves* class power plant, were calculated to make 36.5 to 37 knots, and special attention was paid to hull strength.[7]

Two weeks later the General Board asked the Bureaus to look at a bigger ship, mounting five 5-inch guns and ten tubes with light ballistic protection either for engineering or control spaces, or both. An alternate concept was to feature three quadruple torpedo tubes on the centerline.[8] Three new schemes were outlined along these lines and sent to the General Board on 26 December 1939.[9] All three, unlike the earlier designs, were based on a flushdecked hull for improved stability, midship freeboard, and hull strength. The Board requested further development of the third of these new schemes, a 5-gun, 10-tube flushdecker with a more powerful engineering installation. These were discussed into January 1940, and on the 9th the General Board forwarded its proposed characteristics for the 1941 program:

A flushdeck hull, displacing about 2,050 standard tons.
Five 5-inch/38s, with at least one 1.1-inch quadruple AA gun mount and four .50-caliber AA machine guns.
Two quintuple torpedo tubes, with space reserved for four spare torpedoes.
Two depth-charge tracks, with four single side-throwing depth-charge projectors.
60,000 horsepower, at least 38 knots trial speed, and 6,500 miles endurance at 15 knots, four months out of dock. Split arrangement of boiler and engine rooms, with a main generator in each engine room; either generator to be capable of handling the anticipated battle load. An emergency Diesel generator to be located outside the engineering spaces.
Pilot house, 5-inch gun director, and decks and sides in way of machinery spaces to have $\frac{1}{2}$-inch to $\frac{3}{4}$-inch ballistic plating.[10]

On 27 January 1940 the Secretary of the Navy approved these characteristics. Out of the early proposals, raised-forecastle enlargements of the *Benson/Gleaves* design, had emerged the outline of the new destroyer class which would, in the minds of many, come to epitomize the American destroyer of World War II.

A preliminary design plan for 'US Destroyer No. 445' was drawn by 12 February,[11] and the General Board recommended that this be used as the basis for design development. The pace of war in Europe was intensifying, and on 17 May the design Bureaus recommended that, in the interest of rapid procurement, the eight destroyers then authorized under the regular 1941 appropriation be built

to the *Gleaves* design and that the construction of the new DD-445 type be deferred until its design was fully developed.[12] The General Board felt that a modest number of the *Gleaves* class could usefully be included in the current program for the sake of maintaining production, but that the fleet was already reasonably well provided with destroyers of this type. On the other hand, 'immediate and urgent need' existed 'for destroyers of increased ruggedness and seaworthiness, armament, speed and protection as embodied in the design of 445 class.' After a small number

of additional *Gleaves* class ships were built, the Board considered that all future destroyers should be of the DD-445 pattern and that this program should be expedited as fully as practicable.[13]

On 1 July 1940 the General Board passed the word to CNO and to the technical Bureaus about the results of *Gleaves'* preliminary acceptance trials. To avoid the perils of instability under heavy sea or loading conditions, the Board of Inspection and Survey was 'strongly of the opinion' that forward topweight should be reduced as far as possible

Saufley (DD-465), possibly running trials. Her
depth-charge tracks and after AA gun tub are empty;
though reloading davits for three K-guns can be seen to
starboard on the main deck, the projectors themselves
do not seem to have been installed. Early *Fletcher*s, with
high gun tubs aft, have the same bulky appearance as
early *Benson*s and *Gleaves*.

Conway (DD-507) 'digs her heels in' in this photograph
taken in August 1943: *Fletcher*s seem to have tended to
'squat' in the water when accelerating or steaming at
high speeds. Besides a 40 mm twin on her after
deckhouse, *Conway* has a second twin on the fantail.
The *Fletcher*s modified to carry seaplanes had their
single 40 mm twin mount located here, and some other
ships of the class had a second 40 mm mount located at
the stern in a tentative early effort to improve the class'
AA capability.

in the new DD-445 class. It suggested that this could best be done by substituting a twin 5-inch gun mount on the forecastle in place of the two singles which had been standard since the *Farragut* class, reducing the height of the forward superstructure and lowering the 5-inch gun director. The General Board looked into this, including the thought of adding a 1.1-inch quadruple AA mount forward of the bridge. This would have given the new class what, for the time, was an unusual amount of close-in AA firepower forward; a sketch shows a ship with a two-level bridge/wheelhouse structure, a single dual-purpose twin 5-inch gun mount, and a 1.1-inch quad with director and four .50-caliber machine guns between the 5-inch mount and bridge. This was little enough by even the standards of a couple of years later, but it was evidence of forward thinking at a time when a 'one-point-one' and four machine guns was considered a total short-range AA battery for a destroyer.[14] This proposed arrangement of forward armament foreshadowed the configuration later adopted for the wartime dual-purpose rearmament of the *Porter* and *Somers* classes.

The Bureau of Ordnance saw no insurmountable problem in lowering the gun director in the new ships, but a twin 5-inch dual-purpose mount would be heavier than the two singles it would replace and would not be adequately trainable by hand if power were lost, something that many officers thought essential. A hit cutting the power leads to a twin mount would put two guns out of action, and BuOrd felt that, 'for these reasons, a twin mount should never be placed on an unprotected ship' such as a destroyer. Although twin mounts were in production for battleships, carriers, and cruisers, these had heavier gun shields and a lightweight weather shield would have to be designed for destroyer use. This would prevent delivery of a destroyer twin mount in time for installation in the first 2,100-ton ships if it were adopted.

The Mark 37 director would need no modification to control a twin mount, but the associated computer and other fire-control instruments would have to be altered, delaying things further.[15] The Bureau of Ships also saw problems; visibility from the lowered wheelhouse (as destroyer bridges were then designed, this was the ship control station for the officer of the deck) would be hampered; the wheelhouse could be lowered a foot and a half, but no further. Too, the elimination of an entire deck level of the forward superstructure would displace such things as the radio and coding rooms, which could not be adequately accommodated elsewhere. The four machine guns would have to be eliminated,

not so much for lack of room for the guns themselves although the space forward of the bridge would be crowded, but because the guns' crews would require berthing and messing space which could ill be afforded, and the added magazine requirements would encroach on space allocated to stores.[16] This, incidentally, demonstrates how small alterations to small ships can have large effects and, also, how modifications to a warship are not merely a matter of figuring out where to bolt the new hardware.

The General Board took the Bureaus' objections into account, also noting that the rate of fire of a twin 5-inch mount was 'appreciably less' than that of two singles. The thought of 'serious delays' in construction also loomed large in their thoughts; the Board thought it best to stay with the design already approved, and the Secretary of the Navy agreed.[17] On 28 June and 1 July 1940 the orders for the first 25 ships of the *Fletcher* class had been signed,[18] and circumstances dictated that they should go forward as expeditiously as possible. The contract design for the *Fletcher* class displayed the silhouette that came to be their hallmark, with five 5-inch guns (Mounts 53 and 54 open, the other three closed), one 1.1-inch quadruple AA mount aft, and four .50 guns forward. Two depth-charge tracks and four K-guns were provided. Stowage for four reload torpedoes was included as in the *Porter* class, although, as in the *Porter*s, no quick-reload mechanism was provided. (In the typically confusing fashion of emergency procurement, the lead ship of the class, *Fletcher* (DD-445), was one of the second group ordered on 1 July 1940.)

By now France and the Low Countries had fallen to Hitler, the three-year Spanish Civil War was over and the Sino-Japanese War was three years old. Air power was very much in the news and on the minds of military and naval planners. As work progressed on the *Fletcher*s and continued on the destroyers of earlier pattern being built to supplement them, discussion of improvements went on. The original *Fletcher*s had been designed with the same bridge structure built into the *Sims*, *Benson*, and *Gleaves* classes, a round-fronted wheelhouse with open wings, designed primarily for its aerodynamic qualities at higher speeds. This was all right for a service whose orientation lay in the direction of formation torpedo attacks on a surface battle line. For ships whose expected mission might lie more in the direction of antiaircraft defense, it was inadequate. On 29 May 1941 the Bureau of Ships recommended installation of bridges with all-round vision. Models were built and inspected and approval was recommended. By

January 1942, a sketch design had been worked out for a new *Fletcher* bridge which met this need. The new design provided a boxy structure for the wheelhouse, captain's sea cabin, chart room and radio room. A radar room was included, something that had not been provided for in the original *Fletcher* design. An open bridge around the upper level gave room for the command and lookout spaces considered essential if the destroyer was to live and operate in the same world as the aircraft.[19]

The process of improvement went on. The Navy-developed 1.1-inch quadruple AA gun and the Browning .50-caliber machine gun had been, hitherto, the only close-in air-defense weapons available, but better things were on their way. On 24 December 1941 the Secretary of the Navy approved a recommendation, by CNO and the General Board, that the four .50-caliber guns specified for the class be replaced by 20-millimeter Oerlikon-designed automatic shell guns. To reduce topside weight, thought was given to removal of the two wing tubes from the quintuple torpedo-tube mounts then being fabricated to make triples out of them. This, the Bureau of Ordnance estimated, would mean a saving of some 6,000 pounds per mount.[20] The loss of torpedo capacity was apparently not thought acceptable, since nothing more seems to have been heard of this idea. By early 1942, installation of a 40-millimeter Bofors-type twin gun mount was projected as standard in place of the 1.1-inch mount. The Bureau was directed, by the Chief of Naval Operations, to substitute an additional 40 mm twin for one quintuple torpedo tube and two 20 mm guns. CNO quickly changed his mind, pronouncing the one 40 mm mount sufficient if the four Oerlikons were increased to six: 'With this arrangement of close-in antiaircraft guns, it is considered that, for a fleet destroyer, the retention of two quintuple torpedo tubes is more desirable than the installation of one additional 40 mm twin mount, particularly if such installation causes the loss of two 20 mm guns.'[21]

CNO now prescribed that 1.1-inch and .50-caliber guns, with stowage for four reload torpedoes, be omitted from 'such of the subject ships now building which have progressed so far that no extensive changes can be made in the contract design superstructure and director tower' on a 'not to delay' basis. These ships were to get a twin 40-millimeter and six 20-millimeter guns, with a light director for the 40-millimeter mount. Later ships, those not so far advanced as to create problems, were to receive two twin 40s with directors and four 20s, and have their 5-inch director lowered about six feet.[22] The Bureau of Ships thought it would be difficult to accommodate two 40 mm mounts in the new ships, centerline space being thoroughly occupied. It suggested placing the two mounts abreast of the after stack on the main deck or, if anticipated inclining tests showed adequate stability in these ships, on platforms one deck higher. BuShips noted that the added guns would require enlargement of crew and magazine space, and recommended that the second 40 mm mount be omitted.[23] In a further quest for economy in topside weight, ballistic protection for the wheelhouse was reduced from 30-pound to 10-pound STS.[24] BuShips wished to do the same to the Mark 37 gun director shields. Ordnance demurred, arguing that 'the 5″ director of these ships constitutes a singularly important and yet derangeable unit in a location which is not only fully exposed but also a focus for straffing [sic] fire. It is doubtful whether it would be practicable to restore to service, without at least the services of a tender, a director whose computing elements have been penetrated by fragments or bullets.'[25] CNO recognized the special nature of the protection desired for the gun director, but opined that the increase in close-in gun power feasible if topweight were reduced was worth the possible hazard.[26] The Secretary of the Navy sent CNO's proposal to the General Board for comment; it would seem that the Board took a differing view of the need for director protection, since gun directors in all but very late production *Fletchers* received the recommended $\frac{3}{4}$-inch STS shielding.[27]

As completed, beginning in mid-1942, the first *Fletchers* differed considerably in appearance from even their immediate predecessors. Nearly thirty feet longer than *Gleaves* and a little over three feet beamier, their combination of a flushdecked hull with noticeable sheer and two prominent capped stacks went to create what was to be a standard profile for war-built American destroyers. Earlier *Fletchers* got the aerodynamically-designed bridge introduced in the *Sims* class, with rounded front and open wings; the redesign of bridges would not make itself felt until later production. Five 5-inch/38s went along the centerline in a 2–A–1–2 arrangement like that tried in early-construction *Sims*, *Benson*, and *Gleaves* class ships, but here all five were in gunhouses. No stability problems were to dictate the removal of any of them, thanks to the more generous proportions of the hull on which they were mounted. Depth charge tracks and side-throwing launchers were in their usual locations. One 1.1-inch quad AA mount (in some of the earliest ships) or a twin 40 mm mount was placed between the elevated 5-inch guns aft, firing from a platform above the after deckhouse. Two 20 mm guns

were installed on each side of the midship superstructure on the main deck with two more forward of the wheelhouse. Two quintuple torpedo tube mounts went amidships. Machinery, as in the *Gleaves* class, was relatively high-temperature; 850 degrees at 565 psi for full power with an additional 10,000 horsepower over *Gleaves*. A class of ship had finally come to fruition which would perform well under the urgent demands of war. Its most conspicuous defect was the inadequacy of its close-in antiaircraft defense.

The Bureau of Ships attempted to remedy this problem by suggesting the fantail as an appropriate location for the second twin 40 mm mount desired, and a small number of ships had this done. The forces afloat were something less than enthusiastic since the fantail position could be quite wet and subject to blast from the after 5-inch. The problems associated with this arrangement soon became apparent to the Bureau and a new directive was issued to install two twin 40 mm mounts on raised platforms to port and starboard of the after stack in the ships then building.[28] This arrangement was originally intended to replace the AA mount on the after deckhouse, but in practice it came to supplement it.

Some more or less 'standard' (insofar as such a term can be applied to large numbers of ships during a world war) antiaircraft configurations began to show themselves in the *Fletcher* class as the war went on. The earliest *Fletchers*, as we have seen, commissioned as a rule with one twin 40 mm mount — or a quad 1.1-inch machine gun in a few cases — and six 20 mm guns. As with earlier classes, the forward 20 mm mounts were later supplemented by an additional gun, mounted on an elevated platform to fire over the top of the 5-inch guns. The addition of two more 40 mm twins amidships, while retaining the after-deckhouse guns,

An aerial view of *Thatcher* (DD-514) at Boston, 28 February 1943. Like *Conway*, she has a 40 mm twin between Mounts 53 and 54 with another 40 mm at her stern. Pairs of 20 mm guns are on the main deck amidships, with three more in a two-level arrangement forward of the bridge. *Thatcher* has the round-fronted 'high' bridge seen in the *Sims* and *Benson/Gleaves* classes, and the elevation of her Mark 37 director above the top of the wheelhouse allows room for another 20 mm gun.

was prescribed by the Vice Chief of Naval Operations in February 1943. Four more 20 mm guns were to be added to make a total of ten or eleven. In June 1943, VCNO directed the replacement of the forward three 20 mm guns by a pair of 40 mm twins, reducing the nominal 20 mm battery to seven guns. By this time a suitable design for a standard-type Combat Information Center (CIC) acceptable to the forces afloat had been drawn up, and the Bureau of Ships ordered installation of one of these in each *Fletcher*. All of this, of course, depended on the ships' operating schedules and on the availability of shipyard space and material, so any of these alterations were accomplished in a piecemeal fashion and many variations on basic themes were observed to exist at any time. By December 1944, however, 157 out of 166 active *Fletcher* class ships were listed as mounting five 40 mm twins and seven 20 mm guns. One more had the five 40 mm mounts, but only five 20 mm guns. Five more had the earlier arrangement of three twin 40s. Two still had a twin 40 on the fantail with a second mount on the after-deckhouse; another ship also had these, with two more 40 mm twins amidships. This seems to be the greatest degree of wartime standardisation of close-range AA armament achieved in the *Fletcher* class.

The advent of the *kamikaze* brought with it a corresponding increase in attention to AA defense, and in 1945 a new configuration was developed. The ordeal of Okinawa pounded home the need for better air-defense, and shipyards began to replace the waist 40 mm

was considered no more than a temporary expedient. Well into the postwar years, the quad-mount configuration was listed as 'temporary', with the earlier arrangement of five 40 mm twins and ten tubes listed as the 'ultimate' armament.[29] Those *Fletchers* that had been so fitted retained their increased AA batteries in the postwar years as the likelihood of need for heavy torpedo armament was reassessed.

Many *Fletchers* received expanded bridges and tripod foremasts during the Korean War (1950-53), and a pair of forward-firing *Hedgehog* antisubmarine projectors was made 'ultimate' armament for the class in lieu of the forward 40 mm twins. Most of the class still retained their original ten tubes, except for those which had received the late-war or early-postwar quad-40 mm modification. During the 1950s the rapid-fire 3-inch/50-caliber twin AA mount began to come into service to replace the 40 mm gun. Certain *Fletchers* had one 5-inch gun removed and had their 40 mm and 20 mm guns replaced by three twin 3-inch mounts with directors. Some *Fletchers* lost their second forward 5-inch gun, which was replaced by a *Hedgehog* and, later, by a Weapon *Able* heavy-depth-charge projector; these ships were reclassified as Escort Destroyers (DDE). The program for Fiscal 1960 included the Fleet Rehabilitation and Modernization (FRAM) refit of three *Fletchers*; this involved lightweight super-structures and an extensive over-haul, designed to extend their useful lives. Money for modernization of additional *Fletcher* class ships was diverted to modernization of newer *Allen M. Sumner* and *Gearing* class destroyers.

The *Fletcher* class has long since gone from the US Navy's active inventory, though a number of them still serve in foreign navies. A few remain in the possession of the US Navy, refugees from the mothball fleets chosen to have their watertight compartments welded shut so that they can be used as static targets for missile tests. But the fate of these few ships seems sealed and it is almost certainly only a matter of time before they are either sunk as a result of a particularly damaging hit or sent to the scrapper. A 4-gun *Fletcher* with 3-inch/50 AA guns, *The Sullivans* (DD-537) has been memorialized at Buffalo, New York. The 5-gun *Kidd* (DD-661) will be preserved at Baton Rouge, Louisiana and another 5-gun ship, *Cassin Young* (DD-793) has been acquired by the Department of the Interior's National Park Service and is now at Boston National Historical Park. Appropriately enough, she is berthed just across the pier from the old frigate *Constitution*, epitomizing a different time and technology but a shared spirit.

Top
The 'low-bridge' *Ammen* (DD-527), *circa* 1943. She has 40 mm twins on deckhouse and fantail, with 20 mm guns amidships and forward. 'Low-bridge' *Fletchers* did not have the additional 20 mm gun on the wheelhouse, since this would interfere with visibility from the gun director.

Center
Dyson (DD-572) on 8 May 1943. She has received the first large-scale AA refit given to the *Fletcher* class, and has an additional pair of 40 mm twins on elevated platforms to each side of her after stack. The fire-control searchlights, originally on platforms built out from the second stack, have been relocated to the forward one and their former place has been taken by Mark 51 40 mm gun directors. Pairs of 20 mm guns amidships have been retained; an elevated centerline platform forward allows high-bridge and low-bridge ships alike to mount a third forward-firing 20 mm gun. The heart-shaped bulwark on *Dyson*'s fantail surrounds three more light AA guns. This arrangement of three 40 mm twins and ten 20 mm guns became the standard mid-war configuration for the *Fletcher* class although, as always, there were exceptions.

twins in this class with quadruples and the single 20 mm guns with twin mounts. The forward bank of torpedo tubes was replaced by a small deckhouse supporting two radar-equipped directors for the new Mark 63 Gun Fire Control System, which made blind firing possible for the guns it controlled. (Gun Fire Control System was a nomenclature, introduced during the war, referring to the entire complex of components which made up a specific type of fire control installation.) By November 1945, 50 *Fletchers* had received the new modification, though some still had their 20 mm singles and 32 ships out of the fifty had older-type Mark 51 gun directors, without radar, installed for lack of the newer Mark 63s; their entire close-in AA battery was still without provision for blind firing. In long-range terms, this battery

Top, center, and bottom
A detailed three-view pierside study of *Abner Read* (DD-526) on 13 June 1943. A low-bridge *Fletcher* seen here in the AA configuration described for *Dyson*, page 73, she was lost off the Philippines in November 1944. Her radars are SC-3, SG, and Mark 12. The large T-shaped device seen amidships is a torpedo crane, used for loading and unloading torpedoes from the tubes. A second such crane can be seen near the forward stack. *Abner Read*'s depth-charge tracks each hold eight 600-pound 'ash cans'; five more are in a stowage rack convenient to each track. K-guns, seen forward, fire 300-pound charges and still use the older-pattern can-shaped Mark 6 instead of the newer, streamlined, Mark 9. (See also pages 2/3.)

Chauncey (DD-667) exhibits the 'classic' *Fletcher* profile. Her 40 mm guns are still controlled by Mark 49 directors. The boxy low bridge of later *Gleaves* and *Fletcher* class ships promoted stability by bringing topweight down, and also gave better all-round visibility for ship and gunnery control.

Marshall (DD-676), one of a group of 'repeat *Fletcher*s' contracted for in the summer of 1942, is seen here as delivered on 15 October 1943. Canvas-covered 20 mm guns can be seen at her stern, but her 40 mm guns do not appear to have been installed. Oddly enough, she lacks any provision for light AA guns forward.

Converse (DD-509) at sea in 1943. She has received her midship 40 mm guns, but still has an early-model SC radar. A centerline 20 mm gun tub has been added forward, but the earlier 20 mm mount on the wheelhouse top has been kept. Close-range AA defense abeam and astern in the *Fletcher* class was reasonable for the time, but forward short-range firepower was criticized.

Young (DD-580) at Charleston, 1943. Forward 20 mm guns have been replaced by two twin 40 mm mounts; their Mark 51 directors are located atop the pilot house. This combination of five 40 mm twins and seven 20 mm guns became the next 'standard' rig for the *Fletcher* class, and many ships carried it through the end of the war.

A highly-detailed view of the bridge of *Nicholas* (DD-449), taken at Mare Island on 17 January 1944. *Nicholas* has just received her forward-firing 40 mm guns, and their directors have been installed in 'pulpits' jutting forward from the top of the wheelhouse. Uppermost is the Mark 37 gun director, with its Mark 12 radar antenna. Below this, in the cylindrical supporting structure, is the ship's fire-control station. Leads from the director run to the plotting room, belowdecks, where the associated computer and stable element are located. On top of the pilot house, abaft the shrouded 40 mm directors, are elevated platforms for semaphore signaling, signal searchlights, and 'sky lookout' stations with supports for glasses. On the navigating bridge, just below, the central structure contains wheelhouse, charthouse, and captain's sea cabin. On the open bridge wing is a pelorus, with a Mark 27 torpedo director aft. The level below the navigating bridge contains radio rooms. Senior officers' quarters, radar rooms and 5-inch and 40 mm handling rooms were located below this at main-deck level with the Combat Information Center (CIC), where the incoming information was collected, plotted and evaluated.

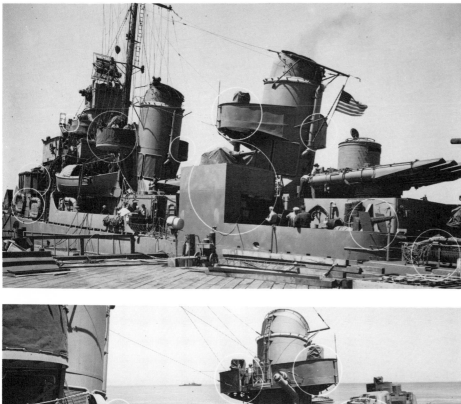

Top and center
Cony (DD-508) on 29 June 1943, illustrating details of the ship's gun and torpedo installation.

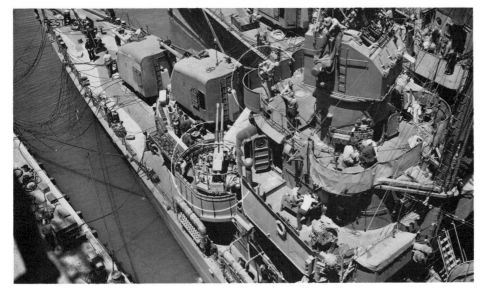

Schroeder (DD-501), 25 July 1943. This photograph gives a comparable look at bridge and forward 40 mm guns; note the Mark 51 gun director and Mark 27 torpedo director, often canvas-covered in many photographs.

Above
Stevens (DD-479) on 1 December 1943. Originally one of the *Fletcher*s built to catapult aircraft, she has been reconfigured to conventional destroyer appearance. *Stevens* has the five 40 mm twins prescribed at this time, with 20 mm guns on her fantail and amidships. The forward 'pulpits' for 40 mm gun directors are prominent; many variations exist in details of gun and director installations, depending on the time and place of installation.

Right
Claxton (DD-571) seen at Mare Island, 13 May 1944, in a new coat of pattern camouflage. An open walkway has been installed around the front of her early-pattern 'high' bridge. 'Kill' marks, tallied on the side of her Mark 37 director, have been neatly painted around during this refit.

Opposite and opposite inset
These detail views of *Bush* (DD-529)(16 June 1944) and *Norman Scott* (DD-690)(14 October 1944)(inset) show the variation possible in ships of the same basic design and armament configuration. The apparent additional height of *Norman Scott*'s director above the wheelhouse is explained by the presence of a canvas 'dodger' around *Bush*'s director.

Top
Kidd (DD-661), seen in 1944-vintage camouflage off
Leyte in the fall of that year. This low-bridge *Fletcher* is
one of only three ships of this once-numerous class to
survive as memorials in the United States.

Bottom right, and opposite top and bottom
Three detailed views of *Kidd*, taken at Mare Island on
8 February 1945. She has just received forward-firing
40 mm twins, and her depth-charge tracks have been
modified to take the faster- and straighter-sinking Mark 9
depth charge. Search radars are SC-3 and SG, with
Marks 12 and 22 on *Kidd*'s gun director.

The ongoing process of wartime destroyer AA improvement was capped, in the *Fletcher* class, with a final configuration which deleted five torpedo tubes to make room for substitution of a pair of quadruple 40 mm gun mounts for the midship 40 mm twins previously carried.

Top left
Howorth (DD-592) is seen on 2 July 1945 with this modification. 20 mm twin mounts have been substituted for her original singles amidships and aft, but she is, otherwise, little altered.

Top right and left
Two photographs of *Isherwood* (DD-520) illustrate the installation of 40 mm quads on outboard platforms which have been moved slightly forward of the after stack; the forward bank of torpedo tubes has been replaced by a small clipping room for 40 mm ammunition, on top of which are installed two directors for the new Gun Fire Control System (GFCS) Mark 63; the antennas for the radar equipments associated with this system are mounted on the guns. DBM radar intercept and TDY jamming antennas are located on a stub mainmast mounted just aft of Mount 53.

Opposite
The final photograph, taken of *Miller* (DD-535) on 29 August 1945, provides details of the installation of 40 mm quads, 20 mm twins, and an ECM antenna rig.

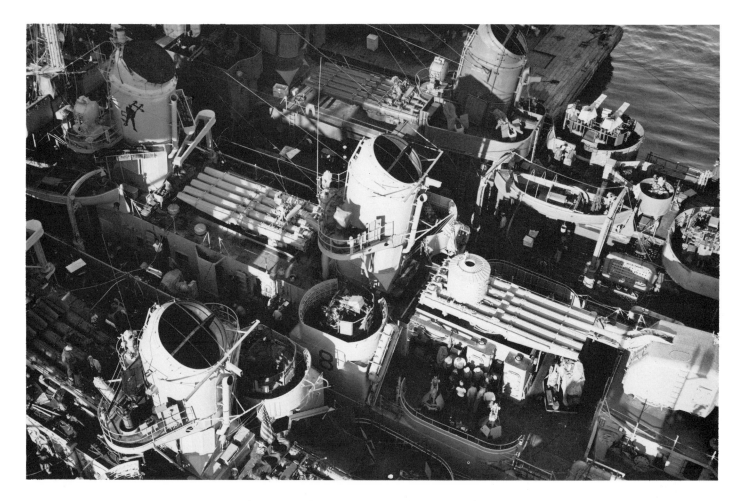

Top above, bottom left, and opposite
Three unusual views of *Mertz* (DD-691), moored
outboard of a *Fletcher* class sister ship and inboard of
the *Allen M. Sumner* class destroyer *Mansfield*
(DD-728), taken on 29 November 1945. In combination,
these photographs provide a detailed side-by-side
comparison of the physical aspects of the *Fletcher* and
Allen M. Sumner classes. Neither of the illustrated
*Fletcher*s has received the late-war 40 mm quad
modification; by V-J Day one *Fletcher* in three was
equipped with it. Postwar plans called for reversion to
the earlier arrangement of ten tubes and twin 40 mm
mounts in ships given these anti-*kamikaze* rearmaments,
but this did not actually take place.

Opposite top
In this 1957 photograph *Owen* (DD-536) has been somewhat altered — 20 mm guns and one depth-charge track, as well as K-guns, removed, with a new tripod mast supporting postwar radar antennae and forward 40 mm mounts replaced by *Hedgehog* antisubmarine projectors — but she retains her original five guns, with five torpedo tubes and radar-controlled 40 mm quads along with her after 40 mm twin.

Opposite bottom
This view of *Cowell* (DD-547) shows her with 3-inch 50-caliber rapid-fire AA gun mounts, introduced during the 1950s, in place of her midship 40 mm quads. Mount 53 and the after 40 mm twin mount have been replaced by a third twin 3-inch gun mount. Many active postwar *Fletchers* received this 3-inch AA modernization and became what were popularly called 'four-gun *Fletchers*'.

Top left
Cony takes heavy seas over her bow in May 1958. Like her sister ship *Cowell* (DD-547), she has received 3-inch AA guns. She has also had her superfiring forward 5-inch mount replaced by Weapon *Alfa*, an ahead-throwing antisubmarine rocket launcher, during her modification to an Escort Destroyer (DDE). Some *Fletchers* were converted to DDEs in a postwar program aimed at producing anti-submarine ships capable of coping with high-performance undersea craft by installing new A/S ordnance in existing destroyers.

Bottom
Radford (DD-446) was one of only three *Fletchers* to be modernized under the Fleet Rehabilitation and Modernization Program (FRAM) to extend her useful life. She has two 5-inch guns, with a Weapon *Alfa* launcher forward. The boxy structure aft of her stacks is a hangar-flight deck combination designed for use with the Drone Anti-Submarine Helicopter (DASH), a remotely-controlled helicopter developed to carry and launch antisubmarine homing torpedoes upon command from the ship. The helicopter did not prove a success, and the aviation facility was never put to its intended use.

Above
Other former American warships still sail on under other flags. The Peruvian destroyers *Guise* (DD-72) (left) and *Villar* (DD-71) (right), the former *Fletcher* class *Isherwood* (DD-520) and *Benham* (DD-796), take part here in Operation *Unitas XIX* during 1978.

Opposite top
Hazelwood (DD-531) did not receive a FRAM modernization, but was fitted with a prototype flight deck and aluminum helicopter hangar. From 1958 through 1964 she carried out extensive tests of this destroyer helicopter installation.

Opposite bottom
Howorth (DD-592) plunges to the bottom in March 1962, after serving as an experimental torpedo target off San Diego. Many old destroyers and destroyer escorts have made their last contribution in this manner, aiding in the development of new antiship ordnance.

14

Experimental Variants

**You cannot have everything. If you attempt it, you will lose
everything. . . . On a given tonnage . . . there cannot be the highest
speed, *and* the heaviest battery, *and* the thickest armor, *and* the
longest coal endurance. . . .**

Rear Admiral Alfred Thayer Mahan

As high-pressure, high-temperature steam plants passed into service in the *Mahan*, *Somers*, and *Gleaves* classes, development of still more advanced engineering systems went on. The old destroyer *Dahlgren* (DD-187) was refitted as an engineering experimental ship in 1939 with new General Electric geared turbines and a pair of Babcock and Wilcox boilers designed for 950 degrees at 1,200 psi.[1] Trials with *Dahlgren*, completed in 1940, 'proved . . . that 1200 p.s.i. and 950° F. was entirely feasible and urgently required.'[2]

On 24 February 1940 the Bureaus of Engineering and of Construction and Repair asked the Secretary of the Navy to approve construction of one ship of the 1941 program 'for the development of an advanced design of this type vessel.' This was approved on 18 March.[3] On 7 June the Bureaus asked for authority to construct one of the *Fletcher* class with a Diesel propulsion system. This had been advocated for some years, both in the United States and abroad, for reasons both technical and military; Germany had used Diesel plants in its *Deutschland* class *Panzerschiffen*. 'The advantages of this system', the Bureaus said, '. . . are mainly of a military rather than an engineering nature.' The proposed power plant would be Diesel-electric and would, they thought, make better internal subdivision possible. Smokepipes would be replaced by much smaller Diesel exhaust stacks; it might prove possible to vent exhaust out the sides instead of through the deck (as was done in many wartime Diesel-engined ships). Upper decks would be clearer without the encumbrance of large stacks, simplifying the installation of AA guns. It is clear that this prototype Diesel destroyer was seen as possibly leading the way to 'Dieselization' of combatant ships in general, since the Bureaus speak of the desirability of exhausting engines below the protective deck, a feature of battleships, carriers, and cruisers; they also mention the possibility of a flushdecked aircraft carrier. 'From an engineering . . . as well as a military point of view, the elimination of all piping under pressures will be', they concluded, 'a very great improvement.'[4]

CNO felt that the military advantages of a successful Diesel installation were of 'such importance that approval . . . is strongly recommended', and the Secretary gave the Diesel prototype his blessing on 15 June 1940.[5]

Construction contracts for the two experimental ships were signed with Federal Shipbuilding and Drydock Company, of Kearny, New Jersey, on 1 July 1940. DD-452, named *Percival*, was to have four General Electric geared turbines with four new Babcock and Wilcox 'ultra-high pressure' boilers. *Watson* (DD-482) was to have a General Motors Diesel-electric plant; since there would be no boilers to power turbogenerators, *Watson*'s five 125-kilowatt, 450-volt ship's service generators were also to be Diesel-powered. Both plants were to generate 60,000 horsepower, as in the case of conventionally-powered *Fletcher* class ships.[6]

Pearl Harbor put a new face on things, and theoretical considerations, no matter how intriguing, had to be put aside. Wartime needs delayed work on the projected machinery; by the middle of 1945 neither engineering installation had been tested. The Chief of Naval Operations felt that the design of large, high-speed Diesel engines had not attained the necessary reliability, and proposed to install advanced steam plants in both destroyers. Also, since production of the *Fletcher* class had by then been completed, CNO wished to build the two experimental ships to the newer *Gearing* design with several modifications that were thought deserving of service testing. These involved moving the two forward 5-inch twin gun mounts seven feet further aft, increasing main-deck sheer to allow about two

feet more freeboard at the bow, and an increase in bow flare. Bridge arrangement and other hull and battery features would be much the same as in standard *Gearing* class ships.[7]

The Fleet Maintenance Division drafted a memorandum to Admiral King for signature by the Vice Chief of Naval Operations. This held that construction of two identical experimental ships would not be worth the money and effort involved, and recommended that only one such ship be built with the other being completed as a 'stock' *Gearing* class destroyer.[8] This was apparently routed back through BuShips for comment, since a BuShips memo of 18 July 1945 urged support for the Bureau's recommendation for two experimental-steam destroyers, 'as we think the engineering data and experience fully justify this course.'[9] VCNO's comments were rewritten, and went forward on 20 July concurring with BuShips' request for two experimental ships, remarking in conclusion that there was 'considerable merit in having two . . . units from which to obtain good service experience and engineering data.'[10] Admiral King's headquarters approved this on 7 August 1945, only a week before V-J Day brought the war to an end. Both *Watson* and *Percival* remained on the agenda for only a short while; the contract for both was canceled on 7 January 1946.[11] It would seem that *Watson* was dropped from serious consideration before *Percival*. A Secretary of the Navy memorandum of 15 December 1945 cites only DD-452 as 'an experimental Destroyer with a propulsion plant of advanced design which has been already completed and is under tests at the boiler laboratory in Philadelphia; its main feature is the cyclo-therm boiler. Abandonment of this project without service tests would be negative economy in the long run.'[12] Any such considerations had to give way to postwar cutbacks, and new engineering plants had to be put off until the completion of the experimental *Gearing* class destroyer *Timmerman* (EDD-828, the 'E' prefix denoting her status as an experimental ship) in 1952.

Thought had been given to the use of aircraft from destroyers as early as 1923, when the flushdecker *Charles Ausburn* (DD-294) was equipped with a forecastle cradle for a Curtiss TS-1 float-equipped biplane fighter which was to be hoisted off and onto the ship for water take-offs and landings. *Charles Ausburn* went to sea with the Scouting Fleet in the fall of 1923, but nothing seems to have come from this; the arrangement must have been very topheavy, if nothing else. Another flushdecker, *Noa* (DD-343) was modified during 1939 to carry a floatplane abaft her funnels, again with a boom to lift the aircraft to and from the water. During 1940 *Noa* conducted some operations with a Curtiss SOC-1 Seagull observation seaplane. These seem to have been satisfactory enough for the Navy Department to approve the inclusion of aircraft-carrying destroyers in the current construction program.

As approved on 27 May 1940, the new two-year building program included the first 26 ships of the *Fletcher* class. These were to be built 'in accordance with contract plans and specifications now in course of preparation, except that 6 of these destroyers are to be fitted for catapults in lieu of guns.'[13] This was not quite as drastic as it sounded. The plane-carrying ships were to be conventional *Fletchers*, except that a quintuple torpedo tube, 5-inch gun, and 1.1-inch quadruple AA gun mount located abaft the second stack were to be omitted, and in their place a turntable seaplane catapult and aircraft-handling boom were to be installed. The Bureau of Ordnance was quick to point out that the only close-in AA armament provided for in this concept consisted of four .50-caliber machine guns forward of the bridge, and urged that 'the maximum number' of machine guns also be mounted aft for protection against dive bombers approaching from astern.[14]

Other reaction was less than enthusiastic. The Commander in Chief, United States Fleet, did not care for the loss of gun and torpedo firepower involved in the modification, and suggested that it be rescinded. The Bureau of Aeronautics looked to the difficulties involved in catapulting and recovering floatplanes from ships the size of destroyers, and held that 'the advantages to be gained from the necessarily limited operation of the aircraft do not warrant the necessary sacrifice of other features.' War Plans repeated these objections, adding that it felt 'that the price necessarily paid in loss of other valuable military characteristics is unjustifiably great.'[15]

These criticisms notwithstanding, catapult installations were ordered for six *Fletchers*, DD-476 through –481. Five of these were so completed.

The first catapult *Fletcher*, *Pringle* (DD-477), was placed in commission on 18 September 1942. By April 1943, *Stanly* (DD-478), *Hutchins* (DD-476), *Stevens* (DD-479), and *Halford* (DD-480) had followed suit, in that order. *Pringle* escorted a convoy from mid-Atlantic to Halifax in January 1943, and seems to have been the first of these ships to use her catapult operationally. *Halford* and *Stevens* had short periods of Pacific service in 1943 with their catapults installed, *Halford* escorting a South Pacific military convoy and both ships participating in carrier strikes.

Hutchins and *Stanly* seem to have made no service use of their catapults. *Leutze* (DD-481), the last of the group, never received her catapult.

The *Fletcher* aviation installation included the catapult, with a handling crane mounted to port. A tank for aviation gasoline, surrounded by a carbon dioxide-filled cofferdam, was installed on the main deck at the after end of the superstructure. Light bombs and depth charges were stowed in the magazine space provided for the deleted 5-inch gun. The embarked plane — a Vought OS2U King-fisher two-seater monoplane — was intended to be used for reconnaissance, gunfire spotting, and antisubmarine patrol, and was operated and supported by a pilot and two maintenance men.[16]

The headaches involved in this installation apparently far out-weighed its benefits. After visiting *Stevens* and talking to her officers, Rear Admiral G. J. Rowcliff, of the General Board, wrote that he believed 'that this installation would be of extremely limited usefulness on account of the difficulties of stowage, handling, service, launching, and recovery. It would appear that use would be limited to messenger or quick-reconnaissance work of a special nature under favorable conditions of use, operating by stealth or without much opposition.'[17]

Admiral Rowcliff was apparently not the only one who doubted the catapult destroyer's value. The Commander in Chief, Pacific Fleet, recommended that aviation equipment be removed from all destroyers; Admiral King agreed with this, and on 15 October 1943, the Bureaus were directed to remove aircraft equipment from these ships and replace it with normal destroyer ordnance. Completion of *Leutze* (DD-481) had been delayed and she was still under construction; she was, accordingly, completed as a standard *Fletcher* with five guns, ten tubes, and no catapult.[18] The marriage of aircraft and de-stroyer had undoubtedly looked much better in 1940 — when aircraft-carrying ships were relatively scarce — than it did by 1943, when difficulties had been proven in actual service and new carriers, as well as battleships and cruisers (both of which types operated seaplane units), were entering service. The destroyer aviation unit was recognized as a clumsy expedient, and disposed of when its lack of utility was demonstrated. In another generation the development of effective light-weight helicopters would return aviation to the destroyer Navy, but this was still years away.

Still another experimental destroyer project had a short life and never even approached fruition. Construction of four experimental ships (DD-503–506) was directed on 9 September 1940. The first two of these — given the names *Stevenson* and *Stockton* — were to be small ships, displacing some 750 to 900 tons, and inspired by Britain's 'Hunt' class of small antisubmarine destroyers. DD-505–506 (*Thorn* and *Turner*) were to be 1,100–1,150 ton ships, with characteristics to be formulated by the General Board which had for some time been discussing the idea of the small, mass-producible destroyer. All four were ordered from Federal Shipbuilding on 16 December 1940, but were canceled on 10 February 1941. In their place four *Gleaves* class destroyers (DD-645–648) were ordered, and the names originally assigned to DD-503–506 were given to them.[19]

Pringle (DD-477), one of the *Fletcher* class ships completed with four guns and a catapult. Her after tubes, 40 mm gun tub, and forward superfiring 5-inch gun have been omitted to make room for a cruiser-type powder catapult with a simple plane-handling derrick. Aviation gasoline was stowed at main-deck level at the after end of the superstructure. The 40 mm twin mount, for which there was no place forward, is accommodated at *Pringle*'s stern. This destroyer-aviation experiment was fairly short-lived, and those *Fletchers* which received catapults had them eventually removed. The aircraft on the catapult is the ubiquitous Vought OS2U Kingfisher, used in battleships and cruisers as well as for training and coastal patrol.

15

The Allen M. Sumner and Gearing Classes

It has ever seemed strange to me, how weapons and warships — the tools of death — are the loveliest things man has made.

Poul Anderson, *The Sign of the Raven* (New York: Zebra Books, 1980), 182

The last generation of wartime American destroyers was not a new design, but a development and improvement of the *Fletcher* class. As early as 1942, as will be seen further on, thought was being given to a new design of large destroyer. Development of the new type, however, was expected to take some time (it was still going on when the war ended three years later), and the DD-692 concept was outlined as a more powerful modification of the basic *Fletcher* hull. As with so many ship designs, it was conceived as a compromise with increased hitting power obtained at some sacrifice of speed and steaming radius.

The *Fletcher* class was hardly on its way before the Bureau of Ships began work on what it termed 'large destroyers'. The General Board, discussing improvements in AA batteries for destroyers in May 1941, remarked that it might be possible 'to widen the ... 2050 ton destroyer [*Fletcher*] at a small sacrifice of speed and thereby obviate the need for fixed ballast and insure stability and buoyancy that will permit adherence to proper military characteristics.'[1] BuShips drew two sketches for a modified *Benson/Gleaves* at 1,810 (standard) tons, with four 5-inch/38s and two twin 40 mm AA mounts; only five torpedo tubes were included in one of these sketches, and the two 40 mm mounts were echeloned between the after stack and the after 5-inch guns, a close-in AA configuration ultimately embodied in the DD-692 design. Rear Admiral Howard, Chief of the Bureau of Ships, remarked that, 'The removal of the after quintuple tube allows the after battery to be separated so that not only are the arcs of fire greatly improved, but there is not the same possibility of destruction or being put out of action by a single bomb or projectile.'[2]

On 28 October 1941 the General Board held hearings on what was presented as a question of improvements to the *Fletcher* type destroyer, referred to as the '2,100-ton' type. BuShips had drawn up six sketches featuring dual-purpose 5-inch/38 twin gun mounts combined with singles in various combinations. Captain G. L. Schuyler, representing the Bureau of Ordnance, supported inclusion of as many 5-inch guns as possible, remarking that, 'The 5-inch guns are not being played up enough for anti-aircraft use. The Bofors and Oerlikons, to defend one's own ship against dive bombing attack is about all they will do. If another ship in the formation is attacked they are expected to contribute little if anything. ... The ships themselves might not be the targets. There might be a horizontal attack right over a number of boats like these, and in that case everything you might have sacrificed by taking off 5-inch to crowd on more Bofors is doing rather a selfish job to protect the ship itself and not doing anything for others. I would like the whole six 5-inch guns on there.'[3] The Fleet Maintenance Division of the Office of the Chief of Naval Operations had previously written to the General Board, recommending adoption of what amounted to a 6-gun *Fletcher* with three 5-inch twins, two quad 40 mm mounts (one forward and one aft), and four 20 mm guns; both 5-inch and 40 mm directors should be equipped with radar.[4]

By October 1941, seven concepts had been outlined. All were 369-foot offspring of the *Fletcher* hull, though some were a foot beamier, and all were slightly heavier. Batteries included four to six 5-inch guns, two or four 40 mm twins, and five (1×5), ten (2×5), or six (2×3) tubes. Two depth-charge tracks and six K-guns were standard, as was a 60,000-horsepower plant and 6,500 miles endurance at 15 knots (this last requirement was a step toward greater realism after the low radius speeds prescribed when defining the desired characteristics for earlier

destroyers). Extensive splinter protection was also allowed.

In forwarding its sketches to the General Board, the Bureau of Ships explained that 'when the characteristics of the DD-445 Class were established in January 1940 the importance of air attack was recognized and some features were incorporated in the design to provide both active and passive defense against this form of attack. Since that date, however, the seriousness of air attacks has been emphasized increasingly by experiences of ships in the present war. Some degree of protection against splinters and ... fragments is now generally considered essential for ... personnel ... topside .... Active defense with heavy machine guns against dive bombing attack to the maximum degree practicable is a necessity — with the so-called 'four-cornered' arrangement of heavy machine guns being considered very desirable. It is now generally accepted that some sacrifices in other characteristics are warranted even in destroyers in order to attain these features; whereas this was not the case in January 1940.' The Bureau went on to say that 'torpedo attack has been considered to be the primary function of destroyers, with speed and a 5″-gun battery provided to permit driving through destroyer opposition to push the attack home. The essence of torpedo-boat design since its inception has been to sacrifice durability and any form of protection for speed. This was carried over into destroyer design and speed is still the dominant influence in such design. ... The importance of the manifold duties of destroyers other than torpedo attack is gaining emphasis in the present war ... .' BuShips cited a General Board opinion to the effect that current conditions seemed to demand two types of destroyers, one an offensive type capable of operating with the battle fleet and heavily armed with guns and torpedoes, and the other a 'sea control' type designed to protect waters already under general control from submarines, aircraft, and — to a lesser extent — surface raiders. The *Fletcher* class fell into the first of these categories.

Early-wartime developments such as radar, faster major warships, and heavy air opposition all tended to make the classic destroyer mission of torpedo attack against heavy ships less likely to happen and more difficult to achieve. 'It appears desirable', the Bureau continued, 'to re-assess the weight which should be given to the various elements of total displacement of destroyers and particularly in the distribution of the total weight of the armament, as between torpedoes, 5-inch guns, depth charges and close-in AA defense, and the weight of the control for the battery.

The arrangement of the battery to disperse the risks of damage and minimize the ill effects of any single hit and gain maximum sectors of effective fire for each gun or tube must also be considered.' BuShips cited its schemes as showing 'the variety of solutions which can be developed for the DD-445' hull. It was not essential, they thought, that all destroyers be so configured, 'but manifestly the more nearly a standard arrangement — with all the elements of the battery represented — can be approached the greater will be the assurance that a commander afloat will have available a destroyer capable of accomplishing the mission in view, even though that destroyer may not be as well-fitted for the task as a specialized design might have been.'

In earlier studies leading to the design of the *Fletcher* class and of proposed improvements to the *Benson/Gleaves* classes, 5-inch dual-purpose twin mounts had been rejected by the General Board. This was principally due to an anticipated slower rate of fire from a twin mount as compared to that from two singles, and to the fact that twin mounts could not be effectively trained by hand — something that had been much on the minds of many officers since the design of the *Farragut* class and the first consideration of the 5-inch/ 38 had begun. It was time, BuShips felt, to reopen the question of a more efficient gun arrangement, and some of its sketches included twin gun mounts. The first sketch — Scheme B — was a 5-gun, 10-tube modified *Fletcher* with a heavier close-in battery. The arrangement of guns and tubes was thought 'congested', and other schemes represented proposals to remedy this. The Bureau thought that any of these proposals would approx-

imately equal the steaming radius of the *Fletcher* class and that all should be able to turn up trial speeds of at least 37 knots. Four schemes could be accommodated by the unaltered *Fletcher* hull, while the other three would require an additional foot of beam for adequate stability. Two sketches — Schemes B-I and B-II — omitted one quintuple tube to allow a better arrangement of the guns and 'in line with the thought that effective destroyer torpedo attack is of decreasing probability in modern warfare.'

Of the designs outlined, the Bureau felt that 'the scheme which appears . . . to meet the requirements for modern destroyers . . . to the greatest degree, is Scheme B-II, which carries a powerful main battery, one quintuple tube, full depth charge armament, is well protected by heavy machine guns against dive-bombing attacks, and at the same time has its battery arranged so that there should be little interference between AA machine guns and 5″ guns.' In silhouette, dimensions, and many details this design was a *Fletcher* 'look-alike'. The principal difference was in its armament. Three dual-purpose 5-inch twins were arranged 2-A-1, with five torpedo tubes between the two stacks. Two twin 40 mm mounts were in echelon abaft the after stack, with two 20 mm guns forward of the bridge. 'The advantage of having a strong 5″ battery (four guns) located forward appears to be of great importance for destroyers which, of necessity, depend upon high speed and volume of their own fire for security during an attack. Also, . . . it is not looking too far into the future to consider the improvement of anti-aircraft fire which the introduction of radar promises. If air targets can be brought

under effective fire by 5-inch guns early, the provision of four of such guns on the forecastle becomes increasingly attractive.' BuShips recommended that Scheme B-II be adopted for any ships yet to be ordered, since the requirement for an additional foot of beam made its armament too heavy for hulls already laid down. Procurement of adequate numbers of destroyer-weight 5-inch twins would have to be undertaken and, to avoid delays in completion of badly-needed destroyers, construction of ships of the new design should not be undertaken until the twin mounts were available. Ships already in the program, the Bureau advised, should be completed as 5-gun destroyers.[5]

BuShips reiterated its recommendation a few days later. 'Having in view again the developments in anti-aircraft defense through the use of radar, and the advantage of a powerful 5-inch battery bearing ahead for any offensive action, the Bureau considers that the design with three twin 5-inch mounts offers advantages which outweigh the moderate increase in displacement associated therewith.'[6] In November 1941, a modification of Scheme B-II was sketched in reply to a request from the General Board. Additional room was provided for the new lowered — and lengthened

Barton (DD-722) off the coast of Maine during trials, 28 December 1943. This early *Allen M. Sumner* class ship has the armament designed for her class: three twin 5-inch/38 dual-purpose gun mounts arranged 2-A-1, two quintuple torpedo tubes, two 40 mm quads echeloned abaft the second stack, and two 40 mm twins on the elevated platforms between bridge and forward stack. 20 mm guns are mounted forward, on the stern, and next to the after 40 mm quad. The design of *Barton*'s bridge, though angular, is similar in concept to that of early *Fletchers* with a closed wheelhouse and open wings. This came under criticism for its lack of forward visibility, and was soon modified.

— bridge structure now being planned by moving the forward 5-inch mount — Mount 51 in US Navy parlance — six and a half feet forward on the forecastle and moving Mount 52, the superfiring forward mount, along with it and bringing it six feet forward. The original design for B-II had included only three K-guns, to port of the after-deckhouse; as modified, three more were added to starboard as was now customary for new destroyers. An alternate design, also requested by the General Board for comparison, had one 5-inch twin forward and three singles aft.

The Board had felt that the superfiring 5-inch mount in Scheme B-II was so close to the 5-inch gun director that damage would result if the guns were fired at extreme train and high elevation, and the new alternate concept was proposed to alleviate the problem. BuShips calculated that moving the two 5-inch mounts of Scheme B-II forward would place the gun director almost entirely outside the harmful blast pattern and provide acceptable operating conditions for the director.[7]

The General Board took issue with BuShips, preferring the upgunned *Fletcher* design drawn up as Scheme B.[8] The Bureau was asked to draw a modification of Scheme B with the two single forward guns moved forward (as had been done with the twin gun mounts in the modified B-II) and two more 20 mm guns added. BuShips, in the meanwhile, had constructed models representing Schemes B and B-II, and had used them to illustrate its points in several informal discussions with representatives of the Office of Naval Operations and of the Commander in Chief, US Fleet. The participants in these talks liked the 6-gun battery of B-II, agreeing that 'six 5″/38 cal. DP guns in twin mounts all of which can be used to develop a heavy concentration of fire forward [the after mount was designed to train 60 degrees forward of either beam] would be by all means the most desirable main battery for a destroyer of this size . . . .'[9] On the other hand, B-II provided only five tubes and two 20 mm guns, and the ten tubes and four 20 mm guns of Scheme B were judged preferable. It was then agreed that the 5-inch battery of B-II and the torpedo and 20 mm armament of Scheme B should be combined into a new design, Scheme B-VII. This came closer to the ultimate DD-692 design with three 5-inch twins, ten tubes, two twin 40 mm mounts, and four 20 mm guns. The Bureau of Ordnance had commented that 'excessive emphasis has been placed on blast effect on the 5″ director station, and . . . the advantage of the added separation of No. 2 twin mount from the director is less important than the resulting disadvantage from crowding the forward twin mounts too closely

together.'[10] This was in line with BuShips' original thinking, and the spacing of forward gun mounts and gun director was restored to approximately the same dimensions as in the first B-II design. The Bureau felt that, with two torpedo-tube mounts included, things were somewhat crowded topside in B-VII as compared with B-II but, if ten tubes were thought essential, the new sketch would be 'a workable scheme'. 'If subsequent developments in the present war', the Bureau continued, 'indicate that one quintuple tube would be sufficient for this type, the after tube . . . could be omitted, with consequent improvement in the arrangement of the AA machine guns in that part of the ship.'[11] Instead of the interrupted superstructure of the *Fletcher* class, a continuous deckhouse extended along the main deck and provided weather-sheltered access to machinery spaces and other belowdecks compartments, a feature later judged 'extremely practical' after service experience.[12] BuShips pointed to the 'much more powerful, particularly in forward fire,' gun battery of Scheme B-VII as compared to the Scheme B preferred by the General Board, and recommended that B-II or B-VII be adopted, depending primarily on the number of torpedo tubes finally judged essential. 'Early decision', the Bureau concluded, 'in this matter will permit early completion of the necessary design work and early introduction of the new type into the building program.'[13]

The Bureau of Ordnance favored the B-VII design, remarking that its 20 mm fire ahead at low angles would be 'perhaps slightly weak' and assuming that fire control radar would be included. BuOrd did not advise an attempt to substitute the contemplated 5-inch/54-caliber gun, then under development, for the existing 5-inch/38, and thought the B-VII 'the type of which the armament approaches that best suited for all purpose destroyers.'[14] (Twin 5-inch/54s were planned for the *Montana* (BB-67) class battleships, canceled in 1943; singles armed the *Midway* (CVB-41) class carriers commissioned in 1945.)

The General Board sent a set of draft characteristics to BuShips on 24 March 1942. These called for a trial speed of 38 knots, something which the Bureau felt could not be achieved without an enlargement of the design which 'would require so much change that the ship could no longer be considered a mere development of the present 2,100 ton destroyers, but would become a complete new design, approximating a small cruiser rather than a destroyer in its major characteristics.' It was probable that such a ship could not be built at some of the shipyards now working on *Fletcher* class ships. BuShips recommended a 36.5 knot ship without the internal torpedo

bulkheads desired by the General Board, which 'would materially increase the size and displacement of the ship.' The General Board had also specified an auxiliary power unit for each 5-inch gun mount, but the Bureau thought that, since each of the two main turbogenerators would be capable of carrying the battle load and the 100-kilowatt diesel auxiliary generator was to be able to power the 5-inch gun director and one twin mount, this was as much weight and space as could reasonably be given to electrical power.[15]

The General Board held hearings in mid-April 1942, and generally accepted the pattern laid down in Scheme B-VII. On 24 April the Board forwarded the proposed characteristics to the Secretary of the Navy. These defined the new design as a 2,200 (standard) ton ship, 'preferably of the flushdeck type of rugged construction; designed to maintain high speed in heavy weather and to accompany battleships, carriers, and cruisers,' with the now customary divided engineering plant, not less than 36.5 knots trial speed, and a 6,500 mile radius at 15 knots. The battery was to consist of three 5-inch twin mounts, two 40 mm twins, at least four 20 mm guns, ten tubes, two depth charge tracks, and six K-guns.[16] Admiral King endorsed the design, recommending that the new ship and the destroyer escort (DE) be the only destroyer type ships laid down for the present (referring to proposals to build improved *Gleaves* type destroyers) since 'the current and prospective material and production situations will not allow any further diversification of destroyer types.'[17] On 11 May 1942 the Secretary approved the characteristics for the DD-692 class, and on 7 August the first block of ships was ordered; more were contracted for on 14 June 1943. By the beginning of 1944 the first of the '2,200-tonners' were going into commission, and most of the program had been completed by 1945.

As with the *Fletcher* class, changes were being made long before the first ships were completed. A full scale mockup of the designed bridge was built at the Philadelphia Navy Yard in November 1942. Representatives of Washington offices and the forces afloat looked the mockup over, and the bridge

Opposite top
Charles S. Sperry (DD-697) in August 1944, wearing Pacific pattern camouflage. Note her arrangement of 20 mm AA guns on the fantail, to starboard at the after end of the deckhouse, on a platform to the port side of the second stack, and forward of the bridge. The arrangement of after 5-inch mount and 40 mm quads gave them excellent fields of fire.

Opposite bottom
Soley (DD-707) seen from overhead; note the improved arrangement of her bridge with an open forward walkway.

configuration was given final approval in January 1943. In March a BuShips plan to increase the close-in AA armament to four 40 mm twins and eleven 20 mm guns was approved by the Vice Chief of Naval Operations who cited the demonstrated need for the greatest possible number of light anti-aircraft guns and the fact that it had been found practicable to substantially increase the close-in batteries of the *Fletcher* class. VCNO considered it 'particularly important' that the two forward 40 mm gun mounts be equipped with radar and with gun directors.[18] On 8 June 1943 VCNO authorized installation of two 40 mm quad mounts on the after superstructure in lieu of twins in response to a recommendation from Service Force, Pacific Fleet, that the 40 mm batteries of the new ships be augmented.[19]

Another proposed change, this time in the location of the Combat Information Center (CIC) on the superstructure deck below the bridge, was approved by VCNO in September 1943, even though it would delay the building program by some five months. This, again, was the product of strong representations from the forces afloat, whose experience with early CIC installations in the Pacific had convinced them that radar indicators should be located in CIC, and that the CIC itself should be placed as far as possible from the noise and shock of gunfire.[20] With four 5-inch guns forward in the new ships, this would be even more critical in the DD-692 class than in the *Fletchers*.

The next problem to arise was that of steaming endurance. Operations at task force speeds in the enormous reaches of the Pacific placed a premium on cruising radius. It was being found, though, that at heavy wartime displacements and high formation speeds, ships were coming nowhere near their original

Top
Collett (DD-730) at Boston, 7 August 1944. In spite of her pattern camouflage many details of superstructure, AA battery, and electronics stand out satisfactorily.

Center
The *Gearing* class were identical to the *Allen M. Sumner* class in all but length and fuel tankage. *Leonard F. Mason* (DD-853), seen here in 1946 after completion, shows the slight increase in funnel spacing that distinguishes the *Gearing*s. Like other units of these classes, she has had a third 40 mm quad substituted for her after torpedo tubes; radar countermeasures (RCM, known today as ECM) antennas are mounted on her stacks. *Leonard F. Mason* is painted in the overall haze gray introduced into the fleet late in the war; her funnel caps have not been painted a contrasting peacetime black, and her bow number is still in small wartime characters.

Bottom
Gearing (DD-710) on 21 May 1945, in bicolor camouflage. The lighter gray of her upperworks permits a closer examination. Her after tubes have been removed, but the third 40 mm mount has not yet been fitted.

Kenneth D. Bailey (DD-713), as delivered on 30 July 1945. Like *Leonard F. Mason* opposite, she has been completed with her third quad 40 mm mount. The distribution of AA guns and dual-purpose 5-inch weapons in these classes made them good antiaircraft ships for their time. *Allen M. Sumner*s and *Gearing*s show their family resemblance to the *Fletcher* class when seen in profile.

specification radii. This had to be remedied. Admiral King and the Bureau of Ships looked at the *Fletcher* program and concluded that 'no worthwhile improvement in fuel capacity is practicable in the DD-445 class destroyers. On the basis of the urgent employment of all vessels of this class and near completion of the program ... no changes are now contemplated for this class. This also applies to vessels in the first part of the DD-692 class destroyer.' BuShips suggested that lengthening the ships fourteen feet and adding fuel tanks between the forward and after halves of the engineering plant would add 168 tons of fuel capacity and boost radius by 30 per cent. King approved this plan, directing that it be implemented as soon as possible, but without seriously interfering with destroyer completions.[21]

This decision effectively divided the '2,200-tonners' into two distinct classes, deceptively similar in appearance and most military characteristics but dissimilar in fuel capacity and, thus, in cruising range. These were the *Allen M. Sumner* (DD-692) and *Gearing* (DD-710) classes, often referred to in contemporary documents and publications as the 'short hull' and 'long hull' 2,200 ton destroyers.[22] It was calculated that, where the *Allen M. Sumner* class would be capable of 3,300 miles at 20 knots, the 'long hull' *Gearing* class would be able to steam 4,500 miles at the same speed.

As with any other new design, the 2,200-ton destroyers ran into their share of problems. Propeller shafts were supported by two struts which projected from the hull, and vibration at high speeds tended to crack the forward of the two. These ships were built with twin rudders, the first American destroyers to have them, and quick turns created stresses which the struts could not handle. Steps were quickly taken to strengthen the propeller struts in existing ships, and some later ships got an additional strut arm in an effort to cope with the side forces created. This did not correct the situation, and heavily reinforced single struts were finally adopted. The three-bladed propellers installed on the first 2,200-tonners were replaced by 4-bladed screws on later ships, again to combat vibration.[23]

Besides the problem of propeller-shaft struts, Admiral King found other things to criticize in the new ships, and wrote that since 'this class represents in all probability the last of our present destroyer building program' it was 'essential that we get a satisfactory ship'. King felt that 'we must take time out to review the design features of the class and not go ahead with the production of the class which includes so many unsatisfactory features.' Preferring to accept a temporary delay in delivery of the class 'in order ultimately to get a better destroyer', King directed VCNO to take corrective steps at once.[24]

The bridge structure presented another headache. The Navy Board of Inspection and Survey, after trial of *Barton* (DD-722) in late December 1943, showed that visibility for the conning officer was inadequate and that the Bureau of Ships should look into this for the entire class. A series of trials, studies and recommendations followed, and another full

scale mockup was constructed at Boston Navy Yard in May 1944. The final result of the study was a bridge similar in general arrangement to that of later *Fletcher* class ships.

The first 2,200-tonner completed was *Barton* (DD-722), placed in commission on 30 December 1943. By the summer of 1944 adverse comments were being heard, and on 8 July 1944 Admiral King asked the Naval Inspector General to investigate the allegations of deficiencies.[25] The Inspector General found much to criticize. He felt that it should have been evident from examination of the first mockup in 1942 that the projected bridge would be too low and crowded, but nothing was done until after *Barton* had been delivered for service in early 1944. The sonar compartment, originally located on the bridge deck, made the rest of the bridge too congested and turned out to be too small to accommodate adequately the sonar equipment installed in the ship. Living quarters for officers and men were crowded thanks to the addition of electronics and fire control gear during the design and construction process. The dimensions of the ships being what they were, very little could be done about this. Increases to the ships' AA batteries during this time increased displacement, affecting speed and radius, but again, nothing was done to remedy the situation except for the lengthening of the *Gearing* class to carry additional fuel. Even this, the Inspector General pointed out, was not done until after the first ships were delivered and their short cruising ranges 'forced the issue'. The Bureau of Ships had not anticipated the effect of faster turning, with twin rudders, on the propeller shaft struts, and this also had to be corrected after some ships had been completed. Inadequate planning, he concluded, had resulted in about a month's delay in completion of 20 to 25 ships; last minute changes would add $235,000 to $250,000 to the cost of each ship. (It should be emphasized that these were 1944 dollars.)

The Inspector General felt that at least some of the confusion was due to the unrealistic terminology being used. Trial speed had little real meaning to the operating forces, and standard displacement, that artificial legalism born of the Washington Treaty, was meaningless. Nomenclature should be revised to show 'the actual battle condition capabilities of vessels, and fleet reference publications should be changed to show this. "There is no point", the Inspector General interjected, "in calling a vessel that displaces 3200 tons and that makes 34.5 knots a '2200 ton, 36.5 knot destroyer.'" The real problem, he felt, lay in the fact that the existing Navy Department organization did not 'provide a single agency or group (preferably small) with definite authority to determine and prescribe the military characteristics of ships in accordance with the requirements of strategic planning and tactical usage,' that would follow those characteristics through the BuShips design process without constant changes 'until a reasonable experience in sea operation has demonstrated the necessity or desirability' of such alterations. The recommended organization should be set up within the Office of Naval Operations, and should control the formation of ships' characteristics not only in the planning and construction stages, but throughout the service life of the resulting ships. Much of this had, in previous years, been within the purview of the General Board, but now a new organization was called for, with executive authority which the General Board did not have. This would result, early in 1945, in the establishment of the Ship Characteristics Board under the Chief of Naval Operations.

In spite of the assorted deficiencies laid out before him, the Inspector General was able to conclude that 'while the DD-692 class may not be all that every one in the Navy desired, it is still the outstanding destroyer in existence as regards fire power, maneuverability, sound and ship control, and the ability to perform all of a destroyer's tasks. It is a bit overloaded with guns, equipment, and personnel and can only make 34½ knots top speed, and cruise 3,300 to 3,866 miles at 20 knots. However, officers interviewed, including DD captains, would not consent to removing any sizeable amount of equipment to reduce

weight.' He could also note that 'after interviewing ten ... Commanding Officers of this class, a Squadron Commander, and many officers experienced in destroyer characteristics, it was the consensus of opinion that the present armament is the best of any destroyer in service, effective and adequate.'[26]

Rumors continued to circulate. Some of the new ships had their forward 5-inch mounts damaged by seas coming over the bows; the forecastle deck of *Walke* (DD-723) was damaged while that ship was steaming at 17 knots in moderate seas with three sister ships, none of which was damaged. Destroyer captains interviewed during the Inspector General's investigation described their ships as 'bow heavy'. An examination of some of the class showed them to be trimmed by the stern from 6 to 12 inches; this was increased, to an extent depending on speed, when the ships were underway. The officers' opinion was apparently caused by the weight of the two twin 5-inch gun mounts, with their ammunition, on a bow of *Fletcher* dimensions; the new ships did not tend to lift themselves out of a wave as readily as did earlier ships, giving the impression that forward weights of bridge structure and guns were pulling the ships down by the bow.

By October 1944 stories about the DD-692 class had spread far afield. A Pacific Fleet destroyer squadron commander could then write that he had 'for the past four months, ... been in the unique and unenviable position of having to defend his ships against a variety of unfavorable com-

ments, some of them unfounded criticisms and some of them the insidious damnings of faint praise. There seems to persist in too many minds (outside the ships themselves) a prevailing feeling that "2,200-tonners are fine ships, but ——." It is time for these rumors to be scotched.' Calling the new ships 'the finest destroyers that this or any other nation has ever launched', this destroyer commodore pointed to their heavier 5-inch, 40 mm, and 20 mm batteries, bigger depth charge capacity, twin rudders for maneuverability, and enlarged auxiliary electric power plant. He liked their newly designed CIC and what he termed 'an excellent combat bridge with ... a spacious open bridge conning station providing unrestricted air and surface visibility in any direction.' The 330 degree arc of fire for the after 40 mm guns was a plus, along with the provision for 5-inch and 40 mm gun-control radars. The DD-692 class destroyer was called 'an unusually stable gun platform lacking the snap roll characteristics so disturbing in some earlier types and

Opposite
Walke (DD-723) alongside a *Fletcher* at Mare Island, 26 March 1945. Elevated, circled, tubs contain canvas-covered Mark 51 40 mm directors. *Walke*'s K-guns are provided with streamlined Mark 9 300-pound depth charges. A comparison of *Fletcher* with the newer classes shows how the adoption of twin 5-inch mounts permitted a heavier gun battery while allowing ample deck space for torpedoes and light AA guns.

Bottom
Ault (DD-698) heads for Japan with the fast carrier striking force, July 1945. Like the flushdeckers of the 1920s and 1930s, these '2,200-tonners' largely epitomized the destroyer navy for years after the war ended.

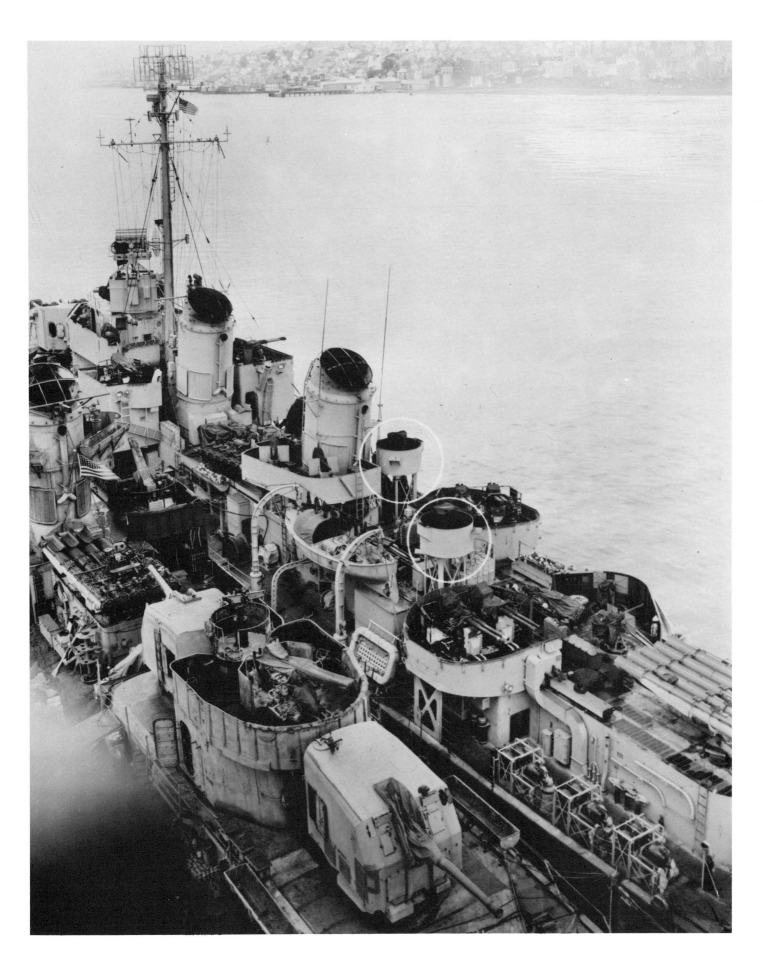

unusually dry weather decks in the vicinity of the [40 mm] auto weapons.' Also singled out for praise was the provision of special risers and manifolds forward and aft, connected to the ship's fire main to permit one of these destroyers to come alongside a burning ship and pass across as many as eight hoses to help extinguish the blaze. 'Little else', he finished, 'need be said. Comments derogatory to these ships are obviously unfounded and it is hoped that none of the unfortunate impressions recently in circulation will prevent the assignment of the 2,200-ton destroyers to tasks which will employ their full combat ability.'[27]

The Commander in Chief, Pacific Fleet, found it necessary to step into the debate. In a general letter he took notice that 'unfavorable comments about the 2,200-ton class of destroyers have been circulating in the Fleet. Most of these criticisms are based on rumor, and are undoubtedly the result of early difficulties, which are common in any new type ship. Unsatisfactory construction details of the bridge, failure of the intermediate shaft struts, low performance level of the originally installed echo ranging gear and other minor defects, have now been corrected. ... Derogatory rumors concerning cruising radius, speed, vibration, behavior in a seaway, effectiveness of sound gear, etc., are unwarranted.

Although these ships have not been tried in battle, their potentialities indicate that they will prove to be the finest destroyers that have ever joined the Fleet.'[28] While no one could accuse Admiral Nimitz of understating his case, especially with regard to the steaming radius of the first ships of the class, the corrosive effect of wartime rumor on the forces afloat certainly had to be countered.

As completed, the *Allen M. Sumner*s and *Gearing*s were tactically similar except for the added length — and range — of the 'long-hull' *Gearing* class. Both classes were armed with the same 6-gun, 10-tube battery and mounted two 40 mm quads on the after-deckhouse, with two 40 mm twins on elevated deckhouses to port and starboard just abaft the bridge. This arrangement was backed up, as was by now customary, with 20 mm guns, depth-charge tracks, and K-guns. Electronic suits and fire control were basically the same as in the *Fletcher*s, except that the new class' design had made internal provision for radar, the first American destroyers to do so. Engineering plants in all these ships were so generally similar that a common basic training text could be published for the *Fletcher*, *Allen M. Sumner*, and *Gearing* classes.[29] In the hope of preventing complete loss of power in case of a torpedo hit, in all three classes the

forward fire room and engine room could be operated together as a completely independent plant, as could the after fire room and engine room. Athough there were many differences in arrangement between the *Fletcher* class and the later ships, the basic principle was identical throughout. Where the *Fletcher* class had two 290-kilowatt turbogenerators with a 100-kilowatt Diesel emergency generator, the 2,200-tonners were built with a pair of 400-kilowatt turbogenerators and two 100-kilowatt emergency Diesels to handle the increased power requirements imposed by electronics and power-operated gun mounts. One of the two main generators could carry the entire ship's battle load if necessary.

The inevitable changes were made or proposed. The Bureau of Ordnance recommended that five spare torpedoes for the after tube mount, with a 'roller loader' arrange-

ment for quick reloading, be added to the DD-692 and –710 design at an estimated cost of eleven and a half tons of topside weight. This, the Bureau believed, would encourage destroyer captains to fire 10-tube initial salvoes instead of holding one loaded tube mount in reserve; '. . . in the early stages of an engagement', BuOrd suggested, 'our advantage in radar should be exploited to its maximum, and ... the firing of full torpedo salvoes will immensely increase the probabilities of decisive damage to the enemy.'[30]

The Bureau of Ships was unenthusiastic. Reload torpedoes could not be accommodated in any ships earlier than the *Allen M. Sumner*s and *Gearing*s, and even here the addition of reloads would reduce speed and radius, cut down the existing reserve of damaged stability, and add to the displacement of 'vessels which are already heavily overloaded.'[31] The Chief of Naval Operations agreed, and dropped the idea with the remark that reloads might be considered in 'the design of new construction Destroyers that might follow

the 2,200-ton type.'[32]

Antiaircraft modifications followed through 1945 as ships of both classes continued to go into service. The *kamikaze* began to make its appearance late in 1944, and the suicide counter-offensive swelled to a furious pitch during the battle for Okinawa. Considerations of stability had to be balanced against the need to survive air attack. The after bank of torpedo tubes was removed from many 2,200-tonners during 1945 and replaced by a third quadruple 40 mm mount. Single 20 mm guns were replaced, when possible, by twin mounts. As with the *Fletcher* class this was not considered 'ultimate' armament; the Bureau of Ordnance planned an eventual return to the original 10-tube configuration.

A major late-war development was the radar-picket *Gearing* modification. This conversion combined the early-warning and fighter-direction functions in one ship. Destroyers had been used for fighter direction as early as the Gilberts operation in late 1943, but these were not special ship modifications.

Destroyers also came to be used for radar picket work at this time but, again, this involved no special equipment; a picket destroyer was simply a standard ship placed along the axis of expected enemy approach and given radar-guard duties. The two functions were first combined in the *Fletcher* class *Kimberly* (DD-521) during the assault on the Gilberts, and destroyers occupied several picket and fighter-direction stations in the summer of 1944 during the capture of the Marianas. During the first carrier strikes on the Tokyo area in February–March 1945 a destroyer picket line operated between Task Force 58 and Honshu, and worked with a Combat Air Patrol (CAP) of fighters to protect the carriers from attack. In several instances the picket ships were able to identify enemy planes attempting to approach the task force with returning strike planes; these might otherwise have gone undetected, with the chance of fatal results. The serious damage inflicted on carriers *Bunker Hill* (CV-17) and *Franklin* (CV-13) off Japan in 1945

These four photographs allow a detailed comparison between the late-war *Fletcher* configuration and the 5-tube and 10-tube *Allen M. Sumner* pattern.

Top and bottom left
These views show *Mansfield* (DD-728) alongside *Mertz* (DD-691); they should also be compared to those of *Mertz*, taken at this time, which appear on pages 96–7.

Opposite top left and right
In these views *Hyman* (DD-732) is moored 'Chinese fashion' beside a *Fletcher* which has just had 40 mm midship quads and 20 mm twins installed. The stern view of *Hyman* illustrates the concentration of gunfire available for use against aircraft coming in from astern or either quarter.

emphasized the importance of stopping such attackers. In April 1945, tactical instructions including procedures for radar picket destroyers were issued by the Fast Carrier Force. Throughout the Okinawa campaign destroyers and destroyer escorts were used on picket duty, and their ordeal is a familiar part of the story of the Pacific war. The Japanese quickly realized the significance of the picket line of 'small boys' interposed between Okinawa and the suiciders' airfields, and the picket ships were subjected to the full fury of the Divine Wind. Twelve destroyers and one destroyer escort were sunk off Okinawa; and 57 DDs and DEs were damaged, some so severely that it was a wonder they stayed afloat. Navy planners realized that the invasion of the Japanese home islands, planned for October 1945 under the code name *Olympic*, would make the Okinawa campaign seem like a pleasant outing in the country. *Olympic* was to have been an amphibious assault on Kyushu. Operation *Coronet*, planned for 1946, would have involved a landing on the Kanto Plain in central Honshu, near Tokyo. Naval planners anticipated continuing, large-scale *kamikaze* resistance. If effective fleet antiair defense had been essential before, it would be even more so in the months to come; the radar-picket *Gearing* was part of the answer.

Twenty-four *Gearing*s were modified during the summer and fall of 1945. The original plan called for removal of the forward torpedo-tube mount. In its place was installed a high tripod mast bearing antennas for the height-finding SP radar, hitherto used only by bigger ships, as well as an aircraft homing beacon, IFF, (Identification, Friend or Foe) and a complete RCM (Radar Countermeasures, the original US Navy term for Electronic Countermeasures — ECM) installation. Each ship retained its own air-search, surface-search, and fire-control radars, but had its radio and CIC spaces considerably enlarged to accommodate the additional men and equipment needed to keep track of the aerial

picture and to keep in touch with tactical command and orbiting fighters.

Chevalier (DD-805) was the first picket ship to complete conversion in May 1945. After trials and picket training she visited the Naval Gun Factory at Washington, DC, for detailed inspection by representatives of the various Bureaus and offices of the Navy Department. Other ships followed as quickly as possible, although the end of the war in August eliminated their original purpose. By this time the remaining torpedo-tube mount in nearly all of the ships had been removed, as in 'standard' *Gearing*s, to make room for a third 40 mm quadruple mount. Because of their expected importance in *Olympic*, the picket destroyers were given preference in assignment of the new Mark 63 Gun Fire Control System which, with its associated radar, would permit blind firing of the 40 mm battery.

The specialized picket ship remained in use for nearly two decades after the end of World War II. In March 1949, they were formally classified as Radar Picket Destroyers (DDR). During the Korean War *Eugene A. Greene* (DD-711) received a new-pattern DDR modification, with expanded CIC facilities and the new AN/SPS-8 medium-range air-search and heightfinding radar. The existing 'Okinawa DDRs' were refitted to this standard, losing their tripod mainmasts, and twelve more *Gearing*s were modified to DDRs. Nine of these ships were equipped with TACAN air-control electronics in the late 1950s. When these ships underwent FRAM modernization in the early 1960s they lost their SPS-8 radars, reverting to a Destroyer (DD) classification.

As some of the *Gearing* class were converted to picket ships, a number of *Allen M. Sumner* class destroyers were converted to Light Mine Layers (DM). As we have noted, the first DM's were modified flushdeckers intended to plant moored minefields in enemy waters or to lay drifting mines in the path of a hostile battle line during a fleet action. By World War II the notion of tactical minelaying seems to have been largely discarded, although drifting mines remained in the ordnance inventory.

The laying of moored fields, though, was very much a part of the war at sea in all theaters. In the Pacific area the converted destroyer was a natural choice for work in the hotly-disputed waters of the Solomons chain, as it would later be in other areas where enemy surface or submarine opposition might be expected. On 20 February 1943 the Com-

mander, Service Squadron Six, Pacific Fleet, pointed to the inadequacy of the Pacific mine-laying force, eight flushdeck DMs and four smaller minesweepers modified to lay mines. Although this force was useful for planting defensive fields, it lacked 'the speed and strength to properly conduct an offensive mining operation in enemy waters.' The old DMs were slow, the removal of one boiler to increase fuel capacity having brought their speed down to about 25 knots, and old age was manifesting itself in general deterioration and structural weakness. New mines, with

Henry A. Wiley was ordered as an *Allen M. Sumner* class destroyer (DD-749), but completed as a fast minelayer (DM-29). Torpedo tubes have been removed and mine tracks installed to each side of the main deck; in this photograph she is carrying to a load of dummy moored drill mines. She has the two 40 mm twins and two quads common to her class, but K-guns have been moved to the after end of her superstructure deck to clear the way for mine tracks; depth-charge tracks remain at the stern, but have been moved closer together.

bigger explosive charges, were considerably heavier than those of the prewar years, and the old ships could carry fewer of them. Their armament of 3-inch or 4-inch guns was 'too light to be effective against the type of opposition normally expected in offensive operations.' The existing concept of DM operations called for the ships to begin their approach at nightfall, steaming at their maximum sustained speed to reach the target area and plant their mines shortly after midnight before retiring at high speed, and the old flushdeckers were no longer suited for this kind of work. Since the new destroyer building program would 'shortly be fairly well in hand', conversion of four new destroyers to light minelayers was requested.[33]

This proposal met a cool reception on its way up the chain of command. The Commander, Service Force, pronounced the existing DMs 'barely satisfactory as regards speed and gun power, and deficient in carrying capacity', but felt that the existing need for destroyers and escort ships was so great that any diversion was unjustified. The entire question, he felt, was one for higher command since any such conversion would depend on future plans for offensive minelaying operations. Since offensive minelaying should normally be carried out under cover of a protective screen, heavy gun armament was unnecessary.[34] Admiral Nimitz concurred in this,[35] but the Vice Chief of Naval Operations held that 'when carrying out offensive mining missions, fast surface minelayers will not normally be screened and should have a reasonably heavy gun armament.'[36] Admiral King replied that no new destroyers could be spared at that time for conversion, and that offensive aerial minelaying was being developed to an extent that might lessen the need for fast surface minelayers. He did, however, think it 'entirely possible that an urgent need for such new minelayers will develop', and directed the Bureau of Ships to design suitable minelaying configurations 'with particular emphasis on plans for quick, temporary and limited conversion of destroyers for the purpose of carrying out a special mining mission.' King also agreed with VCNO that future DM armament should be designed for unscreened operations.[37] VCNO passed King's directive to BuShips, specifying designs for 'temporary and limited conversions retaining a maximum gun battery and involving a minimum of structural change. 'Minelaying equipment should, if possible, be prefabricated and interchangeable, suitable for quick conversion, and adaptable for use with different types of surface-laid mines.'[38]

ComServRon Six had apparently not received a reply to his original recommendation when he addressed a second inquiry on 10 May 1943, emphasizing the limited number — eight — of the old flushdeck DMs available. Their age, which made extensive upkeep necessary, and their slow speed, combined with 'the constant demand for antisubmarine and other escort duties, makes it difficult to obtain sufficient of these ships at any one place or time for an offensive mining operation without plans so far in advance as to be unsatisfactory.' He proposed conversion of four ships and, possibly for the long run, eight, on a not-to-delay-completion basis, arguing that 'the need for more, new and faster light mine layers is of prime importance.' When not actually engaged in mine planting they would still 'be almost equally as valuable as DDs on escort duties' and would thus not represent a loss to the fleet's escort capabilities.[39]

As before, ComServRon Six's request climbed the command ladder. ComServPac had changed his mind in three months; he now concluded that 'the picture has changed somewhat' since his earlier recommendation that nothing be allowed to interfere with the provision of destroyers and escorts, and 'now believed that the time has arrived when definite plans should be made towards providing additional fast minelayers.' The increasing use of DMs, the distances involved in Pacific operations, and the age and material condition of the old flushdeckers combined to suggest 'that not less than four new fast minelayers be provided at the earliest practicable date.'[40] Admiral Nimitz still felt that 'the existing shortage of destroyers precludes such conversion' at that time;[41] Admiral King agreed, adding that 'no further action in this regard is contemplated at this time.'[42]

The Bureau of Ships went ahead with its studies of possible DM conversions. Nine schemes were drawn up, three for the *Gleaves* class and six for the *Fletcher* class; each set of schemes involved provision for progressively heavier mine loads at the expense of more extensive removals of guns and depth charges. All loads were 'based on a strict weight and moment compensation', since the wartime AA batteries 'installed on all destroyers have increased their displacement and decreased their stability to a point which makes it unwise to allow weight additions without complete compensation.' The most extensive *Gleaves* conversion would have accommodated 54 Mark 6 moored mines at a cost of the after 5-inch gun and all depth charges. If depth charges and one 5-inch gun, plus 20 mm guns and one torpedo-tube mount, were removed from a *Fletcher*, then up to 84 Mark 6 mines could be carried. BuShips thought it practicable to prefabricate mine tracks and associated gear for *ad hoc* installation at advanced bases as needed.[43] The Fleet Maintenance Division of the Office of Naval Operations pronounced the maximum-capacity *Fletcher* conversion 'the only plan offering sufficient promise to warrant further development',[44] and COMINCH approved completion of the design and fabrication of equipment for conversion of four ships.[45] Plans were drawn, and Mare Island Navy Yard was directed to prepare working drawings and fabricate four conversion 'kits' for *Fletcher* minelayer conversions.[46]

In December 1943, the Commander, South Pacific Force, Admiral Halsey, again pointed out that the flushdeck DMs were 'so old and in such poor material condition that they cannot be relied on' and that a new DM was necessary, while holding that an alternative was preferable to the conversion of new destroyers to minelayers.[47] Commander Destroyers, Pacific Fleet, also believed it 'a misuse of new destroyers to convert them to minelayers' and suggested that the older *Porter* and *Somers* classes would be better suited to DM use. Their large hull and ample deck space would enable them to carry 90 Mark 6 mines if their superfiring forward 5-inch twin mount were replaced by a twin 40 mm mount; this would also improve their AA capability, since the 1,850-tonners had 'always been considered ... deficient in antiaircraft defense.' Conversion of four of these destroyers, ComDesPac believed, would be preferable to 'crucifying new ships' for the purpose and should be carefully considered.[48] The Commander in Chief, Pacific Fleet, considered the *Fletcher* conversion concept satisfactory, but agreed with his destroyer commander's opinion.[49] The Bureau of Ships was asked to look into a 1,850-tonner DM conversion,[50] and a group of officers from Service Squadron Six took a close look at *Selfridge* (DD-357). Removal of the ship's K-guns and torpedo tubes, with some minor rearrangement, would enable one of these 'leaders' to carry 120 mines. Their large fuel capacity gave them a 'highly satisfactory' radius, while their sustained speed in tropical waters was 31.5 knots. Sheer aft increased freeboard at the stern by nearly three feet, and a trough would have to be cut into the main deck astern to allow the proper slope to the mine tracks. This was thought a minor point, but the amount of work involved did make it desirable that any conversion be permanent rather than temporary, and ComServRon Six strongly recommended this.[51]

Destroyers, Pacific, and ServRon Six agreed that any 1,850-ton DM conversion should be permanent. All depth-charge gear should be removed, since depth charges could easily be carried on mine tracks if the ships were required for escort duty. Torpedo tubes should also be removed; if stability warranted, a pair of 40 mm twin AA mounts with directors should be installed in their stead.[52] COMINCH now proposed to convert the *Somers* class *Sampson* (DD-394) and *Warrington* (DD-383) with the *Porter* class *Phelps* (DD-360) during forthcoming overhauls, provided a detailed study then in progress produced a 'feasible and desirable' conversion plan.[53] Asked whether future needs justified this conversion, Admiral Nimitz's reply was to the point: 'NEGATIVE. CONSIDER NUMBER OF FAST LIGHT MINELAYERS THIS AREA NOW ADEQUATE. SUBJECT VESSELS MORE VALUABLE AS DD'S THAN AS DM'S.'[54] While this exchange was going on, BuShips had been at work on modification plans and, on 14 June 1944, forwarded the results to CNO. This study had been combined with the projected modernization of the 5-inch batteries of the *Porter* and *Somers* classes, already completed in *Selfridge* (DD-357), scheduled for *Clark* (DD-361) and *McDougal* (DD-358) in the near future, and to be authorized for the rest of both classes. As completed, the proposed 1,850-ton minelayers would have mounted two dual-purpose 5-inch twins, three 40 mm AA mounts (three twins in the *Somers* class, two twins and a quad in the *Porter*s), and six 20 mm guns, with a capacity of 97 Mark 6 mines.[55]

By June 1944, the battle for the Marianas was in full swing. Admiral Nimitz, who in April had thought the existing DMs adequate, now reversed himself in another message to Admiral King: 'AFTER CAREFUL CONSIDERATION, NOW ANTICIPATE NEED FOR 12 FAST (35 KNOT) DESTROYER TYPE MINELAYERS TO BE READY FOR SERVICE IN PACIFIC BY FEBRUARY 1945. RECOMMEND CONSIDERATION BE GIVEN TO CONSTRUCTION OF THESE SHIPS UTILIZING 2200 TON DESTROYER HULLS NOW UNDER CONSTRUCTION.'[56] (By February 1945, the Philippines would have been recaptured and the Iwo Jima operation underway.) Admiral King replied that time prevented any extensive redesign of the DD-692 and DD-710 classes. A conversion could be accomplished in general accordance with existing plans, but this would involve removal of the after 5-inch gun mount. As an alternative, King suggested a conversion of twelve *Fletcher*s.[57] Nimitz recommended the 2,200-ton conversion, but with a 120-mine capacity and all torpedoes removed.'[58]

King, accordingly, directed the conversion of twelve *Allen M. Sumner* class destroyers to

'heavy DMs' with the 'largest practicable' mine capacity up to a maximum of 125 and with no torpedo battery. 'Subject to stability considerations with largest mine capacity' the ships were to have 'maximum anti-aircraft gun power aft in the ultimate armament and such anti-aircraft gun power aft as an interim armament as can be completed without delaying delivery.'[59] The material Bureaus were ordered to complete twelve ships then under construction as DM-23 through –34. This *Robert H. Smith* (DM-23) class was to retain the three 5-inch twins, two 40 mm twins and two 40 mm quads of the *Allen M. Sumner* class, with eight 20 mm guns (three on the stern being omitted) and two depth-charge tracks without extensions. Instead of six deck-edge K-guns, four were to be installed on the after end of the superstructure deck. As far as possible, the 'remainder of original DD char-

acteristics and equipment' were to be retained, and structural changes were to be kept to a minimum.[60]

All twelve of the *Robert H. Smith* class were in commission by the end of October 1944 and saw action in the Pacific. All kept their original 40 mm battery through the end of the war, but light AA armament included a variety of 20 mm guns as well as .50 and .30-caliber machine guns. Two of the class were severely damaged off Okinawa, and after V-J day they were both scrapped. Active DMs had a third quad 40 mm mount installed after the war ended, following the general pattern of their parent destroyer class. Four ships were still active when the Korean War began and another was reactivated in 1952. The last two were placed out of commission in 1958, the US Navy's last active surface minelayers.

Top right, top left and opposite top right
Detailed views of the destroyer minelayer *Adams* (DM-27) taken on 2 July 1945. *Adams* has two 40 mm quads with four K-guns where her after torpedo tubes would have gone, as had *Henry A. Wiley* (DM-29).

Bottom left
Tolman (DM-28) in heavy seas. 2,200-tonners were more seaworthy than their smaller ancestors, but even they could make heavy weather of it.

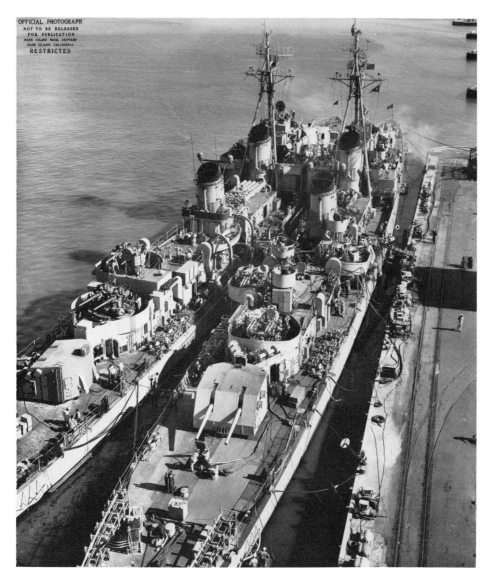

Opposite top left
Detailed view of the destroyer minelayer
Robert H. Smith (DM-23) taken on 27 June 1946. Her
K-guns are on the main deck, whence they must be
moved when mine tracks are to be used; this had to be
done to accommodate a third 40 mm mount.

Opposite bottom
Chevalier (DD-805) was one of the *Gearing*s selected, in
1945, for conversion to a radar-picket destroyer. Seen
here on 29 August 1946, she has had her torpedo tubes
suppressed and is equipped with a high tripod mainmast
supporting a Type SP height-finding radar. Internally,
she is fitted with expanded CIC, communication, and
fighter-director facilities.

Opposite top right
Midship details of *Chevalier*, 6 September 1946. The
curved antenna on a pole topmast above her SP is a Type
YE radio homing beacon. In the tub at the left of the
photograph is a GFCS Mark 63 40 mm gun director;
twin 5-inch practice loading machines are between the
forward stack and the short searchlight tower.

Top left
Stickell (DD-888) is seen here on 28 September 1950.
Like other war-built destroyers, she has received a
tripod foremast to support heavy new radar antennae.
Stickell still retains her late-war 40 mm battery; her
sister ship moored alongside, has two new 3-inch/
50-caliber rapid-fire AA mounts aft and two
3-inch singles forward. *Stickell's* torpedo directors are
still on her bridge wings; her neighbor has had 3-inch
directors mounted in this position, and her torpedo
directors have been moved to a new platform on the after
stack.

Bottom left
A close view of the forepart of *Richard B. Anderson*
(DD-786) after installation of her tripod foremost. The
larger antenna is part of an SPS-6B air-search
equipment; above it is smaller SG-6 surface-search and
zenith (overhead) warning antenna. The Mark 25
fire-control radar, its dish-shaped antenna seen on the
Mark 37 director was designed to replace the late-war
Mark 12/Mark 22 combination.

Opposite
Rowan (DD-782) in the Pacific, 1958. Many active destroyers had fixed *Hedgehog* launchers installed to port and starboard of their bridges during the 1950s; the performance of postwar submarines called for increasing effort to counter them.

Top left
Epperson (DDE-719), completed in 1949 as an antisubmarine escort destroyer with a trainable ahead-throwing *Hedgehog* launcher in place of Mount 52.

Center left
Fechteler, one of an improved generation of radar-picket destroyers modified in the early 1950s. Unlike the earlier 1945 conversions, they were redesignated as DDR on conversion. *Fechteler* has an SPS-8 height-finding radar aft; the 'box' abaft it is the director for a GFCS Mark 56, a radar-equipped system capable of controlling 3-inch and 5-inch guns. Like *Richard B. Anderson* (DD-786), *Fechteler* has SPS-6B, SG-6, and Mark 25 radars forward.

Bottom left
Gyatt (DD-712) is seen here after her 1956 modification and redesignation as the Navy's first guided-missile destroyer (DDG-1). Her after superstructure was modified to stow *Terrier* surface-to-air missiles for the launcher installed in place of her after 5-inch guns, and a British-designed Denny-Brown fin stabilization system was installed.

Top and center
Charles P. Cecil (DD-835) after her **FRAM Mark I** modernization. FRAM alterations were intended to add five to eight years to ships' useful lives and gave them new superstructures, DASH facilities, and trainable Mark 32 antisubmarine torpedo tubes (the small triple mounts seen forward of the bridge). Some ships received fixed tubes for conventional torpedoes. The box-like launcher between the ship's stacks fires the ASROC antisubmarine missile. A number of variations in appearance can be seen among FRAMmed destroyers.

Bottom
Rough water refueling operations often make for spectacular ship photography, as is evident from this post-World War II shot of *Forest Royal* (DD-872) in the Norwegian Sea.

16

Gearing and Sumner Postscript

Only since the First World War have navies built destroyers large enough really to do what they have long been supposed to do.

Lieutenant Franklin G. Percival, USN, letter to the *United States Naval Institute Proceedings*, (November 1935)

Of the final classes of destroyers produced during World War II, 222 ships were originally ordered with 54 being canceled or never completed. Many were not finished in time to see war service: thirty-one were commissioned in 1946 and two more followed in 1947. Two *Gearing*s were commissioned in 1949 as prototype escort destroyers (DDE); another two were finished as offensive hunter-killer destroyers (DDK), with new rapid fire 3-inch/50-caliber guns, later replaced by less than successful 3-inch/70s. Six more *Gearing*s had one forward 5-inch mount removed and also became DDKs. The killer-destroyer concept was dropped in 1950 when DDKs were reclassified DDEs. *Gearing* class DDEs, their forward superfiring 5-inch gun mount replaced at first with a *Hedgehog* ahead-throwing anti-submarine launcher and later (in some ships) with a Weapon *Able* launcher, existed as a separate type category until 1962 when existing escort destroyers reverted to DDs. One *Gearing* class ship, *Witek* (DD-848), tested an experimental shrouded propeller installation. Another ship, *Timmerman* (EDD-828), was completed in September 1952 as an 'Advanced Design Destroyer' with two 1,050-degree, 875-psi boilers and two more capable of 2,000 psi at 1,050 degrees. The two engine rooms contained different experimental geared-turbine plants and a 1,000-volt, 400-cycle generating plant was designed for a weight saving of 55 percent over the generator installation of a conventional *Gearing*. *Timmerman* was designed as an 'experimental, lightweight advanced design destroyer developed around experience obtained during the war in destroyer power plant design and operation. Reduction in weight far

beyond anything previously attempted has been incorporated in this ship to determine to what extent steam and electrical equipment can be lightened and yet produce a power-plant of the required ruggedness.'[1] This ship's engineering plant produced 100,000 horse-power at a 104-ton saving over the standard *Gearing* installation, a weight/horsepower ratio of 19 pounds/hp compared to 35 pounds/hp in the standard plant.[2] *Timmerman* was reclassified as a miscellaneous auxiliary ship (EAG-152) in 1954 and in her four-year life carried out extensive tests of her engineering system. She was decommissioned in 1956 and sold for scrap in 1958.

Postwar changes to these classes tended to follow the general pattern of the *Fletcher* class. Although late-wartime planning had envisioned restoration of 10-tube batteries as the postwar standard, the 5-tube configuration, with a third quad 40 mm mount installed, became the pattern as the unlikelihood of large-scale torpedo operations became obvious. Tripod foremasts gradually replaced pole masts on most ships; electronics were updated and, during the 1950s, the 3-inch/50-caliber rapid-fire gun supplanted 40 mm Bofors in the active fleet. Pairs of fixed *Hedgehog* launchers supplemented depth charges.

The *Gearing* class *Gyatt* (DD-712) had her after guns replaced by a twin *Terrier* surface-to-air guided missile launcher and recommissioned in 1956 as the US Navy's first guided-missile destroyer, DDG-712. In 1957 a new numbering system for missile destroyers was adopted and *Gyatt* became DDG-1.

An extensive modernization program was conceived in 1958 when the Secretary of the Navy organized a committee under the chair-

manship of Mr. William E. Blewett, Vice-President of Newport News Shipbuilding and Dry Dock Company of Newport News, Virginia. This 'Blewett Committee' returned its report in November 1958 and in the following month, the Chief of Naval Operations issued a general plan for what was termed the Fleet Rehabilitation and Modernization (FRAM) Program. Two prototypes were selected for modernization under the Fiscal 1959 budget. The *Gearing* class *Perry* (DD-844) received a FRAM Mark I overhaul, designed to extend her useful life eight to ten years. *John W. Thomason* (DD-760) of the *Allen M. Sumner* class was given a FRAM Mark II modernization, calculated to stretch her life by five years.

These FRAM conversions were intended to 'reinforce' an entire generation of World War II-built destroyers, not very old by objective standards and expected to be able to 'steam and steer' for some years to come. Improvements in submarine propulsion and hull form had produced new submarines which made their wartime ancestors look crude; the FRAM program was intended to take advantage of recent developments in antisubmarine sensors and ordnance and enable the active *Fletcher*s, *Allen M. Sumner*s, and *Gearing*s—which still constituted the bulk of the American destroyer force — to hold the line until the new classes of missile destroyers and escort ships projected for the 1960s could join the fleet in sufficient numbers to take up the slack. Construction of new escorts (DE) had resumed in 1951 when Dealey (DE-1006) was laid down. The *Claud Jones* (DE-1033) class followed the *Dealey*s, and the *Bronstein* (DE-1037), *Garcia* (DE-1040), and *Knox* (DE-1052) classes would follow during the 1960s, with the missile destroyers of the *Charles F. Adams* (DDG-2) class.

A FRAM modernization involved removal of all 3-inch or 40 mm guns, depth charges, and wartime-pattern 21-inch quintuple torpedo-tube mounts, as well as nearly all of the superstructure above the main deck. FRAMmed *Gearing*s kept two 5-inch twins, while modernized *Fletcher*s retained two single mounts, and *Allen M. Sumner*s held onto all three twins. Depending on the original configuration of the ships, the original class, and the degree of modernization involved, new armament included various combinations of ASROC launchers, Mark 25 fixed tubes for long-range antisubmarine torpedoes, and trainable Mark 32 tubes for short-range acoustic antisubmarine torpedoes. Except for six picket ships, which retained their DDR identity until 1969 and kept their heightfinding radar installations, all FRAM destroyers received a hangar and small flight

deck for the Gyrodyne DSN-3 Drone Antisubmarine Helicopter (the DSN-1 and-2 were prototypes), a small remotely-controlled vehicle designed to carry and launch two acoustic torpedoes. The aircraft installation turned out to be purposeless, since the DSN proved tricky to control and mechanically unreliable; destroyermen sarcastically dubbed the DASH the Down-at-Sea Helicopter, and it was put to no more than limited use. (In a general recasting of US Navy aircraft designations in 1962, the DSN-3 became the QH-50C.) The flight decks were too light to handle the later manned helicopters developed for destroyer use; they are, however, said to have been useful for exercise or for showing movies! Ships which had been armed with *Hedgehogs* or with Weapon *Alfa* (formerly Weapon *Able*, renamed in 1956 when the International Civil Aeronautics Organisation's new phonetic alphabet was adopted) kept them; some got new AN/SQS-23 sonars, while others had their older AN/SQS-4 sonars updated and received new AN/SQA-10 Variable Depth Sonar (VDS) installations. Hull damping and sound insulation was added to facilitate sonar operation and to cut down ship noise. Habitability, under serious study for some years, was

improved. ECM equipment, new search radars, single-sideband radios, and improved CICs were installed.

The two FRAM prototypes were completed in 1960, and the destroyer FRAM program was complete by 1965. Three *Fletcher*s received FRAM II modernizations, as did 33 *Allen M. Sumner*s under the Fiscal 1960–62 programs. Fifteen *Fletcher*s and seventeen *Sumner*s were dropped from the program in December 1961, and 29 *Gearing*s scheduled to get FRAM II overhauls received the more extensive Mark I. A total of 79 *Gearing*s were given FRAM I conversions; ten former DDE and DDR, as well as the six pickets which kept their classification underwent FRAM II refits.[3] Some of these ships are still active; while *Agerholm* (DD-826), decommissioned in December 1978, was the last of this breed to serve with the fleet, two FRAMmed *Gearing*s serve with the Naval Reserve training force. Others, modernized and unmodernized, serve in foreign navies. No 'as-issued' *Allen M. Sumner* or *Gearing* survives as a memorial, though the FRAM destroyers *Joseph P. Kennedy* (DD-850) and *Laffey* (DD-724) have been placed on display at Fall River, Massachusetts, and Charleston, South Carolina, respectively.

Willis A. Lee, ordered in 1948 and completed in 1954, was one of four ships of the *Mitscher* class projected as large destroyers but redesignated destroyer leaders (DL); the latter designation was soon changed to frigate, retaining the DL type symbol. *Willis A. Lee*, originally DD-929 and redesignated DL-4, represents the culmination of the large-destroyer studies begun as early as 1942 and continued through the end of World War II. Her armament is more in accordance with postwar trends than with wartime thinking; she has two new 5-inch/54-caliber single mounts, two 3-inch/70-caliber twins (an unsuccessful high-performance AA gun), Weapon *Alfa*, one depth-charge track, and four fixed single 21-inch torpedo tubes mounted inside her superstructure. Gun fire control is of a postwar pattern and, besides search radars and aircraft-homing TACAN, she also has an SPS-8 height-finding radar.

17

'Large Destroyer' Studies

I think the world is sadly mistaken when it supposes that battles are won by this or that kind of gun or vessel. . . . The best gun and the best vessel should certainly be chosen, but the victory three times out of four depends upon those who fight them. . . .

Rear Admiral David G. Farragut to Secretary of the Navy Gideon Welles, 8 November 1864

In October 1939 the noted naval architect William Francis Gibbs held a discussion with the acting Secretary of the Navy and two principal officers of the then-merging Bureaus of Construction and Repair and of Engineering. Gibbs suggested that his firm — Gibbs and Cox, of New York City — had in mind the possibility of developing 'a powerful type of destroyer with heavy armament, high speed and optimum sea-keeping qualities and maneuverability in bad weather, provided such a development would be considered desirable by the Navy.' He was told the Navy would welcome such a design, and went to work on it.

Early in December, Gibbs appeared before the General Board to discuss fast-battleship design. Asked if he had conceived a suitable destroyer to operate with fast capital ships, Gibbs advanced his destroyer design. Reasoning that battleships were growing in size and in speed, he advocated a new type of fast, heavily-armed destroyer able to keep up with high-speed battleships in heavy seas and able to use its guns and torpedoes effectively in northern winter weather. Gibbs' concept embodied a full-load speed of 40 knots in favorable weather, with enough of a margin of power to avoid forcing the machinery, and a 9,000-mile radius at 12 knots. Extensive ballistic protection against .50-caliber strafing was included, with 'great emphasis on antiaircraft defense'. Machinery spaces were to be laid out as in the *Benson* and *Gleaves* classes, with staggered boiler and engine rooms. The boiler plant was novel; cruising steam was to come from conventional 850-degree, 450-psi boilers. At speeds above 25 knots, main-engine steam was to be provided by new

900-degree, 1,200-psi boilers proposed by Babcock and Wilcox. Gibbs pronounced this system practicable, and felt that it would be lighter in terms of delivered horsepower, with 'a standard of reliability materially greater than in existing destroyers'. The Bureau of Engineering questioned the flexibility of Gibbs' arrangement, and he redesigned it to permit operation at any speed on any combination of boilers. He argued that his design could steam at speeds of '40.0' knots at 3,318 full-load tons, with better flexibility and higher performance than could be obtained by the *Somers* class. His plant, he told the General Board, would 'insure a standard of ruggedness superior to anything that we have today.'[1]

The General Board expressed its 'appreciation for your clear and interesting exposition' and assured Gibbs that it would, 'in its deliberations and consideration of destroyers and of other types of combatant ships, bear in mind the points you so ably made.'[2] Here the matter rested. At this point the main thread of American destroyer development had not yet reached the required maturity level. The Navy Department had other things on its mind, and seems to have looked on the big destroyer as little more than interesting theory.

In a little over two years things had changed. The *Benson* and *Gleaves* classes had been followed by the big *Fletcher*s, and work was underway on what were to become the *Allen M. Sumner* and *Gearing* classes. After reviewing the characteristics of the *Fletcher* class in the light of wartime experience, the General Board proposed a set of characteristics for a 2,500-ton destroyer to the Secretary of the Navy on 24 April 1942, citing 'the

necessity of having some destroyers which under reasonable conditions can accompany battleships, cruisers, and carriers of the largest size and greatest speed projected for our Navy.' This was to be an enlarged *Gearing*, flushdecked and with the same battery of 5-inch guns, torpedo tubes, and depth charges. The close-in AA armament was puny, even for its time, considering the size of the ship: two 40-millimeter twins and eight 20-millimeter guns. Emphasis was placed on ruggedness of hull construction and inherent stability under all loadings. Extensive splinter and strafing protection was included, with the ability 'to maintain high speed in heavy weather and to accompany the fastest battleships, carriers and cruisers.'[3]

The Commander in Chief, United States Fleet (COMINCH) — Admiral Ernest J. King — concurred, remarking that design development was desirable although no actual construction was warranted until more immediate early-wartime construction needs had been met. The Secretary of the Navy approved the Board's recommendations, with Admiral King's reservation, in May 1942.[4] Commander Destroyers, Pacific Fleet, raised the question again in October 1943. He cited 'the generally accepted concept that a destroyer's paramount duty is, and will be, *offensive* with secondary duty as a screening vessel; that it is the Navy's primary surface torpedo carrier; that antiaircraft guns, as such, are defensive, the greatest importance of which is to fight the ship to the torpedo firing point, and secondarily to protect a convoy against attack; that the destroyer is the nearest approach to the 'all purpose' vessel of any combatant type.' On this basic premise, and taking Pacific destroyer experience into account, he recommended modification of the 2,500-ton concept to emphasize maneuverability, with a tighter turning circle than that of new carriers and battleships. Habitability should be improved, with ventilation systems designed to permit their use during extended periods at battle stations. The new 5-inch/54 twin mount — projected for the battleships of the *Montana* class, canceled in 1943 — should be used, with design stress on high rates of fire at all angles of elevation. At least three quad 40-millimeter mounts (one forward of the bridge) should be provided, with as many 20-millimeter guns as possible. Quick-reloading spare torpedoes were wanted, 'if considered practicable', as was simplicity — hence, reliability — in the engineering plant for distant service using inexperienced wartime personnel. ComDesPac proposed a CIC designed to 'provide a single evaluator with an intimate running survey of the tactical, navigational, and gunnery situation', capable of fighter direction and target designation. Fighter-direction (presumably, height-finding) radar, together with fire-control radar for 40-millimeter AA directors, was also desirable.[5]

COMINCH forwarded these comments to the Atlantic Fleet for their thoughts. Commander Destroyers, Atlantic Fleet, generally concurred with his opposite number from the Pacific. His antisubmarine experience in the North Atlantic showed through when he advocated a closed forward wheelhouse, with open bridge wings and DE-type open conning station abaft and above the wheelhouse. Problems with earlier-construction destroyers were reflected in his remark that 'CIC space should be planned 25% larger than is considered necessary at this time, with a view to future installations of new equipment and rearrangements as necessary.'[6] The Commander in Chief, Atlantic Fleet (CINCLANTFLT) questioned the need for reload torpedoes and called for a radius of at least 9,500 miles at 15 knots.[7]

At this point some discussion of the torpedo armament for large destroyers took place. The Bureau of Ships, comparing the effect of Japanese 24-inch torpedoes with the likelihood of encountering targets which would require outsized warheads to sink them, would go no farther than to recommend 'that every step should be taken to provide the maximum practicable warhead charge for general service use within the limitations imposed by the design of existing torpedoes and existing torpedo launching gear and carriers.'[8] The David Taylor Model Basin, the Navy's hull-design test center, felt that there existed 'a definite need, in the torpedo group, for a much larger and more powerful weapon than any now in use.' It concluded that 'there should be developed a torpedo, together with the ships and aircraft to carry and fire it, which will have the maximum practicable weight and power of charge, using the latest advances in materials and technology.'[9]

The Bureau of Ships now opined, on 22 April 1944, that the time had come to consider building a small number — 'perhaps 20' — ships along the lines set forth by the General Board in 1942. The Bureau advanced a sketch design for a 397-foot destroyer with essentially the same power plant and armament as *Gearing*, but with *Gearing*'s waist-mounted 40-millimeter twins moved forward for better ahead fire and with about another knot of speed. This, the Bureau thought, would be the principal military advantage of the new concept, along with improved ship-control and fire-control arrangements. BuShips asked authority to proceed with design development and to build some ships of the enlarged type if this could be done without disrupting the existing destroyer program.[10] In a second letter to the General Board four days later, BuShips said that its new scheme could better the predicted speed of the *Gearing* class by two and a half knots, with a slight increase in steaming radius at 20 knots.[11] The Vice Chief of Naval Operations (VCNO) recommended that, in view of the difficulties being experienced with the *Allen M. Sumner* class, design development of the 2,500-tonner be continued so that improvements to be made in the *Sumner*s and *Gearing*s might be included in the new design.[12] The proposed ship was an enlarged *Gearing* (2,560 tons standard, 3,270 tons full-load) with one fat stack faired into the bridge structure, and an identical armament. The big ship would have twice the bridge space of *Gearing*, with an additional 200 nautical miles endurance under service loading at 20 knots.

A meeting held in Washington on 19 July 1944 included representatives of the Office of the Chief of Naval Operations (OPNAV), BuShips, and the Navy Inspector General, who had been looking into complaints directed at the *Sumner*s and *Gearing*s. This gathering proposed a look at a large destroyer duplicating the *Gearing* class battery, but with a trial speed at maximum displacement of 40 knots, this to obtain a 'service speed' of 38 knots. Studies of this 'high-speed destroyer' were pursued together with those already being made on the 'large destroyer'. They showed that such a ship would run to at least 450 feet and about 4,000 tons and require at least 80,000 horsepower. Even this big ship would not nearly meet the specified radius requirement of 6,500 miles at 20 knots. BuShips' calculations showed that even a 500-foot, 100,000-horsepower ship would do no better than 39 knots and 5,400 miles. Though the Bureau felt that this scheme might serve as a basis for further development in the directions of speed and radius, it pointed out that this ship was much too big to be considered a destroyer. 'Although its size closely approaches some of the small cruiser classes, in our own and foreign navies, it is in no sense a cruiser because . . . its armament is very light for cruiser duties.' Even the 450-foot schemes were pronounced too large for destroyers. If the Department agreed with the Bureau on this and desired a smaller ship, then some reductions in speed and radius requirements would be inevitable. BuShips offered to study the smallest ship capable of handling an 80,000-horsepower plant, a 425-footer capable of 37 knots on trials and a 'moderate' 3,000-mile radius.[13]

VCNO, writing to COMINCH on 4 October 1944, agreed with BuShips that what had resulted from the 'high-speed destroyer' studies was a hybrid type with the size, but without the power, of a cruiser, unsuited for destroyer work. What was needed, he suggested, was a fresh look at the duties and characteristics of the destroyer type. In the Pacific, destroyers were being used for a variety of offensive and defensive tasks which might be better met by two or more distinct types. Added weapons and control equipment had 'materially' affected the speed, endurance, and stability of destroyers; a 'comprehensive study' of light seagoing warships in the 1,500–8,000-ton range was needed to evolve the 'most efficient combinations of military characteristics in type designs to meet future naval warfare demands.'[14]

While these earlier discussions were proceeding, Admiral Nimitz, the Commander in Chief, US Pacific Fleet (CINCPACFLT) had circularized copies of the BuShips 'large destroyer' proposal to his major striking fleet commanders — Third Fleet and Fifth Fleet — and to his cruiser and destroyer type commanders, ComCruPac and ComDesPac. Third Fleet (Admiral Halsey) felt that the increased effectiveness of aircraft made a battle speed of 30 knots a minimum for all major first-line warships such as carriers, battleships, and heavy cruisers. 'Light forces' (light cruisers and destroyers) should have a battle-speed differential of at least five knots to allow for maneuvering in formation. These battle speeds, Halsey went on, should be attainable under average wartime conditions of loading and time out of drydock. A 4,000-mile radius for destroyers 'would be of great value in planning for and executing long-range operations'. Fifth Fleet (Admiral Raymond Spruance) stressed radius, remarking that the 'almost steady reduction in cruising radii of successive classes of destroyers should be met by changes in design of new construction, so that the required figure of 6,500 miles can be met.' Speed, he said, should not be obtained by sacrificing range or firepower; top speeds of battleships and carriers should be taken into consideration in determining destroyer speeds. The commander of the Pacific destroyer force felt that, when the *Allen M. Sumner*s and *Gearing*s were completed, an adequate number of 'slow destroyers' would then be available for screening the battle line and the fast carriers. What was now needed, he went on, was 'a fast destroyer type which can be used offensively'. These ships would be used for fast strikes into enemy waters, and 'will also be valuable in expediting deployment for battle from a large approach disposition.' Increased displacement would be required for higher speed, but ComDesPac thought this was justified 'in the interest of increasing the offensive capabilities of the fleet'. His proposed 'offensive destroyer' would have the battery of the present *Gearing* class, with such additional torpedo armament as increased displacement might make possible, 'including reloads'. In a moderate sea, the new ship should be able to sustain 38 knots under full-load operating conditions. 'This speed requirement', he concluded, 'is considered necessary in order to insure their ability to operate anywhere else in the world. Since task forces habitually of 35 knots.'

Admiral Nimitz forwarded these thoughts to Admiral King, suggesting that design of new ships be predicated on Pacific requirements, on the assumption that this would insure their ability to operate anywhere else in the world. Since task forces habitually steamed at 18 knots in combat zones, ships' cruising radii should be specified at 20 knots, operating with fully-split plants. Nimitz thought ComDesPac's proposal for a striking-force destroyer 'a challenging one'. Realizing that such speed would require additional displacement unless radius was sacrificed to some extent, he pointed out that the concept was really aimed at a postwar destroyer since such a new ship would take quite a while to produce. 'There is time', he concluded, 'for research and improvements. We must raise our sights to what we obviously need. It is therefore recommended that a destroyer design be attempted that will insure a battle speed of 35–40 knots, with a radius of 4500–5000 miles at 20 knots.'[15]

The Bureau of Ships had continued work on the 425-foot fast destroyer proposed earlier, and on 21 October 1944 sent a sketch to Admiral King. Like its design of April 1944, this looked like an enlarged *Gearing* with 40-millimeter guns mounted forward; the added length permitted provision of five reloads for one of the two quintuple torpedo-tube mounts in quick-reload stowage. The new study provided a steaming radius greater than that of the 'short-hull' *Allen M. Sumner*, but less than that of the 'long-hull' *Gearing*. 'The primary advantage of the new design, therefore,' BuShips went on, 'is a material increase in speed while retaining a very good cruising radius at 20 knots.' The Bureau felt that this was a reasonable compromise concept, suitable as a basis for further discussion and development of characteristics for new destroyers. If the Department planned to put a new design into production on completion of the present program, then its characteristics would have to be established so that design development could proceed.[16]

Admiral King now passed the whole package to the General Board, asking it to produce revised characteristics for a new destroyer design 'such as will best meet the future needs of the Fleet'.[17]

The Bureau of Ships reported, on 4 November, that by rearranging hull spaces and including some additional fuel tankage, the 20-knot cruising radius of the new design could be increased from the originally-proposed 3,900 miles to about 4,500 miles, equal to that of the *Gearing*s, with a speed of about 36.9 knots.[18] The Bureau of Ordnance indicated that the weight and space provided in the 425-foot design would allow inclusion of a second director for independent control of the after 5-inch gun mount as well as an improved system of torpedo control. BuOrd recommended substitution of twin 5-inch/54 gun mounts for the planned 5-inch/38s; though the 5-inch/54 mount weighed 11 tons more than a 5-inch/38, preliminary studies showed it would require fourteen fewer men per mount to operate and service. Although weight calculations — still, as ever, the bugaboo of destroyer designers — were tight, Ordnance felt that 'every effort should be made to include all of the latest developments of armament and that, in addition to this, a fair margin of weight should be reserved to take care of future developments in ordnance and fire control. A weight margin of about 2% standard displacement tonnage is suggested.'[19] BuShips replied that installation of a 5-inch/54 battery would increase displacement by about 50 tons, require a beam increase of about six inches to maintain stability, and cost between one-half and three-quarters of a knot in speed. An increase in waterline length to regain that speed would again increase displacement. An acceptable configuration could, however, be developed if the heavier gun were selected.[20]

Useful input was provided from abroad when the French destroyer *Le Triomphant* came to the United States for overhaul during the winter of 1944–45. 'It has long been known', BuShips wrote to Admiral King, 'that certain European powers have built large destroyers with power plants developing considerably more power than any US destroyer. Reliable performance data on such ships, however, were not available' until the Bureau arranged to obtain speed and fuel-economy information from this *Le Fantasque* class heavy destroyer during her post-repair trials. *Le Triomphant* made 38.92 knots at 3,190 tons; extrapolation from trial data gave an estimated speed of 36.2 knots at the full-load displacement of about 3,680 tons. BuShips concluded that the proposed 425-foot design represented a marked improvement, with a fraction higher speed at a heavier displacement on a lower estimated horsepower figure, and over twice the radius. It devoted 6.4 percent of its full-load displacement to armament, as against *Le Triomphant*'s 3.6 percent. BuShips felt 'that the time is now opportune to develop a new destroyer design with the primary objective of attaining increased speed'. It did not contend that the 425-foot design represented more than 'the approximate degree of improvement in speed which could be obtained in a new design'. The Bureau contended that construction of new-type destroyers along this general line 'would be desirable not only from the standpoint of attaining high speed in a particular class of destroyers, but also from the standpoint of stimulating development in design of geared turbine machinery. Future progress in machinery design cannot be expected unless ships are actually built to incorporate improved machinery as technological developments become available.'[21]

On 10 May 1945 Secretary of the Navy James Forrestal issued an order to the General Board and the technical Bureaus. Among other things, it directed development of designs for four new destroyers which 'should have 24" torpedoes or better, substantially increased radius, and maximum available top speed.' This did not authorize any actual procurement or construction, but was intended 'to take the profits of the experience of this war and keep alive the arts of combatant design and construction. It is realized that paperwork alone will not produce combatant designs assuring superiority for the US nor keep alive the ability to build them, and I will strive to obtain the necessary authority to go ahead with construction of the new destroyers.' Forrestal emphasised that 'this is not a war program', and information concerning it was to be kept to those with a 'need to know'. Though not spelled out in this directive, each of the proposed four new destroyers could be drawn up to a different design, though all were to have the same tactical qualities.[22] In June 1945, a committee of the newly-constituted Ship Characteristics Board rejected the notion that destroyer functions could be best performed by two or more distinct types of ship. After considering the opinions of the Fleet and of the technical Bureaus, the committee recommended that further studies be made on the basis of the BuShips' 425-foot concept, which represented 'the best possible compromise in speed and endurance, at the same time keeping the design in the large destroyer class'. The Bureaus were asked to consider incorporating three twin 5-inch/54 mounts, looking into the possibility of placing two aft and one forward. 40-millimeter and 20-millimeter guns were not to be considered, 'since these guns will be obsolete before the ships are built'; the rapid-fire 3-inch/50 twin mount, then under development as an anti-*kamikaze* close-in weapon, was to be considered in their stead since design of a projected 3-inch/70 gun mount would not be completed 'until the latter half of 1946'. A tripod mast was to be installed to accommodate radar antennae, and fixed torpedo tubes were to be looked into as an alternative to trainable mounts. The Bureau of Ships was specifically asked to report on a concept in which only a portion of the allotted weight was actually used for weapons and equipment, 'using dead weights to provide for the difference to allow for future development.'[23]

The Ship Characteristics Board now circulated copies of the General Board's original April 1942 characteristics among its members, asking them to consider these along with its own committee's recommendations. The Ship Characteristics Board studied the destroyer question for some weeks before sending a tentative set of new characteristics to the General Board.[24]

The new design concept set forth two primary tasks (antiair and antisubmarine protection of fast task forces; torpedo attacks supported by gunfire) for destroyers, with shore bombardment and naval gunfire support of landing forces as their subsidiary tasks. The projected design should, as far as possible, provide interchangeability of weights to allow future changes in armament and equipment, and should allow 40 tons at superstructure-deck level for future installation of such things as 24-inch torpedoes or AA machine guns. The new destroyer would displace about 4,400 tons fully loaded, be 450 feet long with a beam of 46 feet, and be as thoroughly subdivided as possible. It would be, preferably, flushdecked and able to maintain speed in heavy weather and keep up with heavy combatant ships. Special attention was to be given to bow form and structural strength, and to dryness of the forward weather decks. Future armament was uncertain, given the then-existing pace of ordnance development. The characteristics presented called for three 5-inch/54 twins, two forward and one aft; four twin 3-inch/50 mounts, with 'latest design, free-swinging weapons' (at that time, this meant 20-millimeter twins) and two quintuple torpedo-tube mounts and 'the latest designed' antisubmarine weapons. Two 5-inch gun directors were included, with one director for each 3-inch mount. Speed was to be the 'highest ... compatible with other characteristics' (about 34 knots under battle conditions), with a radius of at least 4,250 miles at 20 knots.

A month later BuShips advised the General Board that it should produce a ship along the general lines proposed by the Ship Characteristics Board, with some detail differences, allowing weight for three twin 20-millimeter mounts and splinter protection for ship-control spaces.[25]

The General Board noted that it was still not convinced that the large destroyer, designed to screen fast task forces, was the only such ship that the Navy should include in future programs.[26] Rear Admiral Kalbfus, President of the Naval War College, felt that three distinct types could be developed on the same basic hull; antiair and antisubmarine escorts, and a 'fleet torpedo boat' for surface attack. All would have combinations of single 5-inch/54s with torpedo tubes and antisubmarine weapons. These could, he thought, be interchangeable to suit the needs of the moment; a fast tender, based on the Dock Landing Ship (LSD) concept, could be developed to make such modifications in the forward area.[27] Kalbfus was thinking of fixed or limited-train torpedo tubes; in the meanwhile the Bureau of Ordnance suggested development of a 10-tube mount, apparently using a 5-over-5 arrangement. The Bureau thought this would result in a saving of 3,000 pounds and about 35 feet of critical centerline deck space as compared with two of the conventional 5-tube mounts. In terms of interchangeability, BuOrd pointed out that the weight of one of these 10-tube mounts compared to that of a twin 5-inch/38 gun mount.[28]

On 21 September 1945 the General Board forwarded characteristics for 'a large destroyer whose primary function would be to accompany and screen a fast task force' to the Secretary of the Navy for approval, remarking that it called for a ship some 1,700 tons heavier at full load than the *Fletcher* class, which had embodied the latest advances in destroyer design at the time the United States had gone to war. This concept was, in essentials, the one submitted by the Ship Characteristics Board except for a provision that the two quintuple torpedo-tube mounts be quickly interchangeable with twin 3-inch/50 AA mounts.[29] Admiral King recommended approval of this plan as a basis for a new destroyer class, 'subject to continued effort to provide one or more subsequent classes embodying further improved characteristics as soon as it becomes possible to incorporate 24″ torpedoes or better ... , or substantial increases in speed or steaming radius, or improved adaptability to varied duties by more extensive interchangeability of gun and torpedo armament, and subject to pressing technological development of destroyer armament and equipment, on the basis that 3,200 tons will remain the upper limit of standard displacement for the destroyer type.'[30] Secretary of the Navy James Forrestal approved the modified characteristics on 28 November 1945. (Standard displacement was still being used, for purposes of comparison, years after the Washington and London Treaties had lapsed. The proposed 4,400-ton (full-load) destroyer had a 3,200-ton standard displacement.)

By this time the war was over and postwar retrenchment was well under way. As after previous wars, little money was forthcoming for anything beyond bare-bones operation and maintenance, and the tidying-up of unfinished wartime programs. On 13 December 1945 the Commander-in-Chief, Pacific Fleet, forwarded a lengthy report to CNO which dealt with, among other things, recommendations concerning future destroyer design. After the end of the Pacific war, Admiral Nimitz had appointed several boards to examine the naval lessons learned in that conflict and to make recommendations based on this war experience. One of these, chaired by Commodore Merrill Comstock, met at Pearl Harbor in mid-October to study ship and aircraft types.

Though new developments — the atomic bomb and missiles had been mentioned elsewhere in the Board's report — might 'radically modify methods of conducting war' in the future, there was still a foreseeable need for destroyers. A balanced fleet was still necessary to cope with air, surface, and subsurface attacks. Cruisers and destroyers had to be designed to perform a variety of tasks, including surface combat; screening of carrier or amphibious task forces and convoys; antishipping operations; shore bombardment and gunfire support for amphibious landings; protection of advanced bases; and reconnaissance and patrolling. So varied a menu would demand continuation of the balanced armaments characteristic of most destroyers to the end of the war; the Board felt that, though some officers wanted torpedoes replaced by AA guns, this was going too far and the sacrifice of offensive torpedo armament would be 'premature and unwise'.

Future destroyer designs, the Board continued, should be built with mass production and inexperienced wartime crews in mind. Adequate living space for full complements should be built in, as should fuel tankage sufficient to permit steaming the desired radius at war loading and task-force speeds. Power plants should be able to operate reliably 'over extended periods with relatively inexperienced crews'.

The Board liked such features as interchangeability of gun mounts and torpedo tubes, and felt that ships should be built with a weight reserve for equipment not yet produced. Nimitz thought this latter idea open to question. If this kind of reservation were to be included in a new ship, he thought it 'probable that under the pressure of the proponents of various improvements the reserve would vanish by the time she joined the fleet, at which time the inevitable question of sacrificing some quality for further improvements will immediately arise.' He thought that only in the early design stages might such weight reserves be desirable, to prevent the kind of overloading that had plagued some of the designs of the 1930s. 'It would be false economy', he continued, 'to omit important military [characteristics] from a new ship on the grounds that the weight might be required for unspecified future developments.' (A weight reserve is a feature incorporated in the current *Spruance* (DD-963) class. However, Nimitz' attitude was not so unreasonable; conflicting requirements for speed, endurance, and firepower combined with reasonable size and cost—allowing quantity production— meant ships proportionately more crowded than the cruiser-like *Spruance*s. Reservations, in the context of 1945, could have meant less-than-adequate destroyers.)

The open bridge featured in the *Allen M. Sumner* and *Gearing* classes, as well as in late-production *Fletcher* and *Gleaves* class ships, was pronounced 'desirable' for future construction; all-round and overhead vision was specified. Increased emphasis on damage control, with particular stress on compartmentation, was needed, as well as 'more automatic weapons, effective at increased ranges'.

All of the Board's *desiderata* would require weight increases. This would have to be compensated for by eliminating all characteristics 'that do not contribute to the offensive and defensive power of the ships.' The Board went on to specify that 'reasonable habitability is an offensive characteristic. Ships are only as good as the men who fight them.'

A sustained research program was called for to design and test equipment and make modifications as needed. Special ships should be designated for such work, a task for which the new Operational Development Force had only recently been created. New designs, the Board thought, should be considered experimental and 'a certain percentage of failures must be expected. Seemingly crackpot ideas should be investigated. The aim must be not to gradually improve what we now have but to search for new and better equipment based on new concepts.' Sonar and AA guns were singled out as examples of areas where greatly improved performance was needed. New high-speed submarines, of the streamlined German Walther type (Types XXI and XXIII) were thought to demand underwater detection equipments with effective ranges of ten, or even twenty miles. 'Guns of double or quadruple present velocities and not wholly dependent on initial impulse [apparently a combination of the hypervelocity gun and the rocket-assisted projectile] may be the antiaircraft batteries of the future.'

The Board concluded by presenting its characteristics for a future destroyer. This was to be a large flushdecker with the best possible compartmentation and 'excellent maneuverability', capable of 38 knots top speed and 4,500 miles at 20 knots, both at full war displacement. A gas-turbine plant was suggested as having promise. Four twin 5-inch dual-purpose gun mounts, with 24 40 mm barrels in a suitable combination of quads and twins, would be backed by 20 mm guns or, perhaps, by a more powerful short-range gun if developed. One quintuple tube would fire an improved postwar torpedo. Mark 63 Gun Fire Control Systems would control the 40 mm battery, while the Mark 37 5-inch control system would have an improved computer to take care of higher-performance targets. The bridge would be late-war type, with the CIC below the main deck near the 5-inch plotting room. Living spaces were to be adequate for the full war

complement. A radar-picket version, a type pronounced desirable by the Board with Okinawa fresh in their minds, would have a tripod mainmast for height-finding radar. Admiral Nimitz thought that the 8-gun battery and increased steaming radius desirable, but felt that 'we must give consideration as to whether this can be obtained without increasing the displacement beyond an amount suitable for a destroyer.'[31]

Two years later, the Ship Characteristics Board was still discussing the notion of a large destroyer. By 1947 this scheme had grown to 3,650 standard tons, with one single 5-inch/54-caliber gun and one twin 3-inch/70-caliber mount for what this Board considered the most acceptable combination for surface action, antiaircraft firing, or shore bombardment. Four 20 mm twins were included, 'if for nothing more than harassing effect . . . to cover the remote possibility of complete power failure.' Surface torpedoes were omitted, due to the expected lack of suitable targets; four fixed tubes were included for antisubmarine torpedoes, though anti-surface ship torpedoes could be carried if the situation so dictated. Unlike the 1945 large-destroyer schemes, this one was no longer simply an enlargement of the ships which had fought World War II. It was, in fact, an early step along the way to the missile destroyers of our own time.[32] It eventually resulted in the four ships of the *Mitscher* (DL-2) class, funded in Fiscal 1948 and completed in 1953-54. They were variously classified, first as Destroyers (1948), Destroyer Leaders (1951), and Frigates (1955). Admiral Forrest Sherman, CNO until his untimely death in 1951, is reported to have insisted on their reclassification on the grounds that they were simply too big to be destroyers; we have seen earlier instances of this kind of resistance to any growth of the destroyer beyond a certain level. Although their careers were less than spectacular,[33] experience with them did provide useful lessons which were incorporated into the designs of later classes of surface warships.

Conclusion

After a battle is over, people talk a lot about how the decisions were methodically reached, but actually there's always a hell of a lot of groping around.

Rear Admiral Frank Jack Fletcher, USN

As remarked in the preface to this work, American destroyer construction through the end of World War II can reasonably be seen as forming four 'generations' of development. A progression can be seen from the original '1898 boats' through the *Wickes* and *Clemson* class flushdeckers. The time lag between the *Clemson* and *Farragut* class meant that the new ships would begin a new continuum, a process of renewed development that can be traced from *Farragut* through the *Allen M. Sumner* and *Gearing* classes and into the late-war large-destroyer studies. Through both periods of destroyer construction a clear line of descent can be traced.

If anything has been consistent through the destroyer's brief history (the type, in any true sense, is, after all, less than a century old) it has been change. The ship was originally conceived as a 'torpedo-boat destroyer', the protector of the battle line against torpedo attack by fast surface ships. In short order this function, though retained, had yielded pride of place to the offensive mission of massed torpedo attack. The protector had assumed the role of its quarry. The destroyer concept attempted to strike a usable balance between seaworthiness, speed, and firepower within a size that would make it feasible to produce them in sufficient numbers to accomplish the tasks desired. As we have seen, this combination was still sought for as late as World War II. Seaworthiness enabled a destroyer to keep the seas with the battle fleet and, later, with the fast carrier striking force. Speed gave destroyers the tactical margin they needed to attack or defend a battle line; this again proved valuable when carrier-force screening became a major destroyer mission. Torpedoes were long considered the destroyer's principal strength, even its reason for being; gun armament was also stressed in American destroyers, originally for its defensive value against an enemy's light forces and later because of the need to compensate for the American fleet's lack of cruisers to clear the way for attacking destroyer squadrons with gunfire. When World War II became a true three-dimensional struggle the earlier stress on gun firepower served a new purpose.

When destroyers were first built, their task involved surface action only. World War I brought a new problem, the submarine. The fight against the undersea boat was given to the destroyer and was, in fact, the principal task of the wartime American navy. New devices were developed and installed — hydrophones and depth charges — but these did not replace guns or torpedoes. In 1917, as during the Spanish-American War of 1898, 'destroyer-type' ships were lacking, and a combination of commandeered private craft and mass-produced specialized vessels had to be improvised in short order to fill the gap. Here, incidentally, began a process that was to recur again. New tasks and new equipment were added to the existing ships, a situation that would create its share of design problems in future years; and new ship types were created to perform a specialized function that the destroyer could not completely fulfill because of unsuitability or numbers.

The 'gold-plater' designs of the 1930s were developed with the same basic functions in mind — surface offense and defense, plus antisubmarine warfare, with some air-defense capability, but with new weaponry and control systems, such as dual-purpose gun directors and active sonar, that improved their capabilities. The later addition of radar, with its attendant CIC, and automatic shell-firing antiaircraft guns, represented a further improvement. The process of development can be seen through the wartime destroyer studies and construction programs. Once freed of the early displacement limitations of the post-World War I naval limitation treaties, designers increased the size of new classes by what they judged to be an amount sufficient to accommodate desired improvements, but did not choose to go all-out in pursuit of individual-ship perfection so that ships could be produced in sufficient numbers.

By 1941 American destroyers were once again involved in an antisubmarine war in the North Atlantic. This brought increases in underwater weapons; at the same time, new requirements for individual and fleet air-defense introduced radar and light AA guns. This was less of a problem in bigger new designs than in the treaty-limited earlier ships, where stability margins were thin or nonexistent and compensation had to be thought out and made. The discovery that wartime formation speeds were considerably higher than the estimated 'service speeds' on which endurance had been calculated complicated matters further, and later-war design had to make allowance for this.

Many seem to think of the wartime destroyer as a convoy escort and little more. As even a cursory look at destroyer operations will make clear, this is very much a misconception. Destroyers screened surface and carrier striking forces against submarine and air attack; they carried out shore-bombardment and gunfire-support missions; they fought surface actions, by themselves or associated with heavy warships; and, toward the latter part of the war, they were given radar-guard and fighter-direction tasks. As during World War I, this represented the addition of new functions with little or no diminution of existing ones. It was not until later in the war that the time-honored torpedo capability was forced to give way to the overriding demands of antiair warfare, and tubes were sacrificed to make room for AA guns; this process, which began with the reduction of the torpedo batteries in the *Benson* and *Gleaves* classes from ten tubes to five (10-tube ships of these classes were a rarity by the end of 1944), was carried to its logical conclusion in 1945 when some of the earlier generation of destroyers had their torpedo armament eliminated in favor of amplified close-in AA guns and directors. This final development was not, as might be thought, a sudden change but was nothing more than the final step in an evolution which had begun well before Pearl Harbor. It reflected a combat environment in which the air attacker was everything. The Japanese submarine was a minor danger in the Pacific war, though individual submarines did score notable successes; also, by 1945, the Japanese surface fleet had virtually disappeared and the likelihood of a torpedo action was, to say the least, remote. Under these circumstances it was perfectly logical to remove torpedoes and diminish depth-charge batteries (as was done with some ships) to allow installation of the heaviest AA batteries that buoyancy and stability would permit. Post-emergency plans, it may be noted, called for removal of anti-*kamikaze* additions and restoration of full torpedo capabilities although postwar changes and budgets did away with that idea.

The process of destroyer substitution, carried out during World War I with the construction of submarine chasers and the conversion of yachts and fishing craft for antisubmarine patrol, was repeated during the

132

second global war. As in 1917, there were simply not enough destroyers to go around. A numerous new breed of antisubmarine craft, in many shapes and sizes, was developed for that one purpose. The British Admiralty had worked up a concept for a specialized sea-going antisubmarine escort ship, called the frigate. Orders for these ships were placed in American yards, and when antisubmarine warfare became a major Atlantic responsibility for the United States Navy, production of these ships was diverted, in part, to domestic needs. The American fleet dubbed these destroyer escorts (DE).

The DE was specially designed to fulfil a purpose which the destroyer, conceived for other tasks, was less able to handle. The typical fleet destroyer's design was focused on speed, an essential requirement for surface action or carrier-force screening. To achieve this, a high length-to-beam ratio was made a design characteristic of early and modern destroyers. This, however, denied the destroyer the maneuverability that antisubmarine warfare demanded. 'The turning characteristics of destroyers', a 1943 research report concluded, 'have never been satisfactory. These long, narrow vessels, whose missions demand fast action and agility in maneuvering, turn with radii as large as the heavy units which they screen, and with radii larger than the submarines which they hunt. . . . the tactical diameter of a typical destroyer . . . is out of proportion to its length compared to other combatant vessels.'[1] With a waterline length of 341 feet *Gleaves* (DD-423) had a turning circle of 780 yards at 25 knots with 25 degrees rudder. With the same rudder angle at the same speed, the 600-foot light cruiser *Philadelphia* could turn in 600 yards; the 770-foot aircraft carrier *Yorktown* (CV-5) could turn in an 822-yard circle.[2]

The destroyer escort was well fitted to take over the antisubmarine function. The DE lacked the high speed and surface hitting power of the destroyer but, for this one function, they were not necessary. The DE did have a slightly superior underwater battery (two depth-charge tracks and up to eight K-guns, with sonar and, eventually, an ahead-throwing *Hedgehog* projector). Most importantly, the DE had a turn of speed adequate for antisubmarine work (top sustained speeds for DE classes varied from 18 plus to over 24 knots) combined with a narrower turning circle which enabled it to pursue a dodging submarine in better fashion than a contemporary destroyer. At 25 knots, a *Fletcher* class destroyer could turn 180 degrees in one minute 53.5 seconds with a tactical diameter of 880 yards when the rudder was put over 35 degrees to the right. At 24 knots,

with the same rudder angle, a *Buckley* class DE turned in 410 yards and 70 seconds.[3] Production of relatively-inexpensive escort ships for the specialized antisubmarine function left the fleet destroyer free to operate with the various striking forces, where its speed and offensive gun and torpedo power were put to more effective use and its relative lack of maneuverability was no hindrance. The DE lost its usefulness to a considerable extent after World War II, when a new generation of fast submarines appeared which could outrun these war-built surface ships.

The advent of the Cold War was to bring about a revival of the 'Atlantic-Fleet' philosophy, in which the undersea weapon was a real menace; postwar destroyer armaments reflected this. Postwar destroyers were armed with *Hedgehog* and Weapon *Able* in an effort to produce longer-legged surface ASW ships, and the DE was relegated to such tasks as training and radar-picket work. 'Standoff' weapons—homing torpedoes, but particularly antisubmarine shipboard helicopters and ASROC—made speed less critical, and a new generation of (relatively) smaller destroyer-type ships has been built under the designations Escort Ship (DE) and Guided-Missile Escort Ship (DEG), reclassified in 1975 as Frigate (FF) and Guided-Missile Frigate (FFG), respectively.

A recent study[4] poses four major capabilities as being essential to the performance of a warship: engagement range, the range at which the ship can first bring the enemy under fire; firepower/saturation threshold, the level of fire a ship can maintain, and the number of targets it can simultaneously engage; endurance, the ship's capacity to operate in heavy seas and to steam and shoot without replenishing; and resilience/survivability, the active and passive factors such as protection, compartmentation, redundancy, and damage-control capacity that enable a ship to survive in combat and return to action after damage. Other factors are also noted as being important to specific types; speed, for instance, was essential to the destroyer though less so to the wartime destroyer escort, which gave greater emphasis to maneuverability.

In any of these four major areas the American wartime destroyer could be counted as at least the equivalent of its foreign contemporaries. The 5-inch/38 gun was effective and reliable, and it can be argued that the Mark 37 director, with its associated equipment including radar, was as good as, or better than, anything else of its kind. The gun was capable of a high rate of fire and though divided fire against suicide planes was less effective than concentrated shooting,

foreign destroyers' AA capabilities were no better and, in fact, were in many instances inferior. Torpedo armament was unsatisfactory at first, but improvements in the 21-inch Mark 15 destroyer torpedo increased its power and corrected the accuracy problems that had plagued it during the earlier months of the war. The Mark 28 torpedo director, standard in all ships beginning with the *Farragut* class, was effective and remained in use for years after the war. Endurance was always a problem, but so were the unusual distances that destroyers had to cover in the Pacific theater. The realities of wartime task-force steaming—as opposed to theoretical pre-war calculations — dictated an emphasis on fuel capacity and economy in design and operation alike, although wartime 'split-plant' steaming, required for resistance to damage, consumed more fuel than 'economical' cruising. Heavy weather continued to give destroyers problems, especially when attempting to operate at higher speeds with bigger ships. Wartime 'large-destroyer' studies envisioned a larger ship with better seakeeping ability, but designers and forces afloat tended to reject such an increase in size. While it might be tactically desirable and technically feasible to build a bigger destroyer with the speed, range, and seakeeping ability to make it the ideal task-force ship, how many could be built and manned with the money, resources, and men available? Demands for destroyers were many and varied and, while quality was essential, so also was numerical sufficiency. Adequate numbers of adequate ships seemed a more logical wartime choice than insufficient numbers of superdestroyers, and the ultimate criterion — results — seems to have proven this a good choice. In terms of ability to survive, wartime American destroyers seem to have had as much capacity to stay afloat and resist damage as any ships of their type.

The tools of war, given to the fleet by designers and builders, are always no better than the people who bring them to life. Technical deficiencies in the destroyer navy were often, at least in part, compensated for by the skill and ingenuity of its sailors. Mechanical improvements were only brought to full effectiveness by training, organization, and determination. When Rear Admiral J. J. Clark sent the signal, 'Well done, destroyers. You always deliver the goods' to his screening ships after a successful action off the Marianas in 1944, he wrote what might equally well be considered a verdict on the destroyer force in general, from the designers to the antiaircraft screen. As is usually the case, it was more a judgment on men than on machines.

Appendix A

THE RECURRING PROBLEM OF STABILITY

The first requirement for a warship is that it should float the right way up.

British Admiralty, Naval War Manual (1948)

Of the earlier classes of 1930s destroyers not even the *Porter*s, with their lofty tophamper and heavy twin gun mounts, seem to have had any great difficulty with stability as built. On 22 December 1936 the Bureau of Construction and Repair asked the Board of Inspection and Survey to observe the behavior of new destroyers during trials, and conducted special turning trials of representative ships to obtain further information. From the results of these studies and from the service experience of the *Farragut* class, 'the Bureau [saw] no reason for apprehension about the performance of the subject ships in this regard.'[1]

The first ship of the *Sims* class to be completed was *Anderson* (DD-411), commissioned in May 1939. Her trials and inclining experiments took place during April; these indicated that the ship was about 162 tons overweight, with a metacentric height (GM) about a foot lower than anticipated. On her trials, *Anderson*, at full speed in the trough of a sea with fuel tanks low and a stiff wind, did not respond quickly when her helm was put hard over.[2]

Construction and Repair could not, at first, account for the excess weight. Three Bureaus were involved in the design and construction of ships: Construction and Repair (hull), Engineering (machinery), and Ordnance (weaponry). All three, but especially the first two, had exceeded their original weight estimates. C&R blamed the end result on contractor laxity and on 'a more liberal attitude toward weight restrictions on the part of all concerned since the lifting of the limitations imposed by the London Treaty.' The center of gravity (CG) of *Anderson*'s engineering plant had turned out to be more than a foot higher than originally planned, raising the ship's center of gravity about 0.6 foot and resulting in much of the loss of GM. Overweight of hull and fittings was thought to account for most of the rest.

The Bureau did not question the seaworthiness of the ship in her loaded condition, 'but the stability cannot be considered satisfactory when the vessel approaches an assumed extreme light condition which might occur in certain unusual circumstances of peace time operation or following a prolonged engagement.' Fuel and reserve feed water, it warned, should not be allowed to fall below 300 tons before replenishing unless empty tanks were ballasted with sea water; this would permit a ship to use about 170 tons of her full-load tank capacity before ballasting became necessary. The Chief of Naval Operations was advised to approve an instruction to this effect, to be issued to all ships of the *Sims* class.[3]

The Secretary of the Navy now directed the three material Bureaus to recommend corrections. They approached the problem from the standpoint of weight removal, with as little change in military characteristics as possible. On 5 August 1939 they proposed their solution. To avoid a need to remove any part of the ships' armament, they suggested such other alterations as lowering the after superstructure; removing ballistic protection from the gun director and wheelhouse; and lowering, if possible, the Mark 37 director. A minimum liquid ballasting (fuel, diesel oil, reserve feed water, and potable water) of 250 tons was advised. On the basis of assumptions as to service speeds and fuel consumption, the Bureaus concluded that a radius of 3,500 to 4,000 miles could be had under normal conditions without seawater ballasting. Maintenance of 250 tons of liquid would result in a displacement of 1,933 tons with a GM of 2.36 feet, a range of stability of 61.25 degrees, and maximum righting arm attained at 33 degrees list.[4]

On 5 August 1939 BuCon advised the Secretary of the Navy that a *Sims* class destroyer would be able to operate normally up to 3,500 miles, based on *Anderson*'s trial results at 12 knots and increased by hypothetical allowance for service loading and fouling. The Bureau of Engineering disagreed with BuCon's assumption of service speed, pointing out that an examination of actual operating records showed the average operating speed of *Mahan* class destroyers to be 13.2 knots. At the *Mahan* class' rate of fuel consumption, which should be no different from that of the *Sims* class, no more than about 2,000 miles of steaming would be possible without seawater ballasting. The Bureau thought that this point deserved 'very serious consideration' when coming to a decision as to what needed to be done to remedy the stability condition of the *Sims* class.[5] CNO remarked that Engineering's interjection 'really throws the whole situation back into the open', all the more so since the stability of the new *Benson* class, a development of the *Sims* design, would also be involved. He recommended an immediate investigation by the General Board, leading to recommended changes in characteristics 'to make these vessels satisfactory from an operating standpoint. The question of time is urgent.'[6]

The Fleet Maintenance Division pointed out that from 'an operating standpoint, no measures to correct stability are satisfactory which do not insure to the Commander in Chief and the Commanding Officers that each destroyer unit can and will be able to carry out its mission in war.' To avoid the peril of instability and the drawbacks of salt water in fuel tanks, Fleet Maintenance recommended that Mount 53 and its ammunition be removed and that the two wing torpedo tubes be replaced by one centerline tube. Numerous structural revisions to eliminate or lower weights were also suggested. Instructions had, in fact, already been issued to remove wing tubes and Mount 53 on a temporary basis so that ships could proceed with trials and training until a final decision might be made.[7]

BuCon was also studying the same rearrangement of guns and tubes in an effort to minimize the need for seawater ballasting with its attendant danger of fuel contamination. It also considered adding some fixed ballast in the hope of arriving at the best possible combination of weight reduction or rearrangement and fixed ballast to reduce the need for water ballast to the bare minimum under normal (non-damaged) service conditions.[8] Calculations showed that if the original recommendations for the lowering or removal of hull weights were followed, plus the removal of Mount 53 and reduction of the torpedo battery, minimum liquid loading could be reduced to 150 tons with a higher GM (2.49 feet) and the same range of stability.[9]

The Bureau of Ordnance calculated the effect of several armament configurations on the center of gravity. With the original battery, as designed (five guns, twelve tubes, and a $\frac{1}{2}$-inch gun director shield), this was 14.3 feet (full load), 16.72 feet (light). If the director shield was reduced to light weather plating, this would bring the CG down .05 inch at full load. If, on the other hand, one gun and one quadruple tube were removed as Fleet Maintenance had suggested, the CG could be lowered to 14.15 feet at full load without giving up ballistic protection for the 5-inch gun director.[10] This rearrangement, with the addition of some lead ballast, would improve stability without the need for an expensive and time-consuming reconstruction. The General Board agreed on the need to reduce the torpedo battery and retain splinter protection for the gun director, but recommended that all five guns be retained. The Board felt that rearrangement of fuel tanks and the lowering of all possible movable weights, plus addition of about 60 tons of permanent ballast, would be acceptable. After consultation with the Bureau of Construction and Repair, the Board reconsidered its preference for director armor, recommending that it be deleted for the sake of stability. The Secretary of the Navy approved this final suggestion, and the *Sims* class was completed (or, with respect to the earlier ships, modified) to a 5-gun, 8-tube configuration without ballistic protection for director or wheelhouse.

To bring the Bethlehem *Benson* design up to existing *Sims* class standards about 30 tons of ballast would have to be added. Some lightening of such details as spare-parts stowages would also 'improve stability somewhat'. Calculations for the Gibbs and Cox-designed *Gleaves* class were not yet complete, but there was reason to believe that their weight and stability situation would be no better than that of the *Sims* class, and possibly worse.[11] The General Board concluded that a *Sims*-type modification might be sufficient for the *Bensons*, but that this would not be enough to insure the stability of the *Gleaves* class; additional ballasting and the removal of one 5-inch gun might also be necessary.[12] Construction and Repair advised the General Board that modification of the *Benson* design along the lines approved for *Sims* would give the vessels a metacentric height of 2.43 feet with full ready-service ammunition stowed topside. A 50 percent reduction of ready-service ammunition would bring GM up to 2.48 feet, while elimination of one gun would raise it to 2.68 feet. The Bureau felt that a light-displacement GM of about 2.4 feet would be satisfactory; thus, any of these proposed rearrangements would be adequate.[13]

The Chief of Naval Operations had suggested that, 'during the process of construction, the Material Bureaus bear in mind the desirability of further improvement of the stability conditions of this class of ship and make recommendations ... whenever ... changes would be conducive to this end.'[14] The General Board went on to remark that it understood 'that the transverse stability of vessels subsequent to DD's 409–420 [i.e., the *Benson* and *Gleaves* classes] is probably inadequate and therefore suggests the earliest practicable examination of that question.'[15] On 15 September 1939, the Bureaus of Construction and Repair and of Engineering proposed changes for the *Benson* and *Gleaves* classes along the lines of those already approved for the *Sims* class.[16] The Secretary passed this to the General Board, asking for 'prompt action ... in order that the Bureaus may ... stop further work ... on items that are to be omitted from these vessels'.[17] Weight and stability data for DD-421–444 provided to the Board by Construction and Repair had to be predicted since none of these ships was near completion — DD-409–420 were completed in 1939–40, while DD-421–444 went into commission during 1940–41. The Bureau's calculations showed a serious degradation in stability for the *Benson*/*Gleaves* class ships of the 1938–40 programs; they were, in fact, in more dangerous condition than the ships of the *Sims* class.

Rear Admiral Leary, the head of the Fleet Training Division, explained to the General Board that part of the stability problem came from the superfiring arrangement of the two forward 5-inch guns, which necessitated siting the pilot house above the superfiring gun and raising the gun director, in turn, above the bridge. He suggested that substitution of a twin mount forward and another aft for four single gun mounts could mean a general lowering of weights. The centers of gravity of newer and more powerful engineering plants had also risen, and the Bureau of Engineering's representative told the Board

Condition II (Light Condition)

Class	Displacement	GM	Range of Stability	Maximum Righting Arm
Sims	1,638.8 tons	2.29 ft	60 deg.	0.98 ft at 32 deg.
Benson	1,639 tons	1.95 ft	49.5 deg.	0.6 ft at 30 deg.

The four ships of the *Gridley* class did not undergo the degree of modernization given to their contemporaries; stability problems did not allow them to handle 40 mm guns. In this mid-war view *McCall* (DD-440) has two 20 mm guns forward, two more amidships, and another two on her after-deckhouse.

that a significant lowering of machinery weights could only be brought about by a complete redesign of boilers and turbines. While new configurations were being studied, none of them were at a point where they could be recommended for actual use.[18] It might be remarked, here, that the fall of 1939 might not have been thought of as an ideal time for anything more than prototype experimentation. The Board recommended that, since stability data for the *Gleaves* design would not be available for some time, *Sims* type lightening be approved for interim action until more detailed conclusions could be drawn; the Secretary of the Navy approved this on 18 October 1939.

Commander Destroyers, Battle Force, expressed his concern over the need for alterations in the *Sims* class. 'The fact that so many changes are required to insure adequate stability is serious, and indicates that even after these changes are made DDs 409–420 . . . will go into service with no reserve of stability.' He was more worried about the *Benson*s and *Gleaves*: 'In the case of these . . . ships the situation is so serious as to require sacrifices in military characteristics or radical changes in current conception of the essentials in ship's equipment both as to quantity and details.' He was 'strongly opposed' to deletion of a 5-inch gun, and suggested the use of twin gun mounts instead, as well as reduction or lowering of other weights. Redesign, he thought, would be preferable to a loss of military characteristics.[19]

On 28 February 1940 Construction and Repair was able to advise the General Board that an extensive calculation of weights for the *Gleaves* class had indicated that they would be 'no worse but possibly slightly better' than the *Sims* class without the addition of fixed ballast. The Bureau thought that the maintenance of some liquid ballast, plus a 'moderate amount' of fixed ballast — to be determined after inclining experiments — would provide the needed reserve of stability.[20] The Board agreed with this, and on 19 March 1940 the Secretary approved the 5-gun, 10-tube configuration with ballasting for the *Gleaves* class.[21]

Reports of the trials and inclining experiments were available by the middle of 1940. The Board of Inspection and Survey 'was particularly impressed with the high deck structure and top weights forward' in *Gleaves*, and questioned her stability 'under adverse sea and loading conditions'. It felt that topweight forward should be reduced as much as practicable, and liked the idea of substituting a twin 5-inch gun mount for the two single forecastle guns, with a matching reduction in the height of bridges and gun director.[22]

This kind of redesign of a large class of ships does not seem to have had any appeal at a time when things were rapidly collapsing in Europe and tension was increasing in the Far East; improvements were limited to ballasting and to modifications to the existing design. As late as 5 November 1945 the Bureau of Ships was issuing modified liquid ballasting instructions to the operating forces to improve stability 'after long periods of operation without fueling.'[23]

Other classes also encountered stability problems. Inclining experiment data for *Sampson* (DD-394) indicated that reserve stability in the *Somers* class 'under conditions of extensive damage or during high speed maneuvering in the light service condition of loading cannot be considered satisfactory.' Twenty tons of lead ballast were placed in their bilges; specified fuel tanks were to be kept 95 percent full at all times when at sea; if fuel was taken from any of them, they were to be filled with seawater as soon as they became empty.[24]

The *Benham* class now came in for attention. A BuShips study of the Gibbs & Cox-designed DD-397–399 and -402–408 found that flooding of machinery spaces would have a serious effect on stability, but the reserve available would be enough to get a damaged ship home 'in all but the most unfavorable sea conditions.' (Design details for the last two — DD-400 and DD-401 — of the four *Gridleys* were drawn up by Bethlehem; attention would be drawn to their stability problems later on.)

Any additional flooding of wing tanks on one side would cause the ship to list 'and suffer thereby a further reduction in stability far out of proportion to the quantity of water admitted. Any reasonable measures which can be taken to avoid the possibility of such unsymmetrical flooding are, therefore, extremely desirable.' The Bureau concluded that a 'moderate' amount of liquid ballasting would take care of the damage control problem by preventing asymmetrical flooding and give the ships adequate stability during high-speed maneuvering in heavy seas or under light-load conditions. CNO directed that four fuel tanks, holding 105 tons, be kept filled to the 95 percent level — to allow for the expansion of oil at high temperatures — and refilled with seawater if the oil in them had to be used.[25] As topweights were cut down in destroyers during 1941 to make room for new electronics and AA guns, the commander of a destroyer squadron made up of *Benham* class ships asked CNO to review his stability instructions for the class. BuShips advised against any relaxation of precautions, even though recent modifications had resulted in

some increase in stability, and emphasized the value of liquid loading of wing tanks in reducing list after hull damage in the way of machinery spaces. CNO agreed with this, and ordered that its liquid ballasting instructions remain in force.[26]

The four Bethlehem-designed destroyers of the *Gridley* class — *Gridley* (DD-380), *Craven* (DD-382), *McCall* (DD-400), and *Maury* (DD-401) ran into problems of their own. After Pearl Harbor, as the problem of antiair-defense was being brought home in the most pointed terms, close-range AA batteries of naval ships began to grow. These ships had little margin of stability available to allow for increases in topside weight. Like the ships of the *Bagley* and *Benham* classes, they carried two quadruple torpedo tubes to each side in wing positions. Removal of two banks of tubes would help, but this was not done since it would have left these ships with a torpedo broadside of only four tubes to either beam. With this weight compensation not considered acceptable, none of these ships could receive 40 mm AA guns; as a compromise, eight 20 mm Oerlikons were installed instead. This arrangement, it was thought, would give the ships 'barely acceptable stability characteristics' based on an April 1942, inclining experiment carried out on *Craven*.

In a routine check of stability conditions, Mare Island Navy Yard carried out another inclining experiment with *Craven* in November 1943. This test demonstrated 'a material and unexpected reduction in stability'; BuShips asked Mare Island if this test could be considered reliable, and the shipyard replied that it had been carried out under good conditions and was believed more reliable than the 1942 test on which all stability calculations for these four ships had been based. BuShips concluded that all four ships were suffering from defective stability; remedial action was necessary, and the Bureau asked CNO to order two quad torpedo tubes removed 'at the first opportunity'. While the Bureau felt that Mare Island's figures were correct, it would authorize the inclining of one of the ships as the opportunity presented itself for positive verification. If one of them could be made available at a Navy Yard 'in the immediate future' for inclining, removal of tubes could be deferred until the results were in.[27] The Bureau of Ordnance recommended that the stability of these four destroyers be 'fully investigated' before any battery changes be made, and 'strongly recommended' that a ship be made available for inclining. If stability did prove deficient, efforts should be made to restore it by other means before armament was reduced. If removal of two quad tubes should be decided on, then BuOrd advised that close-in AA batteries be strengthened as far as possible, preferably by installing two twin 40 mm mounts.[28]

Five months later BuShips again wrote to CNO, complaining that the availability of one of the four destroyers had been lost in the Pacific Fleet's operational schedule and that none of the four had been inclined for a check on stability. BuShips pointed out that the ships were continuing to operate with all sixteen of their tubes, and that 'their stability in this condition, as indicated by data available to the Bureau, is not considered satisfactory for safe operation.'[29] CNO endorsed the Bureau's recommendation, asking that the Pacific Fleet either make a ship available for inclining or that two quadruple tubes be removed to alleviate the situation.[30] Admiral Nimitz now ordered that a *Gridley* class destroyer be sent to Pearl Harbor for an inclining experiment. The Vice Chief of Naval Operations advised that modifications be held in abeyance until results of this check could be received and studied.[31]

Craven was again inclined, this time at Pearl Harbor in November 1944. This test showed the previous unfavorable report from Mare Island was correct and that stability was deficient. BuShips and BuOrd had looked at the possibility of removing two quad tubes and relocating the remaining two on the centerline to leave the ships with an 8-tube broadside; this, however, would not do an adequate job of restoring stability. Only removal of two tube mounts, leaving the other two in place, or of one 5-inch gun, would be sufficient.[32]

Gridley, *Craven*, *McCall* and *Maury* finally did have their torpedo batteries halved, the two remaining quadruple tubes being left in their original wing positions. This was still not enough weight compensation to permit installation of 40 mm guns; the four ships ended the war with eight 20 mm guns as their entire close-in AA battery, the only surviving American destroyers so armed.[33]

The general question of destroyer stability received continuing attention from Washington and the operating forces alike. Early experience of North Atlantic convoy escorts led the Bureau of Ships to investigate the problem of ice formation, which not only impaired visibility and hampered the use of weapons but could dangerously affect stability by increasing topweight.[34] During the first months of American participation in the war BuShips took a fresh look at the stability of all new destroyers from the *Farragut* through the *Gleaves* classes, taking into consideration the extensive modifications of 1941–42. At the Bureau's recommendation, the Vice Chief of Naval Operations issued new instructions

calling for minimum liquid ballasting, ranging from 153 tons in the *Bensons* and *Gleaves* to 258-259 tons in the *Somers* class. Specified fuel tanks were to be kept full of oil or water-ballasted to the waterline while at sea; tanks emptied of fuel were to be filled with seawater immediately. All wing stowage tanks outboard of destroyers' boiler rooms were to be kept filled to minimize list in case of hull damage. The Bureau thought that the *Fletcher* class might not require liquid ballasting,[35] but soon afterward decided that wing tanks should be ballasted to minimize list in a damaged condition even though *Fletcher*'s undamaged stability in the light-load condition was pronounced 'acceptable'. Leaving any of the wing tanks empty would raise the undamaged center of gravity and 'introduce the possibility of a large angle of heel after damage'.[36]

By the end of 1942 COMINCH — Admiral King — found it necessary to call attention to 'certain dangerous tendencies which are apparent upon study of the war operations to date.' The 'inclination to overload our ships without due consideration for stability' had reappeared, spurred by urgent demands for new weapons and equipment, principally AA guns and radar. Stability had to be kept in mind, King continued, when 'conducting offensive operations against an enemy whose primary weapon to date has been the torpedo.' The ability of a warship to survive was an essential consideration, and had to receive ceaseless attention from the forces afloat; 'all hands, particularly commanding officers, must be buoyancy- and stability-minded.'[37] The Vice Chief of Naval Operations followed up by reminding the fleet that war allowances of ammunition and other consumables were only to be exceeded for good reason and for short periods; captains and destroyer force commanders had to understand the effect of such overloading on stability and survival.[38]

Wartime conditions continued to exert a harmful effect on the loading — and, hence, the stability — of destroyers. Late in 1943 the Bureau of Ships addressed this in detail, telling COMINCH that most warships were being operated at displacements far in excess of those for which they had been designed, adversely affecting the speed, seaworthiness, and power of survival of the ships involved. COMINCH had issued warnings of this, and the problem was generally recognized in the fleet. Considerable amounts of non-essentials had already been removed, but BuShips felt that there was still room for improvement. The tendency to load ships for any contingency, rather than for probable actual service, meant that innumerable small 'extras' eventually added up to serious overloading. Bu-

Ships thought that this stemmed from a lack of knowledge, on the part of forces afloat, of what actually constituted overloading. Limiting displacements, with corresponding mean drafts, were proposed.[39] VCNO liked the idea of a limiting draft, along the lines of the mercantile Plimsoll mark, since this would give destroyer captains something reliable on which to base their individual calculations.[40] COMINCH thought the Bureau's recommendation offered 'a simple and easy method of preventing dangerous over-loading of combatant ships' and approved it, asking that BuShips expand its studies to provide suggested limiting displacements for all other warship types as well. Admiral King remarked that the values given must be clearly identified as a guide against over-loading 'and do not prevent responsible Commanders from authorizing excessive loadings when service conditions warrant, accepting the adverse conditions resulting.'[41]

BuShips had, in the meanwhile, been working on similar calculations for the remaining extant destroyer classes. Early in 1944, weights and drafts were issued for the *Benson* and *Fletcher* classes, with the 1,850-ton leaders.[42] As this information was approved by Admiral King's office, it was forwarded to the destroyer force commanders who, in turn, disseminated it through their commands.[43] A few months later the Bureau of Ships prescribed a 'Plimsoll mark', to be painted amidships at the limiting waterline on all destroyers back through the *Farragut* class.[44]

As topside weights continued to increase, stability had to be re-emphasized. A new edition of the basic fleet damage-control manual summarized the idea of minimum and maximum service loadings, and warned against overloading. This, it went on, reduced speed and cruising radius. By reducing freeboard it made a ship wetter and less effective in heavy weather; this also shortened the range of stability. Excessive loading increased the longitudinal stresses imposed on the hull girder in a seaway. In rough seas this could lead to 'structural distress or even failure.'[45]

In the late summer of 1944 Commander Destroyers, Pacific Fleet, issued a summary of current ballasting instructions to his flock with the remark that the 'steady increase' in topside loading, approaching the allowable limit for destroyers, made strict compliance with ballasting directives mandatory. These instructions were intended to provide satisfactory stability at light service displacement. Those fuel tanks considered critical to stability were to be kept filled. Should it be necessary to draw fuel from them they were to be emptied as soon as possible and ballasted with

sea water. 'This procedure', ComDesPac went on, was 'mandatory . . . to eliminate free surface effects, maintain an adequate righting moment, [and] reduce list effects in case of damage to the tanks, since most ballasting tanks are off the ship's centerline.' Service fuel tanks, those from which fuel was normally first drawn, were to be kept at least half full for as long as practicable. When the fuel supply dwindled to the point where this could no longer be done, oil should be pumped into the best-protected tanks and the empty tanks immediately filled with salt water.[46] The value of this advice would be brought home to the fleet in tragic terms before the year was out.

A violent typhoon hit the Pacific Fleet on 18 December 1944, while it was operating in support of the invasion of the Philippines in an area some 300 miles east of Luzon. A number of warships, including three destroyers, were seriously damaged. Three more destroyers were lost with nearly all hands. The *Farragut* class had suffered out of all proportion to its numbers. Two of the three ships lost, as well as two of the three severely injured, were *Farraguts*.[47]

Responding to an inquiry from Admiral King, BuShips pointed out that stability criteria for the new *Fletcher* and *Allen M. Sumner/Gearing* classes had been 'deliberately made very materially better than those of any previous destroyers in our service'; recent inclining experiments indicated that, in spite of increases in topside weights, they still retained a 'very appreciable margin' of stability over what the Bureau had determined to be acceptable for earlier classes. The liquid ballasting instructions, mentioned above, were intended to maintain stability as fuel was consumed. There were short periods when this water ballast had to be discharged in preparation for fueling, reducing stability below the acceptable minimum, but this possibility had been 'fully weighed in establishing the criterion for destroyer stability'.[48]

Commander Destroyers, Pacific Fleet, and Commander in Chief, Pacific Fleet, both concluded that the loss and serious damage to destroyers was due to unsatisfactory ballasting and a general failure, on the part of commanding officers and tactical commanders, to realize the danger of their situation and take appropriate and timely measures to alleviate it. ComDesPac reissued his earlier ballasting instructions 'for information and *compliance*', remarking that the recent experience of Pacific destroyers 'should be ample evidence to convince individual Commanding Officers and responsible Unit Commanders of the absolute necessity of ballasting for preservation of sufficient stability during unfavorable sea and weather conditions as well as for

security against listing in case of underwater damage.'[49] Admiral Nimitz emphasized the need for study and initiative on the part of commanding officers. As he phrased it, 'the time for taking all measures for a ship's safety is while still able to do so. Nothing is more dangerous than for a seaman to be grudging in taking precautions lest they turn out to have been unnecessary. Safety at sea for a thousand years has depended on exactly the opposite philosophy.'[50]

A Pacific Fleet circular letter remarked that wartime increases in AA guns, radar, and fire control equipment had led to a situation where 'there are few, if any, ships of our Navy today that have left any so-called "margin of stability".' Weight and moment compensation, with strict adherence to ballasting instructions, was essential, as was avoidance of unauthorized alterations. 'Individual unauthorized alterations are like individual sips at a cocktail party — no one has any appreciable effect, but the aggregate seriously affects stability.' If increases were essential, then sacrifices would have to be made elsewhere in ships to compensate for them. 'WE MUST PAY A PRICE', the letter concluded, 'FOR EVERY ALTERATION TO A SHIP AND THE TIME HAS COME WHEN IT WOULD BE MOST UNWISE TO PAY IT IN FURTHER REDUCED STABILITY.'[51]

On the recommendation of the Navy's Inspector General after an investigation of overloading in the *Allen M. Sumner* class, Admiral King had recommended that an office be established under CNO 'to maintain an effective and continuing control over the military characteristics of naval vessels.' The Secretary of the Navy approved King's proposal, establishing a Ship Characteristics Board whose primary function was to make certain that the military characteristics of new ships 'not only meet, but anticipate wherever feasible, the requirements of all phases of naval warfare.' Particular attention was to be given to displacement and stability.[52]

By mid-1945 the Bureau of Ships had discovered that the limiting displacements it had set during 1944 were too conservative. Actuality had overtaken theory. Reports from the forces afloat, with recent inclining experiments, showed that typically-loaded destroyers exceeded the prescribed limits by wide margins in some instances. The bigger 'fourth generation' ships of the *Benson/Gleaves* and later classes had had their AA batteries and electronic suits considerably increased, and permanent weights in those ships (not including consumables) had grown by as much as a hundred tons apiece since the 1944 limits had been issued. The Bureau thus calculated a new set of limiting displacements, designed to

prevent further weight increases without an 'impracticable if not impossible' attempt to reduce topweight to an earlier standard. This was thought 'simply recognition of the fact that the ships have suffered some loss in power of survival, speed, cruising radius, and dryness. Fortunately, the structural strength in intact condition and the stability characteristics of these ships have not fallen below minimum acceptable values.'[53]

Results of an extensive program of inclining experiments led BuShips to conclude that the *Fletcher*, *Allen M. Sumner*, and *Gearing* classes, as well as all destroyer escorts (DE), had 'reached a condition of loading beyond which it is unwise to continue'. Full compensation had already been prescribed for earlier destroyers, and this was now made an across-the-board requirement for the type.[54] CNO specifically applied this principle to electronic installations, emphasizing 'the importance of making full weight and moment compensation for electronic and other equipment whether intended as a temporary or permanent installation.'[55] This was pertinent at this time in the light of improvements — such as new blind-firing AA directors and IFF installations for 5-inch gun directors, as well as radar countermeasures equipments — then being installed in many ships to counter the *kamikaze* effort. The Ship Characteristics Board, reviewing action taken since 1942 with respect to control of displacement and stability characteristics of naval ships, noted that 'considerable campaigning' had taken place on the subject but that 'much of it has, however, taken place within the confines of the Navy Department; the headquarters organization and ships continue to be overloaded to the jeopardy of their power of survival and the impairment of important ship characteristics.'[56]

The Bureau of Ships, shortly afterwards, defined all destroyers and destroyer escorts as 'Both Weight and Stability Critical'. This meant that any increase in overall weight or rise in a ship's center of gravity had to be prevented. When a weight was added, an equal weight was to be removed from the same, or a higher, level; if this was not feasible, a greater weight was to be removed from a lower level.[57] This concern for stability and survival did not, of course, end with the war but was included in the body of technical and operational experience studied and digested in the postwar years. Enough however, has been summarized here to show that this problem assumed particular intensity in the destroyer Navy and that, from Pearl Harbor through V–J Day, headquarters commands and forces afloat alike devoted particular care and attention to quests for solutions.

Appendix B

DAMAGE AND LOSS IN ACTION

The Fleet that sinks while its enemy floats fails finally and utterly.

Commander Destroyer Squadrons, Battle Fleet, Annual Report, 1925

The effects of war damage on American destroyers was extensively studied by the Bureau of Ships, and it would not be amiss here to briefly summarize its findings.[1]

There are reasonable limits to the amount of damage that any ship — 'unsinkable' or not — can absorb and survive. By comparison to larger warships, destroyers are much more fragile; even the relatively large destroyers of World War II were protected by nothing more than light splinter plating designed to protect machinery and control spaces from fragmentation and strafing. For the rest of its survival the destroyer had to depend on a combination of speed and agility; firepower; good design and sturdy construction; determined crews, carrying out effective damage-control doctrine; and, in so many cases, what can only be described as the hand of God.

'Despite their comparative vulnerability,' BuShips concluded, 'numerous cases of war damage have demonstrated that destroyers are rugged vessels and will absorb and survive an astonishing amount of punishment. This is particularly true of the 2100[2] and 2200-ton[3] classes. Furthermore, it is possible to greatly augment their inherent ability to survive extensive damage by prompt and effective damage control measures.'[4]

'In any consideration of the survival powers of the modern destroyer,' it noted 'the personnel factor must be recognized. The ship as built has proved its ruggedness but many vessels survived unprecedented damage largely due to the high degree of training and the heroic determination of the ship's damage control organization. For the same reasons, several that were eventually lost were enabled to remain in action appreciably longer.'[5]

The United States Navy's wartime damage-control Bible was a manual titled *Damage Control Instructions* (FTP 170[B]), which defined damage control as the maintenance of firepower, mobility, maneuverability, and flotation. This was to be accomplished by taking steps to preserve stability and buoyancy and control list and trim; by fighting fire; by repairing vital systems as rapidly as possible; and by caring for the injured. Destroy-

ers being as small as they were, the crew of a damaged ship could usually do little to patch up serious damage to hull or machinery. Their efforts were thus normally limited to keeping the ship afloat and putting out fires. Though fire was hazardous in that it could cause damaging explosions and interfered with other damage-control work, fire-fighting tools and techniques were developed to such a degree that BuShips could say that 'firefighting techniques so far have been much more efficient than those employed to control flooding. For this reason more destroyer losses are attributable to progressive flooding than to fire.'[6]

The relative fragility of destroyer hulls and their lack of the side protection systems found in bigger ships made them particularly vulnerable to torpedo and mine damage, 'primarily because the under-water ordnance carried a larger explosive charge to a more vulnerable spot' than did a projectile, bomb, or *kamikaze* aircraft. Above-water hits sometimes caused very extensive damage but, since they did not necessarily cause flooding, did not cause the loss of ships in the same proportion as did underwater weapons. 'In the future, efficiency of bombs or of guided missiles or pilotless aircraft may be increased to that of torpedoes through the use of more powerful explosive charges and improved fuzing; however, the most effective attack will remain that which introduces flooding.'[7] This was borne out by the numbers involved. Two hundred and fifty-one war-damage cases involving destroyers were reported to BuShips between October 1941 and August 1945. Of 192 ships hit by bombs, gunfire, or *kamikazes* 162, or 84 percent, survived. Twenty-seven ships out of 48 damaged by torpedoes or mine went down, an underwater-damage survival rate of only 44 percent.[8] This, incidentally, underscores the gradual — and partial — shift in relative importance of the American destroyer's own functions during the war years, from primary emphasis on the anti-surface ship mission to greater stress on the antiair-defense and antisubmarine tasks. The downplaying of the ship-killing torpedo in favor of increasingly heavy gun batteries and

electronic suits was far from total (torpedoes were still ubiquitous in 1945), but it was nonetheless indicative.

Korotkin's examination of 495 wartime instances of loss of non-Soviet destroyer types[9] generally tends to bear out the American experience. He concluded that underwater explosions were the principal enemies of destroyers, causing the majority of losses. A torpedo hit at the bow or stern tended to rupture the hull girder and cause the extremity to break off.[10] Some degree of machinery damage usually resulted from shock, flooding, or both. A destroyer so damaged tended to stay afloat, though left dead in the water. Destroyers, especially later ones, were designed to have a chance to survive a single torpedo hit in the midship section; the *Benson* class, for instance, was calculated to have a good chance of surviving the flooding of any three longitudinal groups of compartments.[11] Losses of destroyers to underwater weapons resulted, for the most part, from structural failure or flooding rather than from fire or explosion. Mines had an effect generally similar to that of torpedoes, though influence mines could explode at some distance from a ship. Their effect varied with the weight of the charge and with the distance and relative position of the explosion with relation to the ship's hull.

Projectiles, as well as aircraft bombs, could cause topside damage and fire as well as flooding. Near misses could have a mining effect on a hull. *Kamikazes* — the first operational antiship cruise missiles — caused the loss of destroyers by flooding, hull failure, and fire, the gasoline which these piloted missiles carried making them additionally dangerous.

Although battle damage could be analyzed, its effect could not always be predicted. The *Sims* class *O'Brien* (DD-415) eventually broke in two after being hit by a single Japanese submarine torpedo. The *Gleaves* class *Kearny* (DD-432) and *Hambleton* (DD-455) took single torpedoes amidships and survived; their sisters *Bristol* (DD-453) and *Beatty* (DD-640) were lost to hull failure, as were the *Fletcher* class *Strong* (DD-468) and the *Allen*

Opposite
A well-handled destroyer could often manage to live
through severe topside damage, such as that inflicted by
suicide planes, off Okinawa, on *Hazelwood* (DD-531).

Below
Some destroyers managed to take fearful amounts of
damage and survive. This artist's impression of the
detonation of a Japanese torpedo plane on the forecastle
of *Smith* (DD-378) off the Solomons in October 1942,
gives some idea of the punishment these ships could
take. Though set aflame by ignited gasoline, *Smith*
escaped loss.

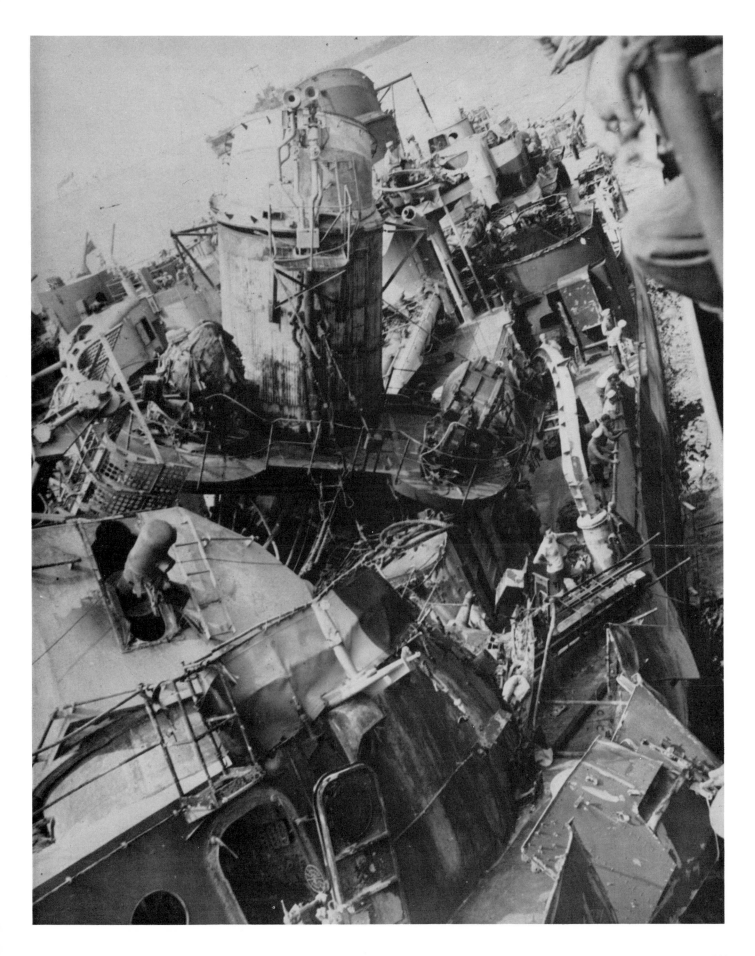

M. Sumner class *Meredith* (DD-726). The more ample hull proportions and heavier scantlings of the *Fletcher* and later classes tended to make them more resistant to hull-girder failure than their predecessors.[12] Only two 'clear-cut' instances were recorded of destroyers succumbing to extensive flooding and capsizing. The *Mahan* class *Preston* (DD-379), lost off Guadalcanal in 1942, and *Johnston* (DD-557), a *Fletcher* sunk at Leyte Gulf in 1944, both had their hulls riddled with gunfire around the waterline. Flooding became uncontrollable, and both ships rolled over and went down.

As has been noted, techniques for fighting fire made more wartime progress than did those for the control of flooding and restoration of stability. This was the result of a number of causes. Better tools helped; the fire main in the *Fletcher* class was served by six installed pumps plus portable gasoline-powered submersible 'handy-Billy' pumps; with all pumps functioning, a ship could operate up to about 30 fire hoses. Ships of the *Allen M. Sumner* and *Gearing* classes had additional pumps and could handle up to fifty hoses at a time. Improved use of foam and multipurpose hose nozzles, combined with a continuing removal of inflammables, made their contribution, while portable oxygen-breathing apparatus (OBA) made it possible for men to do a better job of firefighting without needless risk of asphyxiation. Portable pumps not only fought fire, but also dewatered flooded spaces. All of this would have been of little avail without extensive programs of training which gave crews the knowledge needed to use their equipment effectively under conditions of great stress.

The danger of damage to ship systems from explosive shock had been recognized before Pearl Harbor, but not to an extent suited to coping with the heavier explosive charges of the 1940s. A realization of this brought new programs aimed at 'shockproofing' vital items of shipboard machinery, ordnance, and electronics. Most instances of damage to American destroyers were caused by contact explosions. These, as it turned out, produced little or no shock damage. Most of the shock damage inflicted came from non-contact underwater explosions, which could cause 'extensive and crippling' injury. Where a ship might not suffer hull rupture, she might be left crippled or impaired.[13]

Opposite
The minelayer *Aaron Ward* (DM-34) survived the damage inflicted by kamikazes off Okinawa.

Below
A destroyer could also manage to survive a torpedo hit at bow or stern. *Selfridge* (DD-357) had her bow blown off by a Japanese 24-inch torpedo in the Solomons but, patched up as seen here, returned to the United States for a new bow and came back to the war.

Another testimonial to the American destroyer's ability to take punishment was the ordeal suffered by *Laffey* (DD-724) while on picket duty off Okinawa during April 1945. In this one engagement, the *Allen M. Sumner* class destroyer was attacked twenty-two times by aircraft. The ship was seriously hit nine times, four times by individual bombs and five times by bomb-laden *kamikazes*. In an incredible display of courage and determination, the crew continued to fight and keep the ship afloat — and then brought her home. After repairs in the US, the ship went on to serve into the 1970s.

With the proper training, organization, and discipline, a ship's chances of surviving battle damage were rather good. Many ships, including destroyers, managed to survive fearful injury. FTP 170 was able to conclude that 'aside from cases involving loss from fires or structural failures, war experience has demonstrated that no matter what the list or trim, if the ship does not sink within a very few minutes after damage, there is a good chance of saving her by prompt damage control measures. The cases of loss by bodily sinkage, plunging, or capsizing, several hours after damage have been entirely attributable to progressive flooding.'[14]

In February 1944 CNO asked the Bureau of Ships to calculate the chances of survival of various types and classes of warships when hit by bombs and torpedoes. The Bureau's study concluded that earlier destroyers — 1,500-tonners and the *Benson* and *Gleaves* classes — could survive with two main compartments flooded; flooding of three would 'probably' cause loss. *Benson* class ships, for example, were divided into sixteen compartments by watertight transverse bulkheads. A 660-pound torpedo warhead, if it hit in the middle 65 per cent of the ship, would probably flood at least three compartments 'and, furthermore, probably will destroy enough of the ship's girder to cause breaking in two. Loss, under these circumstances, is almost inevitable.' Besides this vulnerable midsection, another 25 per cent of the ship's length included magazines. A hit in these areas, forward and aft of the machinery spaces, was calculated to have a 50 per cent chance of detonating magazines. These ships' total vulnerability was figured at 75 per cent. Actual war experience to date showed 12 out of 16 destroyers having sunk after being hit by one torpedo — 'a rather close agreement.' In practice, the *Bensons* and *Gleaves* seem to have proven a bit tougher than they were credited with being, beginning with the midships torpedo damage to *Kearny* (DD-432) in the Atlantic in 1941. Later calculations for these ships indicated that they could survive with any three compartments flooded if the ship in question had not been overloaded and wind and sea were not unfavorable.[15] Hits by 250, 500, or 1,000 pound general-purpose (thin-walled) bombs, while serious, were somewhat less so than torpedo hits. These earlier destroyers stood a 91 percent chance of living through a hit by one 250 pound or 500 pound bomb, but only a 30 percent likelihood of surviving a hit by a 1,000 pounder. Three 250 pound or two 500 pound hits still left some chance — 40 and 35 percent respectively — of survival. Conclusions about the effect of near misses were elusive, accurate information being scarce.

The *Fletcher*s, as well as the 1,850-ton 'leaders', were thought capable of surviving with three main compartments flooded. Structural strength of their hulls was superior to that of the 1,500-tonners and hull depth and beam were greater; one torpedo hit was unlikely to cause enough damage to sink one of these ships by flooding, and the chance of hull-girder failure was estimated at one in three. 'It may develop', thought the Bureau, 'that this figure will be even smaller.' These bigger destroyers were considered much more resistant to loss from torpedo damage than their smaller contemporaries, with a loss probability of 0.31. Two hits, except under certain special circumstances, sent the chance of loss up to 0.90. Two or three bomb hits, if the bombs penetrated belowdecks before exploding, could cause flooding and might prove nearly as serious as a torpedo hit. A 1,000 pound bomb should be almost as lethal as a torpedo.[16]

Maintenance of watertightness, especially critical in these thin-skinned vessels, was continually stressed. 'The importance of maintaining the highest degree of water-tight integrity cannot be over-emphasized.'[17] Ships were urged to make frequent compressed-air tests of watertight bulkheads and to guard against any alteration which might compromise their watertightness. While flushdeckers had to go into navy yards for these tests, ships from the *Farragut* class on were equipped with portable air-testing sets and ordered to use them.[18]

A key factor in ship survival was the training of their crews. 'War experience emphasizes that the entire ship's company must be thoroughly educated in damage control principles and methods, and must be properly trained to act in accordance with them.' Damage-control schools were set up to train key officers; firefighting schools were organized for officers and men. Both featured a combination of classroom learning and practical experience. Much attention was given to shipboard damage-control organization; destroyer-force commanders included detailed prescriptions for such organization in the standard battle bills drawn up for the various classes of ships. Captains were encouraged to make casualty drills a regular feature of their ship's operations.[19] The quality designed into ships and their damage-control equipment had much to do with survival. In the final analysis though, as so often proves to be the case in war, the decisive factor was the human one.

Appendix C

ORGANIZATION OF THE DEPARTMENT OF THE NAVY

PART 1: 1934

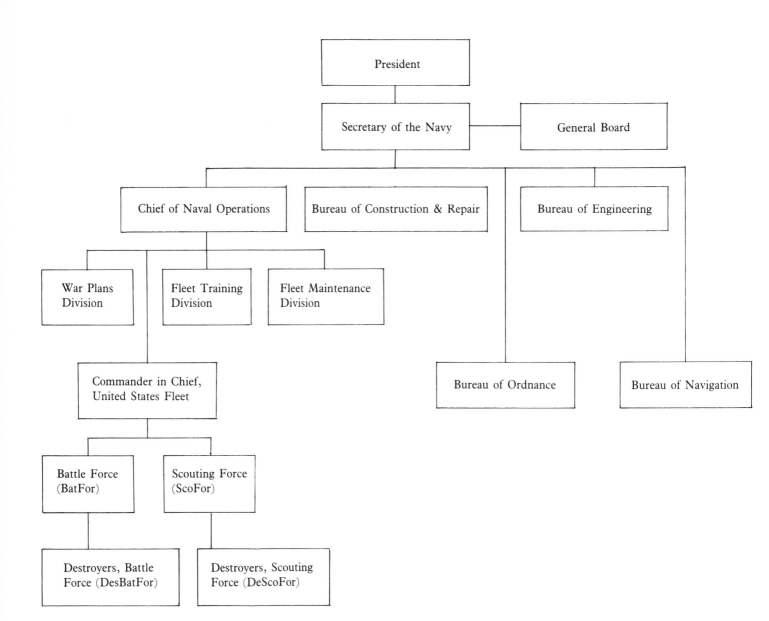

Only major components involved in the destroyer design process are included. The abbreviated titles in parentheses are those officially used. The individual in command of an organization is identified in document references by the appropriate prefix, CH (Chief), COM (Commander), or CINC (Commander in Chief). Thus, the Chief of the Bureau of Ordnance was ChBuOrd; the Commander, Scouting Force, was ComScoFor. The Commander in Chief, United States Fleet, was simply CINCUS. During World War II Admiral King, not liking the sound of the abbreviation, changed it to COMINCH.

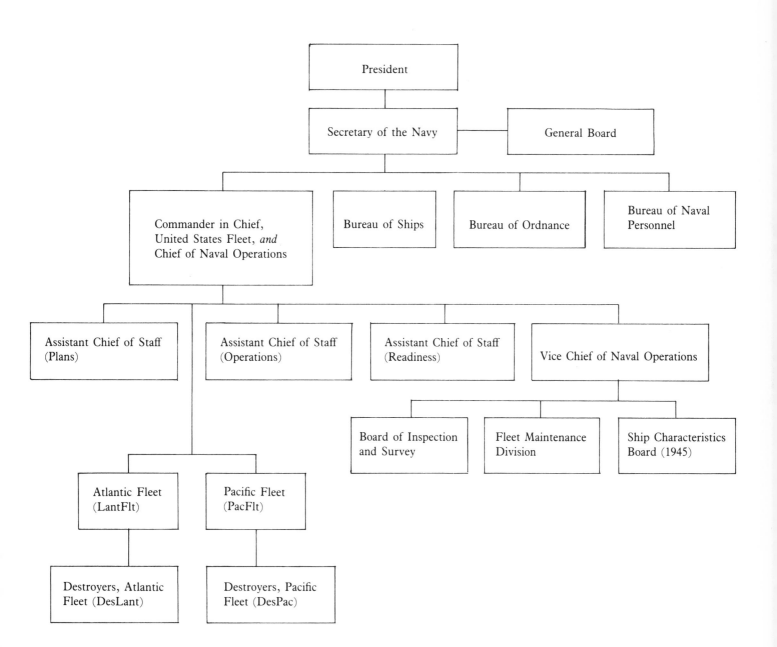

The offices of COMINCH and Chief of Naval Operations (CNO) were combined by order of President Roosevelt on 12 March 1942. As COMINCH, Admiral Ernest J. King commanded the operating forces. As CNO, he was responsible for the 'preparation, readiness and logistic support' of the operating forces and for the co-ordination of the efforts of the various bureaus and offices of the headquarters establishment under the overall direction of the Secretary of the Navy (SecNav). The Ship Characteristics Board (SCB) made its appearance in 1945, during the closing months of World War II.

Appendix D

COMPARATIVE TABLES OF AMERICAN DESTROYER CLASSES, 1931–1945

PART 1: DATA

These tables were compiled to permit a convenient comparison of the basic dimensions and capabilities of the destroyer classes discussed in the preceding chapters. Dimensions and weights are expressed in feet and long tons (2,240 pounds). To convert feet to meters, multiply by 0.3048; to convert long tons to metric tonnes, multiply by 1.016. Armament information is given for each class as of original completion and as existing at the end of the Pacific war in August 1945. By the war's end, particularly in the large war-built classes, many minor variations existed and no attempt is made to reflect them here. The armament of ships and classes can be traced in detail in the Bureau of Ordnance *Armament Summary*.

To save space, armament information is expressed in abbreviated form. All 5-in guns are 5-inch/38-caliber (5-in/38), dual-purpose (DP), or single-purpose (SP), as indicated. All torpedo tubes (TT) are 21-inch. AA gun mounts (20 mm, 40 mm, and 1.1-inch) are identified as single (S), twin (T), or quadruple (Q). All .50-caliber AA machine-gun mounts are singles, and are identified as .50 MG. Depth-charge stern tracks, and side-throwing depth-charge projectors ('K-guns') are indicated by DCT and DCP, respectively. The blocks of hull numbers within each class of ships are specified; ships canceled before completion are in parentheses.

Speeds and endurances are across the board calculations for each class. (Speeds marked thus★ are early-postwar maximums tabulated before extensive alterations and are considered representative.) It is believed the *Gearings'* war steaming speed would be similar to the *Allen M. Sumners'* as they were essentially the same ships except for a 14-foot extension in the *Gearings* for an additional fuel tank, giving them a longer length to beam ratio, tending to add speed, perhaps one knot, but the fuel's weight would tend to detract perhaps one knot. Probably, as the ships were so new at the end of the war the information was simply never published. Postwar war steaming figures are inapplicable to the World War II period because the ships underwent heavy modification, and their engineering plants were growing older.

The set of drawings of American wartime destroyers was prepared by the Office of Naval Intelligence for a ship-recognition manual issued in December 1943.

Sources for Comparative Tables
Ships' Data, US Naval Vessels (Bureau of Ships; editions of 1938, 1942, 1943, 1945).
Armament Summary (Bureau of Ordnance, 1941–45).
FTP-218, *War Service Fuel Consumption of US Naval Surface Vessels* (COMINCH, 1945)
ONI 222-US, *United States Naval Vessels* (Division of Naval Intelligence, 1 September 1945).
James C. Fahey, *The Ships and Aircraft of the US Fleet*. Victory Edition, 1945.
CNO letter Op-22-C(SC) A8-7(3) serial 0129022 of 28 December 1940 to BuShips.
BuShips letter C-DD/S29-1(456) C-EN28/A2-11 of 12 June 1945 to ComDesPac, ComDesLant.
Data tabulation, typescript in General Board file 420-9 (1945), Operational Archives Branch, Naval Historical Center.
ComDesPac Confidential Letter No. 1CL-45 of 15 July 1945.

Class	Ships (DD)	Building Program (Fiscal Year)	Length Overall ft	in	Extreme beam ft	in	Standard Displacement	Limiting Displacement (1945)	Shaft Horsepower	Rated "War steaming" speed 1940	Radius (Nautical miles/knots) (1945)
Farragut	348–355.	1932–33	341	3	34	3	1,500	2,335	42,800	31.7	5,830/14.8 : 2,500/25.3
Porter	356–363.	1934	381	1	37	0	1,850	2,840	50,000	34–34.5	6,140/15.3 : 2,880/25.3
Mahan	364–379.	1934	341	4	35	5	1,500	2,345	48,000	35	6,790/15.2 : 2,880/25.5
Gridley	380, 382 400–401.	1935	341	3	34	8	1,500	2,395	50,000	35.5	5,750/15.5 : 2,810/25.1
Somers	381, 383, 394–396.	1935–36	381	0	36	2	1,850	2,905–2,960	52,000	35	6,490/15.6 : 3,140/25.1
Dunlap	384–385.	1935	341	4	35	5	1,500	2,345	48,000	35	6,100/15 : 2,600/25
Bagley	386–393.	1935	341	3	34	8	1,500	2,325	48,000	35	6,080/15 : 2,600/25
Benham	397–399, 402–408.	1936	340	9	35	6	1,500	2,415	50,000	35.5	5,220/15.4 : 2,510/25.6
Sims	409–420.	1937	348	4	36	0	1,570	2,530	50,000	34.5	5,420/15.7 : 2,580/25.3
Benson	421–422, 425–428, 459–460, 491–492, 598–617.	1938–41	347	10	36	1	1,620	2,575–2,590	50,000	34.5★	5,430/15.3 : 2,780/25.5

Class	Ships (DD)	Building Program (Fiscal Year)	Length Overall ft	in	Extreme beam ft	in	Standard Displacement	Limiting Displacement (1945)	Shaft Horsepower	Rated "War steaming" speed 1940	Radius (Nautical miles/knots) (1945)
Gleaves	423–424, 429–444, 453–458, 461–464, 483–490, 493–497, 618–628, 632–641, 645–648.	1938–41	348	4	36	1	1,630	2,575–2,590	50,000	30.5★	5,790/15.0 : 3,090/25.3
Fletcher	445–451, 465–481, 498–502, (505–506), 507–522, (523–525), 526–541, (542–543), 544–547, (548–549), 550–597, 629–631, 642–644, 649–691, 792–804.	1941–42	376	5	39	7	2,150	3,035	60,000	32.3★	4,790/15.8 : 3,100/25.6
Allen M. Sumner	692–709, 722–741, 744–762, 770–781, 857.	1943	376	6	40	10	2,200	3,315	60,000	32.1★	5,010/15.5 : 2,680/25.3
Gearing	710–721, 742–743, 763–769, 782–791, 805–808, (809–816), 817–853, (854–856), 858–890, (891–926).	1943–45	390	6	40	10	2,200	3,340	60,000	31.3★	5,800/12 : 1,430/31.3

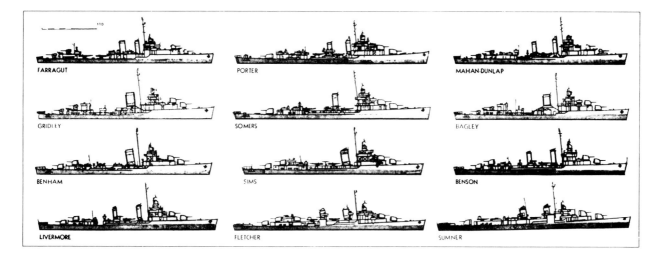

PART 2: ARMAMENT

Class	Original	August 1945			
Farragut (DD-348)	5 × 5-in DP 4 × .50 MG (2 × 4) × TT 2 × DCT	4 × 5-in DP 2 × 40 mm T 5 × 20 mm S 8 × TT 2 × DCT 4 × DCP			
Porter (DD-356)	(4 × 2) × 5-in SP 2 × 1.1-in Q 2 × .50 MG (2 × 4) × TT 2 × DCT	(2 × 2, 1 × 1) × 5-in DP 3 × 40 mm Q 2 × 40 mm T 2 × 20 mm T 2 × DCT 4 × DCP	*or*	(2 × 2, 1 × 1) × 5-in DP 1/2 × 40 mm Q 2 × 40 mm T 2 × 20 mm T 8 × TT 2 × DCT 4 × DCP	*or* (3 × 2) × 5-in SP 1 × 40 mm Q 3 × 40 mm T 8 × TT 2 × DCT 4 × DCP
Mahan (DD-364)	5 × 5-in DP 4 × .50 MG (3 × 4) × TT 2 × DCT	4 × 5-in DP 2 × 40 mm T 5/6 × 20 mm S 8/12 × TT 2 × DCT 4 × DCP	*or*	4 × 5-in DP 2 × 40 mm Q 5 × 20 mm S 2 × DCT 4 × DCP	*or* 4 × 5-in DP 2 × 40 mm Q 2 × 40 mm T 4 × 20 mm T 2 × DCT 4 × DCP
Dunlap (DD-384)	5 × 5-in 4 × .50 MG (3 × 4) × TT 2 × DCT	4 × 5-in DP 2 × 40 mm T 5 × 20 mm S 12 × TT 2 × DCT 4 × DCP			
Gridley (DD-380)	4 × 5-in 4 × .50 MG (4 × 4) × TT 2 × DCT	4 × 5-in DP 8 × 20 mm S 8 × TT 2 × DCT 4 × DCP			
Somers (DD-381)	(4 × 2) × 5-in SP 2 × 1.1-in Q 2 × .50 MG (3 × 4) × TT 2 × DCT	(2 × 2, 1 × 1) × 5-in DP *or* 2 × 40 mm Q 3 × 40 mm T 6 × 20 mm S 2 × DCT 2 × DCP		(3 × 2) × 5-in SP 3 × 40 mm T 6 × 20 mm S 8 × TT 2 × DCT 6 × DCP	
Bagley (DD-386)	4 × 5-in DP 4 × .50 MG (4 × 4) × TT 2 × DCT	4 × 5-in DP 1 × 40 mm T 6 × 20 mm S 16 × TT 2 × DCT 4 × DCP			

Class	Original	August 1945			
Benham (DD-397)	4 × 5-in DP 4 × .50 MG (4 × 4) × TT 2 × DCT	4 × 5-in DP 2 × 40 mm T 4 × 20 mm S 8 × TT 2 × DCT	*or* 4 × 5-in DP 4 × 40 mm T 4 × 20 mm T 2 × DCT 4 × DCP		
Sims (DD-409)	5 × 5-in DP 4 × .50 MG (2/3 × 4) × TT 2 × DCT	4 × 5-in DP 2 × 40 mm T 4 × 20 mm S 8 × TT 2 × DCT 4/6 × DCP	*or* 4 × 5-in DP 4 × 40 mm T 4 × 20 mm S 2 × DCT 4 × DCP		
Benson (DD-421)	4/5 × 5-in DP 6 × .50 MG (2 × 5) × TT 2 × DCT	4 × 5-in DP 2 × 40 mm T 4 × 20 mm S 10 × TT 2 × DCT 6 × DCP	*or* 4 × 5-in DP 2 × 40 mm T 7 × 20 mm S 5 × TT 2 × DCT 4/6 × DCP	*or* 4 × 5-in DP 2 × 40 mm Q 2 × 40 mm T 2 × 20 mm S 2 × 20 mm T 2 × DCT 4/6 × DCP	
Gleaves (DD-423) (*DD-423 class DMS)	4/5 × 5-in DP 6 × .50 MG (2 × 5) × TT 2 × DCT	4 × 5-in DP 2 × 40 mm T 4 × 20 mm S 10 × TT 2 × DCT 6 × DCP	*or* 4 × 5-in DP 2 × 40 mm T 7 × 20 mm S 5 × TT 2 × DCT 4/6 × DCP	*or* 4 × 5-in DP 2 × 40 mm Q 2 × 40 mm T 2 × 20 mm S 2 × 20 mm T 2 × DCT 4/6 × DCP	*or★* 3 × 5-in DP 2 × 40 mm T 7 × 20 mm S 2 × .50 MG 2 × DCT 2 × DCP *or★* 4 × 5-in DP 2 × 40 mm T 2 × 20 mm T 5 × TT 2 × DCT 6 × DCP
Fletcher (DD-445)	5 × 5-in DP 1 × 1.1-in Q 1 × 40 mm T 5 × 20 mm S (2 × 5) × TT 2 × DCT 4 × DCP	5 × 5-in DP 5 × 40 mm T 7 × 20 mm S 10 × TT 2 × DCT 6 × DCP	*or* 5 × 5-in DP 2 × 40 mm Q 3 × 40 mm T 6 × 20 mm T 5 × TT 2 × DCT 6 × DCP		
Allen M. Sumner/ Gearing (DD-692/ DD-710) (*Gearing* DDR) (**Allen M. Sumner* DM)	(3 × 2) × 5-in DP 2 × 40 mm Q 2 × 40 mm T 11 × 20 mm S (2 × 5) × TT 2 × DCT 6 × DCP	6 × 5-in DP 2 × 40 mm Q 2 × 40 mm T 11 × 20 mm S 10 × TT 2 × DCT 6 × DCP	*or* 6 × 5-in DP 3 × 40 mm Q 2 × 40 mm T 10 × 20 mm T 5 × TT 2 × DCT 6 × DCP	*or★* 6 × 5-in DP 3 × 40 mm Q 2 × 40 mm T 8 × 20 mm T 2 × DCT 6 × DCP	*or★★* 6 × 5-in DP 2 × 40 mm Q 2 × 40 mm T 8 × 20 mm S 2 × DCT 4 × DCP

PART 3: DESTROYER PROGRAMS; CANCELLATIONS, LOSSES AND SUSPENSIONS

This table summarizes destroyer authorizations, construction, and losses from the authorization of the *Farragut*-class through the end of World War II. This is expressed in terms of provision of construction funds (AUTH); laydown, the beginning of actual construction (LD); commissioning (COM); loss, to enemy action or other causes (LOST); cancellation (CANC); or suspension of construction at the war's end, with eventual disposal (SUSP). Some ships, heavily damaged and not repaired, became constructive total losses (CTL), and are totaled separately.

This summary should provide a serviceable idea of the programs being funded and of the numbers of ships added to, or subtracted from, the destroyer force during any given period from the relatively leisurely 1930s to the hectic war years. In connection with the design process, it is worth noting that class followed class in such rapid succession that several classes were often being built simultaneously; successor classes were usually designed and undertaken before experience could be gained with completed ships of earlier groups.

Congressional legislation with respect to ship construction dealt in *authorization*, or statement of intent, and *appropriation*, the actual provision of funds as part of the naval program for a fiscal year (1 July through 30 June). Though the symbol AUTH is used in this table for clarity, references here are to the funding of specific blocks of ships. This process became extremely convoluted during the war years; Dr Stephen S. Roberts' 'U.S. Navy Building Programs During World War II' (*Warship International*, XVIII: 3, 1981) is a valuable key.

Fiscal Year (Program)	1931			1932			1933				1934					1935			1936					1937			1938
Calendar Year (by quarters)	1931			1932			1933				1934				1935		1936				1937				1938		
Farragut (DD-348)	5 AUTH			3 AUTH	1 LD	2 LD	1 LD	1 LD	1 LD	1 LD	1 LD	1 COM		1 COM	4 COM	2 COM											
Porter (DD-356)							4 AUTH	4 AUTH		4 LD	3 LD	1 LD							1 COM	2 COM	1 COM	3 COM	1 COM				
Mahan (DD-364)								16 AUTH			2 LD	4 LD	5 LD	5 LD							9 COM	6 COM	1 COM				
Gridley (DD-380)											2 AUTH					2 AUTH 2 LD						2 LD		1 COM	1 COM		
Somers (DD-381)											2 AUTH					3 AUTH 1 LD			1 LD		1 LD		1 LD			1 COM	1 COM
Dunlap (DD-384)											2 AUTH					2 LD								1 COM		1 COM	
Bagley (DD-386)											8 AUTH						6 LD	2 LD						1 COM	5 COM	2 COM	
Benham (DD-397)																10 AUTH		1 LD	2 LD		1 LD			5 LD	1 LD		
Sims (DD-409)																			12 AUTH						2 LD	3 LD	1 LD
Benson (DD-421)																								6 AUTH			
Gleaves (DD-423)																								2 AUTH			
Fletcher (DD-445)																											
Allen M. Sumner (DD-692)																											
Gearing (DD-710)																											
Experimental ships (DD-452, 482, 503–506)																											
Total (by quarters)	5 AUTH			3 AUTH	1 LD	2 LD	4 AUTH 1 LD	20 AUTH 1 LD	1 LD	5 LD	14 AUTH 6 LD	5 LD 1 COM	5 LD	5 LD 1 COM	4 COM	15 AUTH 5 LD 2 COM	6 LD	3 LD	12 AUTH 3 LD 1 COM	2 COM	2 LD 10 COM	2 LD 9 COM	1 LD 2 COM	8 AUTH 5 LD 3 COM	3 LD 6 COM	3 LD 4 COM	1 LD 1 COM

1 *Cassin* and *Downes*, CTL at Pearl Harbor, rebuilt around original machinery, retaining same names and hull numbers.
2 DD-523–525, 542–543, 548–549, re-ordered to speed production as *Gleaves*-class DD-602–605, 611–612, 617.
3 DD-503–506, re-ordered as *Gleaves*-class DD-645–648.

Destroyer construction status chart — Fiscal Year (F.Y.) / Calendar Year 1939–1946. Values: AUTH = authorized, LD = laid down, COM = commissioned, LOST = lost, CTL = constructive total loss, CANC = cancelled, SUSP = suspended. (Class names appear at the right edge of the original chart; shown here in the left column. Line breaks within a cell are shown with "/".)

Class	1939				1940				1941				1942				1943				1944				1945				1946			
Farragut																		1 LOST								2 LOST						
Porter																1 LOST																
Mahan													2 CTL [1]				1 LOST	2 LOST			1 LOST / 1 COM [1]	1 COM [1]			2 LOST							
Gridley	1 COM	1 COM																														
Somers		1 COM	1 COM	1 COM																						1 LOST						
Dunlap																																
Bagley																	2 LOST				1 LOST											
Benham					3 COM	4 COM	3 COM										1 LOST				1 LOST											
Sims	6 LD				1 COM	4 COM	1 COM	3 COM	3 COM							2 LOST	1 LOST	1 LOST			1 LOST											
Benson	2 LD		3 LD		1 LD				2 AUTH / 6 COM	22 AUTH	1 LD / 1 COM	6 LD	12 LD	1 LD	1 LD	1 LD / 1 COM	1 LD / 6 COM	1 LD / 9 COM	2 LOST / 1 COM	2 COM		1 LOST										
Gleaves	8 AUTH / 1 LD	1 LD		3 LD	8 AUTH / 3 LD	2 LD	6 LD	2 LD / 1 COM	10 AUTH / 1 COM	38 AUTH / 2 LD / 3 COM	6 LD / 1 COM	6 LD / 6 COM	9 LD / 4 COM	12 LD / 1 COM	2 LD / 5 COM	5 LD / 7 COM	2 LD / 10 COM	2 LD / 7 COM	2 LD / 7 COM	6 COM	1 LOST / 4 COM	2 LOST / 3 COM	2 LOST	1 LOST	2 LOST				1 LOST / 4 CTL			
Fletcher									7 AUTH	95 AUTH	7 CANC [2]	2 LD	10 LD	10 LD	16 LD	14 LD	29 LD / 3 COM	16 LD / 9 COM	28 LD / 18 COM	24 LD / 19 COM / 1 LOST	14 LD / 30 COM	11 LD / 34 COM	1 LD / 28 COM	14 COM	9 COM	6 COM	2 COM / 4 LOST	2 COM / 1 LOST	9 LOST / 6 CTL	1 LOST		
Allen M. Sumner																		44 AUTH			4 LD	16 LD / 1 COM	18 LD / 10 COM	22 LD / 10 COM	9 LD / 13 COM	16 COM	16 COM	10 COM	1 COM / 2 LOST / 3 CTL		1 COM	2 COM
Gearing																		44 AUTH					3 LD	4 LD	20 LD / 2 COM	20 LD / 10 COM	14 LD / 11 COM	36 AUTH / 14 LD / 20 COM / 36 CANC	20 LD / 20 COM	11 LD / 18 COM / 11 CANC	2 LD / 12 COM	35 COM / 2 CANC / 5 SUSP
Experimental ships									2 AUTH	4 AUTH		4 CANC [3]																				2 CANC
Total	8 AUTH / 9 LD / 1 COM	1 LD / 2 COM	3 LD / 1 COM	4 LD / 4 COM	8 AUTH / 3 LD / 1 COM	2 LD / 8 COM	6 LD / 4 COM	2 LD / 4 COM	21 AUTH / 4 LD / 9 COM	159 AUTH / 2 LD	7 LD / 2 COM / 7 CANC	18 LD / 6 COM / 4 CANC	21 LD / 14 COM	23 LD / 1 COM	19 LD / 5 COM / 2 CTL	20 LD / 8 COM	32 LD / 19 COM / 2 LOST	88 AUTH / 19 LD / 25 COM / 4 LOST	30 LD / 26 COM / 7 LOST	24 LD / 27 COM / 2 LOST	18 LD / 34 COM / 1 LOST	27 LD / 37 COM / 3 LOST	19 LD / 30 COM / 4 LOST	25 LD / 25 COM / 1 LOST	13 LD / 22 COM / 3 LOST	20 LD / 22 COM / 1 LOST	20 LD / 20 COM / 8 LOST	36 AUTH / 14 LD / 22 COM / 1 LOST / 36 CANC	20 LD / 21 COM / 13 CTL / 12 LOST	11 LD / 18 COM / 1 LOST / 11 CANC	2 LD / 13 COM	37 COM / 4 CANC / 5 SUSP

Abbreviations

AA	Antiaircraft
Adm	Admiral
APD	High-Speed Transport (Converted DD or DE)
A/S	Antisubmarine
AsstSecNav	Assistant Secretary of the Navy
BuAer	Bureau of Aeronautics
BuC&R/BuCon	Bureau of Construction and Repair (both were used interchangeably)
BuEng	Bureau of Engineering
BuNav	Bureau of Navigation
BuOrd	Bureau of Ordnance
BuPers	Bureau of Naval Personnel
BuShips	Bureau of Ships (1940 merger of BuEng, BuCon)
CAP	Combat Air Patrol
Cdr	Commander
CIC	Combat Information Center
CinC	Commander in Chief
CinCLantFlt	CinC, Atlantic Fleet
CinCPac	CinC, Pacific (area command)
CinCPacFlt	CinC, Pacific Fleet
CinCUS	CinC, United States Fleet (later COMINCH)
CNO	Chief of Naval Operations
CO	Commanding Officer
ComBatFor	Commander, Battle Force
ComCruPac	Commander Cruisers, Pacific Fleet
ComDesBatFlt	Commander Destroyers, Battle Fleet
ComDesBatFor	Commander Destroyers, Battle Force (title changed 1931)
ComDeScoFor	Commander Destroyers, Scouting Force
ComDesLant	Commander Destroyers, Atlantic Fleet
ComDesPac	Commander Destroyers, Pacific Fleet
ComDesRon	Commander, Destroyer Squadron
COMINCH	Commander in Chief, United States Fleet (formerly CINCUS)
ComScoFor	Commander Scouting Force, United States Fleet
ComServPac	Commander Service Force, Pacific Fleet
ComServRon	Commander, Service Squadron
DCP	Depth-charge projector
DCT	Depth-charge track
DD	Destroyer
DDR	Radar-picket destroyer
Disp.	Displacement (in long tons, 2,240 pounds)
DM	High-Speed Minelayer (converted DD)
DMS	Destroyer Minesweeper (converted DD)
DP	Dual-purpose (British HA/LA)
F	Fahrenheit
ft/sec	Feet per second (velocity)
GB	General Board
Gun mounts	Identified, forward-to-aft, by numbers. 5-inch mounts were numbered Mount 51, Mount 52, and so on.
hp	Horsepower
K-gun	Side-throwing depth-charge projector Mark 6
kts	Knots
Lcdr	Lieutenant Commander
MG	Machine gun
Miles	Nautical miles
mph	Miles per hour
NIRA	National Industrial Recovery Act (major New Deal relief legislation)
OBA	Oxygen Breathing Apparatus
OPNAV	Office of the Chief of Naval Operations
psi	Pounds per square inch
Q	Quadruple (AA gun mount or torpedo-tube mount)
quad	Quadruple
RearAdm	Rear Admiral
S	Single
SCB	Ship Characteristics Board
SecNav	Secretary of the Navy
SP	Single-purpose (gun mount capable of engaging surface targets only)
STS	Special-Treatment Steel (homogeneous armor)
T	Twin
Tons	Long tons (2,240 pounds)
TT	Torpedo tubes
VCNO	Vice-Chief of Naval Operations
VHF	Very High Frequency (radio-frequency band, 30 to 300 megacycles (megahertz), widely used for short-range tactical voice communication, WWII)
ViceAdm	Vice Admiral
VT	Variable-Time; designation applied to the proximity fuze
WDR	War Damage Report (series of BuShips publications individually identified by numbers)

Endnotes

Chapter 4

[1]Lcdr F. S. Craven memorandum, 8 November 1930 to General Board, in General Board File No. 420–9.
[2]*Report of Gunnery Exercises, 1940–41* (Chapter 6, 'Destroyers'), 49.
[3]A theme which recurs through any story of warship construction is the gap between trial speeds, made under optimum loading in good weather, and those actually steamed under service conditions, in varying weather and weeks or months out of drydock. *See* D. K. Brown, 'Speed on Trial' (Technical Topics No 3), *Warship* No 3 (July 1977), 56–61.
[4]Division of Fleet Training, Office of the Chief of Naval Operations, comment in *Report of Gunnery Exercises, 1934–35*, 402

Chapter 5

[1]Rear Adm William D. Leahy, Chief, BuOrd, at General Board hearing, 25 April 1928.

Chapter 6

[1]Vice Adm Harold G. Bowen, *Ships, Machinery and Mossbacks; The Autobiography of a Naval Engineer* (Princeton University Press, 1954), 62. Bowen was Chief of BuEng, 1935 to 1939.
[2]Mr J. L. Bates, BuCon, internal memorandum, 29 December 1933.
[3]Mr J. C. Niedermair, BuCon, internal memorandum, 29 December 1933.

Chapter 7

[1]Bowen, *op. cit*, includes an extensive discussion of this subject written, of course, from his own standpoint.
[2]CO, USS *Somers* (DD-381) letter serial 0476, 10 November 1941 (enclosure to Commander, Task Group 3.6, action report, 12 November 1941 on seizure of German motor ship *Odenwald*).

Chapter 8

[1]General Board memorandum No. 420–9, serial 1680–X, 9 March 1935 to BuCon, BuNav.
[2]BuCon memorandum DD/S1–1 (DF), 12 March 1935 to General Board.
[3]BuNav memorandum Nav-61-IB, 12 March 1935 to General Board.
[4]BuCon internal calculations, 16 March 1935.
[5]General Board letter No. 420–9, serial 1680, 19 March 1935 to SecNav.
[6]BuCon internal handwritten memorandum for file, 28 June 1935.
[7]US Navy, BuOrd; *Ordnance Vessel Register, US Navy* (1 July 1945), 60–61. US Navy, BuShips; *Naval Vessel Register* (25 March 1946), 9, 59.
[8]President Franklin D. Roosevelt memorandum, 28 December 1938 to SecNav, Asst SecNav, CNO.
[9]SecNav letter, 30 December 1938 to the President.
[10]*Ships' Data, US Naval Vessels* (1945), Volume 1 (BuShips, 1945).
[11]James C. Fahey, *The Ships and Aircraft of the US Fleet* (Privately printed, 1939), 15.
[12]Board of Inspection and Survey letter DD/S8–2 (505–S) serial 3433, 11 March 1939 to SecNav.
[13]Asst SecNav Second Endorsement, 5 April 1939.
[14]BuEng memorandum DD-397–437 Speeds (5-3-Dk), 3 May 1939.

Chapter 9

[1]CNO letter Op-23-1-RSM 3/5/35(SC)S1–1(1), 8 March 1935 to BuCon, BuEng.
[2]CNO letter Op-23B-KM 12/20/35 (SC)S1–1/DD serial 1738, 21 December 1935, a multiple-address letter to CINCUS, and ten of his subordinate commanders having destroyers under them.
[3]*See* Chapter 2, page 13.
[4]BuCon letter DD/S1–1 (DP), 25 March 1936 to CNO.
[5]BuCon letter DD-S1–1 (DP) of 25 March 1936 to CNO. Though bearing the same identifying symbols and date as the letter cited immediately above, this is a separate document.
[6]Dr E. Lacroix, 'The Imperial Japanese Navy (1936–41)', *The Belgian Shiplover*, XXVI:2 (1975), 30–31.
[7]Director, War Plans Division, memorandum Op-

12-WG(SC)S1–1/DD, 30 March 1936 to CNO.
[8]Extracts of 'Comments and Recommendations Submitted by Forces Afloat for Destroyers of the 1937 Building Program', dated 31 March 1936; in General Board File No. 420–9, 1936.
[9]General Board No. 420–9, serial 1714, 12 May 1936 to SecNav.

Chapter 10
[1]General Board letter, 9 July 1937 to CINCUS, ComBatFor, ComScoFor, ComDesBatFor, ComDeScoFor, ComDesRon 1.
[2]ComBatFor letter, 14 August 1937 to General Board.
[3]ComDesBatFor letter, 4 August 1937 to General Board.
[4]ComScoFor letter, 10 September 1937 to General Board.
[5]ComDeScoFor letter, 27 August 1937 to General Board.
[6]Cdr R. B. Carney, *Recommendation for New Destroyer Construction*, 26 August 1937.
[7]President, Naval War College, letter DCS/XTYZ 1937–03, 7 September 1937 to General Board.
[8]Adm Thomas C. Hart personal letter, 7 October 1937 to Adm A. J. Hepburn.
[9]'Memorandum in regard to Destroyer Characteristics', 14 October 1937 in General Board file No. 420–9 (1937).

Chapter 11
[1]CNO letter Op-23B-EJM(SC)A1–3/DD serial 042323, 25 May 1940 to BuCon, BuEng.
[2]BuShips letter C-DD/S1–1(370), 6 April 1942 to General Board.
[3]General Board letter No. 420–9 serial 210-A, 18 April 1942 to SecNav.
[4]VCNO letter Op-23B-KLF(SC)DD/S1–1 serial 0160123, 14 May 1942 to BuShips, BuOrd.
[5]Ship Characteristics Board letter serial 0504P43E, 22 November 1954 to CNO.

Chapter 12
[1]CINCUS letter S74/5129, 16 October 1936 to CNO.
[2]CNO Op-13-PS serial 03613, 7 May 1940 to SecNav.
[3]General Board memorandum No. 420–11 serial 1952-A, 12 June 1940 to CNO.
[4]General Board memorandum No. 420–11 serial 1952, 13 August 1940 to SecNav.
[5]Buford Rowland & William B. Boyd, *US Navy Bureau of Ordnance In World War II* (Government Printing Office, 1953), 220.
[6]ComDesBatFor S74 serial 5002, 3 November 1940 to CNO.
[7]ComBatFor First Endorsement, 15 November 1940, to CNO.
[8]CINCUS Third Endorsement, 27 November 1940, to CNO.
[9]Navy Dept AA Defense Board letter Op-22 (SC)CL10/S74-1 QB/AA serial 25878, 25 January 1941 to CNO.
[10]Navy Department, 'Bulletin to the President, 8 July 1941', quoted in US Congress, *Hearings Of The Joint Committee On The Investigation Of The Pearl Harbor Attack* (79th Congress, 2nd Session), 1946, 4355.
[11]For an extended discussion of these developments, *see* Rowland & Boyd, *op. cit.*
[12]CNO letter Op-23B-MLH serial 07023, 27 January 1941 to SecNav.
[13]General Board letter No. 420–9 serial 136–1, 14 February 1941 to SecNav.
[14]Director, War Plans Division, Second Memoran-

dum Endorsement (Document 27650), 20 February 1941 to Fleet Maintenance Division.
[15]CNO Second Endorsement, serial 029323, 24 March 1941 to SecNav.
[16]BuOrd letter S74 A2, 2 April 1941 to CNO.
[17]Navy Department Office of Inventions letter EN1-9 JEM/LB, 7 May 1940 to SecNav.
[18]War Plans Division Memorandum Endorsement serial 22787, 10 July 1940 to Fleet Maintenance Division.
[19]BuOrd letter DD/S1(231) (T11), 26 July 1940 to General Board.
[20]General Board Fifth Endorsement, No. 420–9 serial 1987, 1 August 1940.
[21]BuShips memorandum C-DD/S74(8-19-DKH), 29 August 1940 to General Board.
[22]CNO Op-23B-RLG(SC)L9-3 serial 0145223, 19 September 1941 to BuShips, BuOrd.
[23]VCNO Op-23B-RLF(SC)S80/DD serial 0223223, 30 June 1942 to BuShips, BuOrd.
[24]VCNO Op-23B-RLF(SC)S74-1/DD serial 0520723, 19 December 1942 to BuShips, BuOrd.
[25]VCNO Op-23B-RLF(SC)S74-1/DD serial 0533223, 28 December 1942 to BuShips, BuOrd. VCNO Op-23B-RLF(SC)S74-1/DD serial 012323, 12 January 1943 to BuShips, BuOrd.
[26]BuShips C-DD/S74-1(440), 23 December 1942 to CNO.
[27]ComDesBatFor S11/S74 serial 01250, 18 September 1941 to CNO.
[28]CNO Op-23B-RLF(SC)S74-1/DD serial 0170323, 13 October 1941 to BuShips, BuOrd. CNO Op-23B-RLF(SC)S74-1/DD serial 095023, 25 March 1942 to BuShips, BuOrd.
[29]There were innumerable wartime variations on basic armament themes, both official and otherwise (ships' companies, for instance, often retained .50-caliber guns after 20 mm were installed). There is no attempt to trace these here. Some can be seen in the photographs in this work; others can be found in Hodges & Friedman, *Destroyer Weapons of World War II*.
[30]SCB memorandum No. 15–45, 15 May 1945.
[31]SCB memorandum No. 29–45, 18 June 1945.
[32]COMINCH FF1/S67-5 serial 03765, 8 November 1944 to CinCPacFlt.
[33]Commander, Fifth Fleet, Action Report, Ryukyus Operation, Through 27 May 1945.
[34]COMINCH P-0011, *Anti-Suicide Action Summary* (31 August 1945), 20.
[35]*Ibid.*, 21
[36]A succinct discussion of wartime air-defense developments is found in COMINCH P-0011, previously cited, and in *Anti-Aircraft Action Summary, World War II* (Confidential Information Bulletin No. 29) (COMINCH, October 1945). Rowland & Boyd, op. cit. provide a valuable outline and discussion of wartime developments in guns, ammunition, and fire control.

Chapter 13
[1]General Board memorandum No. 420–9, 29 September 1939 to CNO, BuNav, BuOrd, BuCon, BuEng.
[2]General Board letter No. 420–9 serial 1883-X, 4 October 1939 to CNO, BuNav, BuOrd, BuCon, BuEng.
[3]Statement of the War Plans Division, Office of Naval Operations, before General Board, 16 October 1939.
[4]General Board, *Notes of Meeting*, 16 October 1939.
[5]CNO Op10B-LA (SC)DD/S1 Document No. 19231, 18 October 1939 to General Board.
[6]General Board letter No. 420–9 serial 1833-X, 17 October 1939 to technical bureaus.

[7]BuCon, BuEng joint memorandum DD/S1–1(DP), C-DD/S1 (10–17-DK), 10 November 1939 to General Board.
[8]General Board letter No. 420–9 serial 1833-X, 24 November 1939 to BuEng, BuCon.
[9]BuCon, BuEng Joint Memorandum DD/S1–1 (DP), C-DD/S1(10-17-DK), 26 December 1939 to General Board.
[10]General Board letter serial 1833, 9 January 1940 to SecNav.
[11]*US Destroyer No. 445*, BuCon drawings, C&R Nos. 014626–014627, 12 February 1940.
[12]BuEng, BuCon letter DDA1-3(5–17–DA), DD 445–51/L4, 17 May 1940 to SecNav.
[13]General Board Third Endorsement, GB No. 420–9 serial 1961 ICN of 23 May 1940.
[14]General Board No. 420–9 serial 1968–X, 1 July 1940 to CNO, BuOrd, BuNav, BuShips, Board of Inspection and Survey.
[15]BuOrd letter DD/S1(250)(T11), 26 July 1940 to General Board.
[16]BuShips memorandum C-DD.S29(7–16–DKH) to General Board.
[17]CNO serial 073223, 21 August 1940 to BuShips, BuOrd, BuNav.
[18]BuShips, *Ships Laid Down Since the Washington Treaty by Authorizing Acts* (NavShips 282), 1 October 1945, 10,12–14.
[19]BuShips letter of 29 May 1941 with War Plans Division endorsement of 10 June 1941; BuShips Drawing No. 017015, 15 January 1942, *US Destroyers, DD-445 class; Rearrangement of Bridge structure*.
[20]General Board letter to BuOrd, 31 October 1941; BuOrd letter to General Board, 25 November 1941.
[21]BuShips letter C-DD-455 Class/S74 C-DD/S29–1/300), 22 January 1942 to CNO.
[22]CNO letter Op-23B-RLF(SC)DD/S74–1 serial 024923 to BuShips, BuOrd.
[23]BuShips letter C-DD-445 Class/S74(440), undated, to General Board.
[24]BuOrd letter DD/S1(1278)(PL2b), 27 February 1942 to SecNav via CNO. STS (special-treatment steel) was the term then used for homogeneous (non-face hardened) armor plate. In practice 10-pound STS would be about $\frac{1}{4}$-inch thick.
[25]BuOrd letter, 27 February 1942.
[26]CNO letter Op-23B-RLF(SC)DD/S1–1 serial 072723 of 9 March 1942.
[27]Ordnance Pamphlet (OP) 1060, *Gun Director Mark 37 and Mods* (31 March 1945).
[28]VCNO letter Op-23B-RLF(SC)S74/DD serial 0448923 of 21 October 1942 to BuShips, BuOrd.
[29]US Navy, BuOrd, *Armament Summary* (25 November 1945); *Armament Summary*, Vol. II (Reserve Fleet), (25 July 1949).

Chapter 14
[1]Bowen, *op. cit.*, 125; John D. Alden, *Flush Decks and Four Pipes*.
[2]Bowen, *loc. cit.*
[3]CNO letter serial 018323, 23 March 1940 to BuCon, BuOrd, BuEng, BuNav.
[4]BuCon and BuEng joint letter DD/S1-3(6-7-A), 7 June 1940 to SecNav.
[5]CNO letter serial 92723, 17 June 1940, BuCon, BuEng.
[6]*Ships' Data, US Naval Vessels*, Vol. I (BuShips, 15 April 1945), 186-91, 210-15.
[7]BuShips letter C-DD/S1–1(440–445) of 14 June 1945 to CNO.
[8]Draft memorandum for COMINCH, no date.
[9]BuShips memorandum, 18 July 1945 to Fleet Maintenance Division.

[10] VCNO memorandum serial 0324023, 20 July 1945 to COMINCH.

[11] BuShips record cards in *Percival*, *Watson* source files in Ships' Histories Branch, Naval Historical Center.

[12] SecNav memorandum, 15 December 1945 to Director, War Mobilization and Reconversion.

[13] BuCon, BuEng, joint memorandum FS/A1–3(A), 27 May 1940.

[14] BuOrd letter DD-476–481/S1-1(2/1)(T 11), 30 July 1940 to CNO.

[15] War Plans Division Memorandum Endorsement serial 23509, 15 August 1940 to Fleet Maintenance Division.

[16] 'When Kingfishers Rode Greyhounds of the Sea' (*All Hands*, February 1966, 58-61) includes a description of *Halford*'s aviation installation, by her wartime commanding officer.

[17] Rear Adm G. J. Rowcliff memorandum for file, 10 July 1943.

[18] CNO letter serial 0483223, 15 October 1943 to BuShips, BuOrd.

[19] *Stevenson, Stockton, Thorn, Turner* source files, Ships' Histories Branch, Naval Historical Center.

Chapter 15

[1] General Board serial 153–X to BuShips, 8 May 1941.

[2] 'Improvements in Destroyer Design.' General Board, *Hearings* (6 August 1941), 433.

[3] 'Improvements in 2100-Ton Destroyers.' General Board, *Hearings* (28 October 1941), 511.

[4] Fleet Maintenance Division letter Op-23-1-MFP(SC)A1-3, 11 October 1941 to General Board.

[5] BuShips memorandum C-DD/S1–1 (370), 20 October 1941 to General Board.

[6] BuShips letter C-S1-1(1)(301)C-FS/A1–3, 24 October 1941 to General Board.

[7] BuShips letter C-DD/S1–1 (370), 29 November 1941 to General Board.

[8] General Board letter No. 420–9, serial 136-X, 3 December 1941 to BuShips.

[9] BuShips letter C-DD/S1–1(370), 18 March 1942 to General Board.

[10] BuOrd letter DD/S1 (275)(Re), 30 December 1941 to BuShips.

[11] BuShips letter C-DD/S1–1(370), 18 March 1942 to General Board.

[12] US Navy, Division of Naval Intelligence. ONI 222-US, *United States Naval Vessels* (1 September 1945), 83.

[13] BuShips letter C-DD/S1–1(370), 18 March 1942 to General Board.

[14] BuOrd letter DD-S1(282)(Re), 31 March 1942 to General Board.

[15] BuShips letter C-DD/S1–1(370), 1 April 1942 to General Board.

[16] General Board No. 420–9, serial 210 B, 24 April 1942 to SecNav.

[17] COMINCH Endorsement, 7 May 1942 to SecNav.

[18] VCNO Op-23B-RLF(SC)S80/D serial 098923, 17 March 1943 to BuShips, BuOrd, BuPers.

[19] VCNO letter Op-23B-RLF(SC)S80/DD serial 0230323, 8 June 1943 to BuShips, BuOrd and Bureau of Naval Personnel.

[20] Naval Inspector General FF1 A17 25 serial 02888, 19 August 1944 to COMINCH.

[21] COMINCH memorandum FF1/A5–7 serial 0274, 22 January 1944 to VCNO.

[22] These were completed in staggered production blocks, causing much scrambling of hull numbers; *see* Appendices for details.

[23] COMINCH memorandum FF1/S1 serial 01418, 24 April 1944 to VCNO.

[24] Naval Inspector General serial 02888, 19 August 1944 to COMINCH.

[25] COMINCH memorandum serial 02330, 8 July 1944 to Naval Inspector General.

[26] Naval Inspector General letter FF1 A17 25 serial 02883, 19 August 1944 to COMINCH.

[27] ComDesRon 62, letter FC4-62/A2-15 serial 018, 3 October 1944 to ComDesPac.

[28] Quoted in Air Force, Pacific Fleet, Confidential Letter No. 22CL-44.

[29] *Operation Manual, Main Propulsion Plant; DD-445 and DD-692 Class Destroyers.* BuShips, 1944. Revised Edition, 1946.

[30] BuOrd letter (DD/S75(Rel)), 3 July 1944 to CNO. This letter proposed to fit reload torpedoes to all destroyers with centerline tubes, 'considering weight and space available'.

[31] BuShips First Endorsement, 1 September 1944 on BuOrd letter dated 3 July 1944, 1 September 1944.

[32] CNO letter Op-23-B-PGB (SC)S75-1/DD serial 0531023, 15 September 1944 to BuShips, BuOrd.

[33] ComServRon 6 letter A4-1/DD serial 0027, 20 February 1943 to VCNO. At this time Pacific Fleet minelayers formed a part of ServRon 6.

[34] ComServPac First Endorsement, 24 February 1943.

[35] CinCPacFlt Second Endorsement, 8 March 1943.

[36] VCNO Third Endorsement, 26 March 1943.

[37] COMINCH Fourth Endorsement, 10 April 1943.

[38] VCNO Fifth Endorsement, 17 April 1943.

[39] ComServRon 6 letter A4-1/DD serial 00108, 10 May 1943 to VCNO.

[40] ComServPac First Endorsement, 15 May 1943.

[41] CinCPacFlt Second Endorsement, 21 May 1943.

[42] COMINCH Third Endorsement, 6 June 1943.

[43] BuShips Sixth Endorsement, 25 August 1943.

[44] Fleet Maintenance Division Memorandum Endorsement, 28 August 1943.

[45] COMINCH Second Memorandum Endorsement, 3 September 1943.

[46] CNO letter C-DD/L9-3(814), 8 November 1943 to Mare Island Navy Yard.

[47] Commander, South Pacific Force, Third Endorsement, 10 December 1943 on Commander, Mine Division One, report of Offensive Mining Operation dated 3 September 1943.

[48] ComDesPac letter S1/L9-3 serial 01583, 11 December 1943 to CinCPacFlt.

[49] CinCPacFlt letter Pac-F310-wjh L9-3/DD serial 0151, 13 January 1944 to CNO.

[50] CNO letter Op-23D-MEM(SC)L9-3/DD serial 041723, 25 January 1944 to BuShips.

[51] ComServRon 6 letter S28 serial 069, 13 February 1944 to BuShips.

[52] ComServPac First Endorsement, 13 March 1944.

[53] COMINCH message 051947, 5 April 1944 to CinCPac.

[54] CinCPac message 082316, 9 April to COMINCH.

[55] BuShips letter C-DD/L9-3(814), 14 June 1944 to CNO.

[56] CinCPac message 240333, 24 June 1944 to COMINCH.

[57] COMINCH message 271549, 27 June 1944 to CinCPac.

[58] CinCPac message 012357, 2 July 1944 to COMINCH.

[59] COMINCH memorandum FF1/L9-3 serial 001942, 6 July 1944 to VCNO. 'Interim armament' was the battery to be installed as present circumstances permitted; 'ultimate' armament was the *desideratum*.

[60] CNO letter Op-23D-MM (SC) L9-3/DD serial 0432323, 17 July 1944 to BuShips, BuOrd, BuPers.

Chapter 16

[1] USS *Timmerman* letter EAG152;JJR:gb A10 serial 509, 26 September 1955 to Chief of Information, Navy Department.

[2] *Ibid.*

[3] *Fleet Rehabilitation and Modernization Program* (Bureau of Ships, undated); James C. Fahey, *The Ships and Aircraft of the United States Fleet*, Eighth Edition (US Naval Institute, 1965); Stefan Terzibaschitsch, *Das FRAM-Modernisierungsprogramm der US-Navy* (J. F. Lehmanns Verlag, 1975); S. Terzibaschitsch, 'Fleet Rehabilitation and Modernization,' *Warship International*, XII:3 (1975), 238-252.

Chapter 17

[1] Gibbs & Cox letter 10911/S1(K5-178), 11 December 1939 to SecNav, General Board, BuEng, BuCon.

[2] General Board letter, 5 February 1940 to William Francis Gibbs (Gibbs & Cox, Inc.).

[3] General Board No. 420–9 serial 210–C, 24 April 1942 to SecNav.

[4] VCNO Op-23B-RLF(LG)(SC)DD/S1–1 serial 0160023, 14 May 1942 to BuShips, BuOrd, BuNav.

[5] ComDesPac serial 01259, 23 October 1943 to VCNO.

[6] ComDesLant S1–3/FF13–6 serial 0227, 23 January 1944 to CinCLantFlt.

[7] CinCLantFlt S1(0388), 2 February 1944 to COMINCH.

[8] BuShips C-S75-1(374), 25 March 1944 to BuOrd.

[9] Rear Adm E. C. Kalbfus memorandum serial 272–X, May 1944 to General Board.

[10] BuShips C-DD/S1–1 (420), 22 April 1944 to COMINCH.

[11] BuShips C-DD/S1–1(420), 26 April 1944 to General Board.

[12] VCNO Memorandum Endorsement Op-23B-IGM (SC)DD/S1–1 serial 0250623, 29 April 1944 to COMINCH.

[13] BuShips C-DD/S1–1, 13 September 1944 to CNO.

[14] VCNO memorandum Op-23-B-B-PGB: hg serial 0554223 (SC)S1–1/DD Doc. 135406, 4 October 1944 to COMINCH.

[15] CinCPacFlt A5–7 serial 05425, 6 October 1944 to COMINCH (w/enclosures).

[16] BuShips C-DD/S1–1(400), 21 October 1944 to CNO.

[17] COMINCH/CNO FF1/S1–1 serial 272-A 30 October 1944 to SecNav.

[18] BuShips C-DD/S1–1(400), 5 November 1944 to CNO.

[19] BuOrd (Re1) DD/S1, 10 November 1944 to CNO.

[20] BuShips C-DD/S1–1(400), 10 January 1945 to General Board.

[21] BuShips C-DD/S1–1(400), 23 April 1945 to CNO.

[22] SecNav letter, 10 May 1945 to General Board, BuShips, BuOrd, BuAer.

[23] SCB Report No. 2, 17 June 1945.

[24] SCB Op-23-B-PGB serial 0298523 (SC)S1–1/DD, 6 July 1945 to General Board.

[25] BuShips letter, 7 August 1945 to General Board.

[26] General Board memorandum, 8 August 1945 to COMINCH, BuShips, BuOrd.

[27] Rear Adm E. C. Kalbfus undated holograph memorandum in General Board file 420–9, 1945.

[28] BuOrd S75-2(Sp), 24 August 1945 to BuShips.

[29] General Board No. 420–9 (Serial 272), 21 September 1945 to SecNav.

[30] CNO Op-34E2-Sa(SC)S1–1/DD, 23 November 1945 to SecNav.

[31]CinCPacFlt letter A19 serial 004586, 13 December 1945 to CNO, the report of the Pacific Fleet's Ships and Aircraft Types Board.

[32]SCB Characteristics for Destroyer (DD), [1947].

[33]See 'DL-2 Joins Fleet' (*BuShips Journal*, August 1953, 9–11); Edward C. Fisher, Jr., 'DLs of the US Navy' (*Warship International*, VII:4 1970, 325–349); 'Seagoing Guinea Pigs' (*United States Naval Institute Proceedings*, CIV: 6 June 1978, 74–83).

Conclusion

[1]S. H. Banks & Lieutenant-Commander E. A. Wright, 'Full Scale Turning Trials, DD423 and DD444', (TMB Report 522) Navy Department, David Taylor Model Basin, October 1943.

[2]*Ibid.*

[3]David Taylor Model Basin Report R–167, 'Tactical Curves For Destroyer Escorts, DE51 Class', (December 1943); ComDesPac serial 0591, 17 June 1943 to Destroyers, Pacific Fleet.

[4]US Congress, Congressional Budget Office. 'Shaping The General-Purpose Navy Of The Eighties: Issues For Fiscal Years 1981–1985' (Budget Issue Paper for FY 1980).

Appendix A

[1]BuCon letter DD-397-9, 402–8/S29–1&2(DF), 7 September 1937 to Superintending Constructor, USN, New York.

[2]Bowen, *op. cit.*, 115.

[3]BuCon letter DD-411/S29–1&2(DF), 11 July 1939 to CNO.

[4]BuCon, BuEng, BuOrd, joint letter, 5 August 1939 to SecNav.

[5]BuEng letter, 17 August 1939 to SecNav.

[6]CNO First Endorsement, serial 6149, 23 August 1939 to SecNav.

[7]Fleet Maintenance Division memorandum, 24 August 1939.

[8]BuCon memorandum, 24 August 1939 to General Board.

[9]Naval Constructor Homer N. Wallin internal memorandum, 24 August 1939 to the Chief Constructor (the title of the Chief of BuCon).

[10]BuOrd Sketch No. 84163, Destroyers 409 to 420; Study of Effect of Battery Changes on CG of Ship, 28 August 1939.

[11]BuCon letter serial 1879–X, 28 September 1939 to General Board.

[12]General Board memorandum No. 420–9, 29 September 1939 to CNO, material Bureaus, and CINCUS.

[13]BuCon letter DD-421-2, 425–8/S29–1&2(DF) DD-423-4, 429–44/S29–1&2 serial 1879 of 6 October 1939 to General Board.

[14]CNO Second Endorsement, 19 September 1939 to SecNav.

[15]General Board Third Endorsement, serial 1876, 21 September 1939 to SecNav.

[16]BuC&R, BuEng, joint letter (C&R) DD-421-2, 425–8/S29–1&2, DD-423-4, 429–44/S29–1&2(T), (Eng.) DD-421-2/S29 (9–6–D) of 15 September 1939 to SecNav.

[17]SecNav First Endorsement, 27 September 1939 to General Board.

[18]General Board, *Hearings*; 11 October 1939.

[19]ComDesBatFor letter serial 6744, 28 October 1939 to Commander in Chief, US Fleet.

[20]BuCon memorandum DD-423-3, 429–44/S29–1&2(DK3), 28 February 1940 to General Board.

[21]CNO letter Op-23B-EJM serial 022823, 22 March 1940 to Bureaus.

[22]Board of Inspection and Survey letter serial 3121, 31 May 1940 to SecNav.

[23]BuShips letter C-DD/S29–1(456–5814–5820)C-DMS/S29–1, 5 November 1945 to ComDesPac, ComDesLant others.

[24]CNO letter serial 042923, 1 June 1940 to Commanding Officers, *Sampson*, *Davis*, *Jouett*.

[25]CNO letter serial 0923, 10 January 1941 to DesBatFor, and Destroyers, Patrol Force.

[26]CNO letter serial 0197223, 9 December 1941 to DesLant.

[27]BuShips letter C-DD-382/S29 (456), 13 January 1944 to CNO.

[28]BuOrd first endorsement, 24 January 1944 to CNO.

[29]BuShips letter C-DD/S29–1(814–456), 29 June 1944 to CNO.

[30]CNO letter serial 0408823, 8 July 1944 to CinCPacFlt.

[31]VCNO memorandum serial 0578423, 29 September 1944 to COMINCH.

[32]BuShips letter C-DD/S29–1(456), 7 December 1944 to CNO.

[33]BuOrd, *Armament Summary*, 25 August 1945, 25 November 1945; ONI 222-US, *United States Naval Vessels* (1 September 1945), 99.

[34]BuShips letter FS/L9-3(341), 8 November 1941 to CinCLant.

[35]VCNO letter Op-23B-RLF serial 0290923, 4 September 1942 to ComDesPac, ComDesLant.

[36]VCNO letter Op-23B-RLF(SC) serial 0471823, 5 November 1942 to ComDesLant and ComDesPac.

[37]COMINCH letter FF1/A16–3 serial 03230, 26 December 1942 to all ships and stations.

[38]VCNO letter Op-23-1(a)BH(SC) S78–1/DQ serial 038023, 8 February 1943 to all ships and stations.

[39]BuShips letter C-S29–1(456), 8 December 1943 to COMINCH. Limiting displacements and drafts were proposed for ships from the *Farragut* through the *Gleaves* classes, the *Benson*, *Porter* and *Somers* classes excepted.

[40]VCNO Memorandum Endorsement, serial 0708923, 15 December 1943 to COMINCH.

[41]COMINCH Memorandum Endorsement serial 0113, 9 January 1944 to VCNO.

[42]BuShips letter C-S29–1(456), 23 February 1944 to CNO.

[43]ComDesLant circular letters S29–1/FF13–6, DesLant X–61 (17 February 1944); DesLant X–61, Revision No. 1 (13 May 1944); Revision No. 2 (7 August 1944); ComDesPac Monthly Orders No. 9, Material Item 91 (March 1944); ComDesPac circular letter DD/S29 serial 0990 of 20 May 1944.

[44]BuShips letter C-DD/S29–1(456) C-EN28/A2–11, 4 September 1944 to ComDesLant, ComDesPac. Limiting displacements had not yet been established for the *Allen M. Sumner* and *Gearing* classes.

[45]COMINCH, *Damage Control Instructions, 1944* (FTP 170(B)) (10 April 1944), 5.

[46]ComDesPac, circular letter DD/S29 serial 01660, 22 August 1944.

[47]For a general account of this incident, *see* Samuel Eliot Morison, *History of United States Naval Operations in World War II*, Vol. XIII; *also* Theodore Roscoe, *United States Destroyer Operations in World War II*. Captain C. Raymond Calhoun's *Typhoon: The Other Enemy* (Naval Institute Press, 1981) includes a detailed critique of *Farragut*-class stability problems based on the author's wartime experience in command of *Dewey* (DD-349).

[48]BuShips letter C-DD/S29(400), 23 December 1944 to COMINCH.

[49]ComDesPac, circular letter DD/S29 serial 0478 of 3 February 1945. Italics are as in the original.

[50]CinCPacFlt, *Pacific Fleet Confidential Letter 14CL-45*, 13 February 1945.

[51]Fleet Maintenance Office, Service Force, Pacific Fleet, *Pacific Fleet Maintenance Confidential Letter No. 7–44*, 29 December 1944.

[52]SCB memorandum, 20 July 1945 to Committee No. 9 (Damage Control).

[53]BuShips letter C-DD/S29–1(456) C-EN28/A2–11, 12 June 1945 to ComDesPac, ComDesLant.

[54]BuShips letter C-DD-692 Class/S29–1(5814) C-DD-445 Class/S29–1 C-DE/S29–1, 3 July 1945 to ComDesLant, ComDesPac, BuOrd, Navy Yards, Navy Industrial Managers.

[55]CNO Op-25-C2/grm (SC)S67-1 serial 0137425C, 4 July 1945 to CinCPacFlt.

[56]Senior Member, SCB, memorandum, 20 July 1945 to SCB Committee No. 9 (Damage Control).

[57]BuShips C-S29–1(456) C-EN28/A2–11, 28 July 1945 to Navy Yards and Industrial Managers.

Appendix B

[1]This précis is based largely on two titles in the BuShips' *War Damage Report* series: *Destroyer Report*; *Torpedo and Mine Damage and Loss in Action . . .* (W. D. R. No. 50, 1 May 1945), and *Destroyer Report*; *Gunfire, Bomb and Kamikaze Damage . . .* (W. D. R. No. 51, 25 January 1947).

[2]The *Fletcher* class.

[3]The *Allen M. Sumner* and *Gearing* classes.

[4]W. D. R. No. 50, 11–12.

[5]W. D. R. No. 51, 6.

[6]*Ibid.*, 7.

[7]*Ibid.*

[8]*Ibid.*, 6 Eleven ships were damaged by such 'miscellaneous' agencies as strafing, ramming, suicide boats, or 'unknown' causes.

[9]I. M. Korotkin, *Battle Damage to Surface Ships During World War II* (published in Leningrad, 1960, as *Boevye Provrezhdeniya Nadovdnikh Korablei*; translated, 1964, by US Joint Publications Research Service).

[10]Korotkin, 361; W. D. R. No. 50, 4.

[11]*Damage Control Book, DD-421 Class* (BuShips, January 1953), II(a)2.

[12]W. D. R. No. 50, 6.

[13]United States Fleet, *Damage Control Instructions, 1944* (FTP 170(B)), 13.

[14]W. P. Welch, 'Mechanical Shock on Naval Vessels as Related to Equipment Design.' *Journal of the American Society of Naval Engineers*, LVIII (November 1946), 599 ff.

[15]*Damage Control Book, DD421 Class*.

[16]BuShips letter S-F8/S29(424) serial 08733, 11 May 1944 to CNO.

[17]ComDesPac, circular letter serial 0541, 30 May 1942.

[18]BuShips letter C-DD/S29-8(814) C-EN28/A2–11, 26 April 1942 to navy yards, destroyer force commanders.

[19]*Damage Control Instructions, 1944* (FTP 170(B)), 61–62.

Bibliography

Alden, Commander John D., USN. *Flush Decks and Four Pipes*. Annapolis: United States Naval Institute, 1965. 107 pp., illus. A generously-illustrated history of the 'flushdeck', or 'four-stack' destroyers of the *Caldwell* (DD-69), *Wickes* (DD-75), and *Clemson* (DD-186) classes.

Preston, Antony, ed. *Super Destroyers* (*Warship Special 2*). London: Conway Maritime Press, 1978. 72 pp., illus. Includes a chapter by Norman Friedman discussing the *Porter* (DD-356) and *Somers* (DD-381) classes.

Friedman, Norman. *U.S. Destroyers; An Illustrated Design History*. Profile drawings by A. D. Baker III. Annapolis: United States Naval Institute, 1982, 489 pp., illus. General development of the American destroyer from the steam torpedo boat to the present.

Hodges, Peter, and Friedman, Norman. *Destroyer Weapons Of World War 2*. London: Conway Maritime Press/Annapolis: United States Naval Institute, 1979. 192 pp., illus. In this two-part work Hodges and Friedman discuss, respectively, British and American destroyer ordnance of the period.

Preston, Antony. *Destroyers*. London: Bison Books/Englewood Cliffs, NJ: Prentice-Hall, 1977. 224 pp., illus. General account of the destroyer type from its beginnings to the present.

Roscoe, Theodore. *United States Destroyer Operations In World War II*. Annapolis: United States Naval Institute, 1953. 581 pp., illus., maps. Detailed account of the operations of destroyers and destroyer escorts.

Schofield, Captain William G., USNR. *Destroyers, 60 Years*. Chicago: Rand McNally, 1962. 180 pp., illus. Summary description of destroyer operations and evolution through the Korean War.

Documentary and Official Sources

Rowland, Buford, and William B. Boyd. *US Navy Bureau Of Ordnance In World War II*. Washington: Government Printing Office, 1953. 539 pp., illus. Includes accounts of the development of weapons and control systems used in American destroyers and destroyer escorts.

Records of the Ships' Histories Branch, Naval Historical Center, Washington, DC.

Records of the General Board of the Navy, Operational Archives Branch, Naval Historical Center.

Records of the Office of the Commander in Chief, United States Fleet (COMINCH), Operational Archives Branch.

Records of the Office of the Chief of Naval Operations (CNO), Operational Archives Branch.

US Navy, Bureau of Ordnance. *Armament Summary (1941-45)*.

Index